ISRAEL, A NATION OF WARRIORS

Moshe Katz was born in Cleveland, Ohio, and has lived in Maaleh Adumim, Israel, for many years. He is a graduate of UCLA (BA) and Bernard Baruch Business School (MBA). He served in the Israel Defense Forces (IDF) – Infantry. Katz has over thirty years martial arts experience. He is the founder of Israeli Krav International (IKI) and serves as Head Instructor. In addition to teaching in Israel, he tours the United States, Canada, Europe, Asia, and South America teaching Krav Maga/Israeli Self-Defense.

Visit the website: http://www.your-krav-maga-expert.com

ISRAEL, A NATION OF WARRIORS

Moshe Katz

Israeli Krav Maga International
Maaleh Adumim, Israel

Designed by Sue Schoenfeld

Cover photo by Arie Katz
Chapter icons: © stringerphoto / Fotolia

Israeli Krav Maga International
Maaleh Adumim, Israel

www.your-krav-maga-expert.com

Printed in the United States of America

This book is dedicated to my nephew Arie Katz, a soldier of Israel, and his friends of the 101 paratroopers, who served in the Second Lebanon War.

To my brother Ethan Katz, a soldier of Israel, who served with an infantry combat unit, and battled terrorists.

To my dear father, Rabbi Paul M. Katz, of blessed memory, a soldier of Israel, who served in the Yom Kippur War and whose life was devoted to the people of Israel. His life and character will always inspire us.

And to my dear mother, Mrs. Hannah K. Katz, "A woman of valor who shall find" (Proverbs), whose love has been the cornerstone of my life.

Blessed be God, my rock, who teaches my hands to battle, my fingers for war.
—Psalms

The world does not pity the slaughtered. It only respects those who fight.
—Menachem Begin, *The Revolt*

CONTENTS

PREFACE

One day I was walking in my neighborhood. Walking through the hills of Maaleh Adumim in the Judean Desert of Israel I started humming, for no apparent reason, the tune to the "Jewish Partisans Song," "Do not say this is my last walk..."[1]

My thoughts turned to the forests of Poland and Belarus, 1941. I looked down at my feet and imagined for a moment the feet of the partisans, their mud covered boots trekking through the forests, never knowing if today would in fact be their last day, if this walk would be their last journey in this lifetime, or who among their friends will not be with them tomorrow. In a way I am continuing their walk; in a way I am living their dream.

My thoughts turned to all of them—the partisans, ghetto fighters, defenders of Masada and Jerusalem, cousin Willie at the Battle of the Bulge, Moses and Joshua, Phineas the Cohen, the Jewish Legion, soldiers in the wars of 1948, 56, 67, 70, 73, the Lebanon Wars, the Gaza Wars, counterterrorist units, Jabotinsky and Trumpeldor, King David and Samson.

My thoughts turned to all our people who over the course of our history slung a rifle over their shoulder, or a bow and arrow, or strapped a sword to their side, left their homes, and went off to fight for our freedom. It is because of them that today I can take a walk in my own land—the land where my forefathers walked. I will *never* take this for granted. This book is about these Jewish warriors.

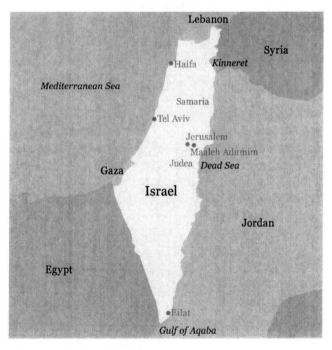

Maaleh Adumim – 7 kilometers (4.3 miles) east of Jerusalem, population approx. 40,000

I took a taxi in Long Island, New York, on my way to JFK Airport after teaching Krav Maga to a group of American soldiers. The driver, Hezi, was an Israeli. He had been living in the United States for twenty-five years. As he helped me with my luggage, he noticed that one of my bags—a green military bag I used while serving in the Israel Defense Forces (IDF)—had numbers on it. He identified the numbers as my military ID and knew the year I had served. It turned out we were the same age. We became good friends.

There was an immediate bond. No longer passenger and driver, we were united by a shared history—we both served; something unspoken took place. The bond goes back thousands of years to the ancient warriors of Israel who battled the Canaanites, the Greeks, and the Romans. This is Israel, a nation united by a dream and a long shared history. Guns, swords or spears, the Tavor rifle, or the slingshot of young David—a warrior nation. We have spent thousands of years fighting to be free.

This book is not about governments. It is not about political leaders. It is not about national policy or international relations. It is not about strategy or questions such as whether or not an attack or a war was justified.

It is about people—ordinary people, people who have been asked to do extraordinary things, and have done so.

The people of Israel have risen to the challenge, neither seeking a reward nor receiving one. Without questions, without hesitation, they left their happy lives and answered the call to arms. And when the fighting subsided, they tried to return to normal lives, with their scars and their traumas. But life in Israel is anything but normal, for this is a nation at war, at war for survival.

When the Jewish people, the people of Israel, began coming home to the Land of Israel, they did not have war on their minds. After being forcibly expelled and driven out of their homeland many centuries earlier, the "wandering Jews," scattered around the world, kept dreaming of returning home, to the small strip of earth simply known as "The Land," The Land of Israel. Individual Jews, small groups, sometimes entire communities, did manage to return to The Land, but not until the 1880s was a more massive return possible.

The Jews had dreams of utopia. They wanted to befriend the Arabs and adapt to the Middle East. Many early photos show Eastern European Jews dressed in Arab garb and riding on camels; they wanted to fit in; they wanted peace. Reality was quite different and the need for organized self-defense soon became apparent. Reluctantly, the utopian Jewish farmers became fighters. It was either fight or be killed.

The symbol of the IDF is a sword (a symbol of war), an olive branch (symbolizing the Israeli desire for peace), and the Star of David (symbolizing Jewish history). Every government of Israel, since its establishment in 1948, has reached out for peace, but prepared for war. The long sought-after peace has proven elusive, perhaps impossible. As the prophet Ezekiel said so many years ago, "Peace, peace but there is no peace."[2]

I recall when I was a young child, people would see my dear mom with four young boys and they would say, "Four boys—four future soldiers." This angered my mother who would say to herself, "Bite your tongue, by the time my boys are old enough to serve, there will be peace." So every mother hopes. Today, many years later, her grandchildren are serving in the army, in combat units, and there is still no peace in sight.

Back in 1967, I was playing with my friend from next-door. His name was Edo, an Israeli born boy. I can picture the day like yesterday. I recall exactly where we stood in our beautiful backyard. We heard the sound of a plane and we both looked up to the sky. I looked up for just a moment, but Edo, he just kept staring. I tried to get his attention, but Edo's eyes were glued to that plane. He watched it until it was totally gone from sight. "What was that all about?" I asked him.

Edo, only six years old, answered simply and to the point, words I still remember to this very day, words I shall never forget, "There was a time when everyone else had planes but we did not. Now we too have planes."

The dispersion and exile and the return, the Holocaust and the rebirth of the State of Israel, the transformation from perceived helplessness to warriors; this is what he was saying. A six-year-old Israeli boy understood it all; summarizing thousands of years of history in just a few words. And I can still see that plane flying away…"There was a time when everyone else had planes but we did not…"

INTRODUCTION

The Beginning of International Terrorism

I was just a child when I was introduced to international terrorism. The year was 1970. My aunt, uncle, and infant cousin Tali came to visit us in Israel. As they boarded their TWA flight back home to New York none of us could imagine the ordeal about to unfold. A few hours later we heard the news—the plane had been hijacked by Arab terrorists and taken to Jordan, fate unknown.

My father, of blessed memory, was in the barbershop getting a haircut when the news was broadcast on Radio Israel. The shock jolted my dad out of his seat. The barber's scissors nicked his ear.

My aunt and cousin would end up spending a week as hostages in Jordan, along with hundreds of other passengers. My uncle, along with some other select hostages, would spend six weeks in captivity. The ordeal would change their lives.

Our Mindset is to Fight Terror

That day the terrorists attempted to hijack four planes as part of their struggle against the State of Israel. This was the beginning, the birth, of international terrorism, the curse that would come to plague Western society in years to come, a cancer we are still fighting today. The Western world had no training in this kind of warfare; no understanding of the terrorist mindset. The Israelis, however, were already veterans of this war.

Of the four attempted hijackings, three succeeded. The only one to fail was the attempted hijacking of EL AL Israel Airlines. Four terrorists tried to board the EL AL flight. Two of them aroused the suspicions of the security staff and were refused entry. The two remaining terrorists, infamous female terrorist Laila Chaled and Patrick Argüello, managed to board the EL AL flight. The rejected terrorists proceeded to book a Pan Am flight, boarded without any difficulty, and hijacked it.

On board the EL AL flight, things did not go as smoothly for the hijackers. The operation had been planned for a team of four. Argüello hesitated. Laila Chaled assured him she had done this before and all would go smoothly. She had hijacked before. This time it did not succeed.

The terrorists stood up and pulled out handguns and hand grenades and announced that the flight was being taken over by the Popular Front for the Liberation of Palestine (PFLP). The general international policy in those days was to cooperate with the hijackers and enter into negotiations, not to resist and endanger the passengers. The crew and passengers of EL AL Israel Airlines thought differently. The terrorists had not counted on resistance and Israeli stubbornness.

The first thing to go wrong for the terrorists was the takeover of the cockpit. As planned, Laila Chaled stood outside the cockpit with a pistol held to a flight attendant's head and a hand grenade in her other hand. She demanded the pilot open the door at once. But the pilot was no ordinary civilian. His name was Uri Bar Lev and he was a former captain in the Israeli air force. No terrorist was going to hijack *his* plane.

Captain Bar Lev refused to open the cockpit door. He would not be the first to blink. Instead, the former combat pilot sent the aircraft into a nosedive. The nosedive had the same effect on the passengers as an elevator going into free-fall. The sudden move knocked the hijackers off their feet, just as Bar Lev had planned.

Then the Israeli passengers went into action. As one passenger put it, "I made a decision that they were not going to hijack this plane. I decided to attack him rather than wait and see what happens. So I jumped him. I got shot in the shoulder."

The terrorist, Argüello, was hit over the head with a bottle of whiskey and then killed in the struggle by his own gun. Laila Chaled was tied up with neckties and belts provided by passengers. The pilot summed up the fighting spirit that day, "I didn't succeed because I was a better pilot. It was only because of my attitude that we were not going to be hijacked. Our mindset is to fight terror."

Israeli Attitude

Here is the key to Israeli self-defense—attitude! It is a resolve to fight terror, not to give in, not to be a victim anymore. This is a universal aspect of Israeli culture born out of the bitter experience of being an unwelcome guest in foreign lands and being surrounded by a hostile Arab population.

The pilot was trained to improvise, to think "on his feet," or in this case, on his seat, in the air. He used what he had available, another key to Israeli self-defense, and came up with a brilliant way to fight back. Equally important, the pilot knew that once the terrorists were on the floor, the crew and passengers, all former soldiers, would respond as warriors; they would unite and fight back. He could count on it without even asking them; for they are part of a warrior nation, this is part of their upbringing, their military training, their lifestyle.

Shortly after 9/11, in November 2002, an Arab terrorist, twenty-three-year-old Tawfiq Fukra, tried to hijack an Israeli flight to Turkey. Somehow he managed to smuggle a knife on board the aircraft. He started swinging his knife at the flight attendant, threatening her. The flight attendant reacted instinctively with evasive techniques designed to buy time and prepare a better defense. She managed to avoid getting cut by using the techniques she learned as part of her basic military Krav Maga training. This gave the flight marshals time to react. They quickly neutralized the threat.

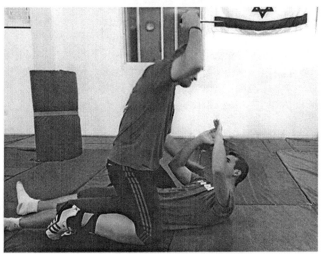

Krav Maga knife defense

The key here, as in the 1970 incident, was that neither she nor anyone else panicked. They made use of what was at hand and relied not only on their own training, but on the preparedness of everyone around them. This is the Israeli mindset.

Nowhere is that mindset more in evidence than in Krav Maga, the native Israeli martial arts system. Krav Maga emphasizes simple, easy to remember gross motor moves, reliance on human instinct, natural body movements, and utilization of whatever one finds available.

Basic Principles of Krav Maga Airline Self-Defense

Be Alert!

Even before boarding a flight, Israelis are on alert. As they are in line checking in, they check out the passengers. If someone notices anything unusual or out of place they will notify the security staff. They never forget that *they* are part of the security staff. Krav Maga expert Itay Gil puts it this way, "You are accountable for your own life, and ultimately you are responsible for safeguarding it."[3]

In 1956, after Egypt violated international law and nationalized the Suez Canal; Israel, Britain, and France took control of the canal in a military operation. After much pressure from the Americans, and assurances of safety, Israel withdrew from the canal. In 1967, when Egypt again violated all agreements and crossed into the Sinai Peninsula, Israel waited for the United States to act on its assurances. No help was forthcoming. Israel realized that one is accountable for his own survival. Written guarantees and promises from others are not to be relied upon. We are accountable for our own safety.

Look for Allies on Your Flight

If you are a trained fighter, if you have skills that can save others, you must assume added responsibility for the protection of others. As you find your seat, and as a fighter, you should *only* take an aisle seat so you can get out and fight if need be; look for allies. You do not have time to interview people as to their abilities and background, but keep an eye open for people who look like they can handle a fight. You will have to rely on your judgment.

Anticipate the Worst Case Scenario

If the worst *does* happen and you have to fight back—then fight you must. In Krav Maga, we stress that you should never make a bad trade. Sometimes in battle people get hurt or die. If the terrorist is threatening one person and demands to get into the cockpit—it is a mistake to give in, despite your desire to save that one person's life. You might be trading one life for the safety of all the other passengers. And even that one life will not be saved if the plane goes down.

Instead, think like a warrior. Fight back. If one hostage gets killed, then that is a tragic consequence of saving one hundred lives. *Don't make a bad trade.* This may be harsh thinking, too much to expect of an average citizen, but Israelis are not average citizens. Who are the Israelis? How did this group of people emerge?

Israel – The Country

The modern State of Israel[4] is situated in the Middle East with the Mediterranean Sea on its western side. It borders with Lebanon to the north, Syrian to the northeast, Jordan on the east.

The population of Israel was estimated in 2014 to be 8.2 million people. It is the world's only Jewish-majority state; 6.2 million citizens, or 74.9% of Israelis, are designated as Jewish. The country's second largest group, Arab citizens of Israel,[5] number 1.7 million or 20.7% of the population (including the Druze and most East Jerusalem Arabs).

In 1967, as a result of the defensive Six-Day War, Israel liberated the biblical lands of Judea, Samaria, the Gaza Strip,[6] and the Golan Heights. Israel also took control of the Sinai Peninsula, but gave it to Egypt as part of the 1979 Israel-Egypt Peace Treaty.

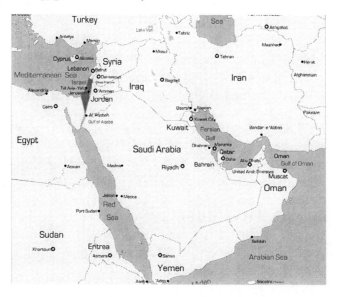

Israel in the Middle East © Ruslan Olinchuk / Fotolia

Since Israel's conquest of these territories, settlements (Jewish civilian communities) and military installations have been built within each of them. Israel has applied civilian law to the Golan Heights and East Jerusalem, incorporating them into its sovereign territory and granting their inhabitants permanent residency status and the choice to apply for citizenship. In contrast, Judea and Samaria have remained under the military government, and the Arabs in this area cannot become citizens. The Gaza Strip is independent of Israel with no Israeli military or civilian presence, but Israel continues to maintain control of its airspace and waters.

Who are the Israelis?

It is important to understand Israelis—who are they? Where do they come from? Some Israelis have direct roots that go back thousands of years, despite all the conquests of our land and the many foreign rulers, they clung to the land and never left. Others can trace their return to Israel to a few hundred years ago. The "newer" returnees came to Israel during the Zionist movement that began in the 1880s.

No matter when they returned—they worked the land, cleared the swamps, fought off the Arabs, and expelled the British troops. Others survived the Nazi war machine, fought in the ghettos and the forests, and then arrived in Israel and fought in several of Israel's many defensive wars. They are not the warm and cuddly type. This is a *fighting* nation.

Israel is a nation comprised of citizen soldiers who are ready to serve at a moment's notice. Israel is a **nation that realizes that if we do not act, we will die**; our history has taught us this. It is a nation that lives by the words of the ancient rabbis who said, "If am not for myself, who will be? And if not now, then when?"[7]

As Israelis, we are taught,

- Do not trust the words of the enemy and hope for the best.
- Do not cooperate with their demands.
- Assume the worst and trust no one.

Prime Minister Golda Meir once remarked about her difficulties in dealing with American Secretary of State Henry Kissinger, "He is a wonderful gentleman; the only problem is that he thinks of the rest of the world as equally wonderful gentlemen."

A nation of warriors is defined as a people with a warrior's mindset, which is very different from a citizen's mindset.

When tragedy strikes, an ordinary citizen responds by saying, "Thank God it wasn't me!" or "Thank God I was not there!" A warrior, whether a police officer, martial artist, fireman or soldier, responds by saying, "I wish I had been there, I could have done something to help those people."

One of my handgun instructors told me that whenever he hears about a terrorist attack he gets down and does as many push-ups as he can. It is his way of saying, "I must be strong. I must be prepared. Next time, perhaps, I will be there and I want to make a difference. I must be ready to act." Being ready to act—a warrior knows there will most likely be no warning, no chance to get organized. Israeli culture stresses the belief in always being ready, in anticipating the next attack, in thinking ahead.

A warrior responds with action. In Israel, when there is the sound of an explosion or gunshots, people run *toward* the sound, not away. They are thinking, "I have military training, I have medical training, perhaps someone needs my help." These people do not consider themselves heroes, just people doing what is right, what is expected of them.

CHAPTER 1

A Warrior Nation Mindset

Many Americans are obsessed with personal freedom. Personal freedom is so important to them that they are often unwilling to take the necessary measures to protect that freedom. If security measures go against their principles of freedom they would rather take the risks than compromise this sense of liberty.

As an example, having a security guard at an airport or store empty the contents of one's bag or pockets offends most American's sense of personal freedom. But that is one of the very measures necessary to protect the personal freedom of every American—including the freedom and security of the person being searched.

In Israel, we are not so sensitive. We have less privacy and we understand the need to compromise our personal freedom in the interest of greater security. As Uri Dromi of the Israel Democratic Institute said, speaking of the Jewish state, "The question of civil liberties is always in the shadow of security." Israelis ask, "If you don't exist, what's the point of having civil rights?" he noted. "The first right is the right to live, and this is what Israelis get in the milk of their mothers. There is security and then, there's democracy. People in America value democracy first."[8]

With a warrior nation, fighting, dying, and sudden attacks, are all par for the course. Americans do not have this mindset, as evidenced by the April 16, 2007, massacre at Virginia Tech. On that horrific day, a mentally ill student, Seung-Hui Cho, killed thirty-two people and injured many others in what was the worst shooting incident in US history.

In two separate shooting incidents, about two hours apart, Cho gunned down terrified students and staff in cold blood. The first victims were shot around 7:15 am; about two hours later Cho came back for more.

There was only one hero that day, an Israeli, Professor Librescu. He was seventy-six years old yet he did what none of the young people, of many nationalities, were able to do.

When he understood that a murderer was on his way into the class, he kept the door shut with his body so his students could escape out the window. He died after being shot multiple times through the door.

William Daroff, director of the Washington office of the United Jewish Communities said, "The first thing that occurred to me about it, besides the tragedy of it, is how his heroism was informed by his experience as an Israeli. He clearly had thought about terrorism as an Israeli and, with a split second to respond after hearing a gunshot, went into autopilot, barricaded the door with his body and gave his students time to flee. Being an Israeli, having that mentality of how to deal with this sort of crisis comes more naturally."

A Warrior's Response

Autopilot; a typical Israeli is alert, like an animal in the jungle, always aware of potential predators. Most humans have lost this animal instinct, but Israelis know that wherever they are, they can be the target of a terrorist attack; we cannot afford to be lax. "The guardian of Israel does not rest and does not sleep"[9] in the battlefield, at home, or on vacation. We are always on guard.

A warrior in battle should never be shocked by an enemy attack. When the attack comes, he should know how to respond. A civilian can be caught off guard. In Israel, the whole nation responds as the combat warrior. Dromi commented about the students' response at Virginia Tech, "The big difference is that for them it looks like out of the blue. For us, it's a sad way of life." Israelis are experienced with war and terror. "Once they have this kind of basic preparedness in the back of their minds, if this happens, people don't fall off their feet thinking that something unthinkable has happened, which is the feeling that people have here [in the United States] today."[10]

Israelis don't wonder, "How could this happen? Why would anyone want to hurt us?" They know the world is a harsh place and bad things happen. They know they must learn how to cope and to protect themselves.

During the Virginia Tech massacre, the young American college students, raised with freedom and liberty, were not able to respond like warriors; they froze like a deer in the headlights. Yet the old Israeli, the Jewish holocaust survivor, had already tasted terror in his life and he knew how to respond. He died as a warrior.

We Are All Always at War

Since the Civil War, America's wars have all taken place overseas. Most Americans have never seen an enemy face to face or had to barricade their homes or worry about being attacked while shopping.

·

In Israel, it is different. The war is everywhere. It is at all our borders, it is overseas where Israeli tourists are targeted (Bulgaria, India, France, Argentina, Germany, Nairobi, United Kingdom, United States), and it is in our shopping malls, cafés, our buses, and on our streets. It is also in our homes and in our kindergartens. Every Israeli is a front line soldier; men, women, children and the elderly. Every home is a mini fortress.

If you were an Israeli, you might find yourself pushing an attacker off the bus or defending yourself against a knife wielding Arab in the Old City of Jerusalem. You might alert authorities and your fellow citizens to a suspicious object while out on your morning walk or to an Arab girl with a large package walking into a crowded supermarket. No one would think you were unusual. The alertness and training of the average citizen/soldier has prevented many potentially deadly attacks.

The Home as a Fortress

The lines between civilian and warrior are blurred at home as well as in public. After the wars in the 1960s and 1970s, a law was passed requiring that each new home built have a bomb shelter large enough to accommodate all members of the household. An apartment building must have a bomb shelter sufficient for all the residents.

Following the first Gulf War in 1990, the law was amended to require new construction to have a "sealed room," one that could be hermetically sealed to protect against chemical weapons. Public education programs teach citizens how to prepare the room and how to use the atropine emergency kit. Every citizen has a personal gas mask. Sealed protective cribs were designed to protect babies. Special programs to train the home guard are part of all high school education, and home security is a required course of study.

To protect against less sophisticated terrorists, most people install metal bars over their home's windows. Many people own handguns and are trained in their use. Houses are indeed mini fortresses. Schools are similarly equipped. Young children are drilled in how to behave during times of combat. In a sense, they are young soldiers in training.

When I drive home at night, I must drive through the barricade set up at the entrance to my town. Several soldiers will be there and I must drive through a short obstacle course while they eye me. They might stop me and ask me a few questions.

When I go to the supermarket or mall, I must stop my car while an armed security guard examines my vehicle, asks me a few questions, and opens the trunk. (I never leave anything in the trunk that might cause me embarrassment.) Before I enter the building, I will empty my pockets, open my bag, and walk through a metal detector with an armed guard at the ready. In day-to-day life, it is hard to forget that the enemy is all around, and that we must always be on high alert.

Refuse to be a Victim

Airline Security

Israeli airline security is like no other. The **last, and only** time an EL AL flight was hijacked was in 1968. This was the first act of terrorism perpetrated against EL AL, Israel's national airline. On July 23, 1968, terrorists, members of the Popular Front for the Liberation of Palestine, boarded an EL AL flight leaving Rome, took over the plane, and landed it in Algiers. Since then no one has succeeded in hijacking an Israeli plane. I believe that EL AL is the safest airline in the world, and Israel's Ben Gurion International Airport is the safest airport in the world. That is why I only fly EL AL.

What is EL AL's Secret?

Part of it is attitude, resolve, stubborn refusal to be a victim, and military training; all working together to create a combat mindset. But there is more to it than that. Americans blindly look for weapons. They are reluctant to profile, believing that goes against an American sense of freedom and equality. We don't have that luxury. We profile and we make no apologies for it.

Simply put, profiling is the best method for spotting, and stopping, terrorists. Even in this age of technology, human instincts and study of human behavior is the key to spotting potential terrorists. No machine can replace a human being. Profiling helps focus extra attention where it is most needed.

In Israel, unlike the United States, not every passenger has to take off his shoes and belt. We believe that if you use a "one size fits all" screening process, you lose your edge. You become machinelike, operating automatically. "Security is first and foremost based on common sense, which is supposed to provide you with the right intelligence, technology and modus operandi," says Pini Shiff, who served for thirty years in the Ben Gurion Airport security division. "It is all about brains, since if you do everything automatic, it won't work."[11]

Another airline employee added, "Profiling makes the biggest difference. A man with the name of Umar (like the terrorist who attempted to set an American plane on fire in 2009) flying out of Tel Aviv, whether he is American or British, is going to get checked seven times."

In the United States, on May 1, 2010, Faisal Shahzad, a Pakistani born terrorist tried to bomb Times Square in New York City, but failed. His name was placed on the "No-Fly List," and yet on Tuesday, May 4, 2010, he was sitting in his seat on his way out of the country. At the last minute someone realized the mistake and ordered the plane back, just as it was about to take off. American authorities downplayed the incident and stressed that in the end he was caught, but they did not address the fact that he got through their security system and nearly flew away.

"Faisal Shahzad was aboard Emirates Flight 202. He reserved a ticket on the way to John F. Kennedy International Airport, paid cash on arrival and walked through security without being stopped. By the time Customs and Border Protection officials spotted Shahzad's name on the passenger list and recognized him as the bombing suspect they were looking for, he was in his seat and the plane was preparing to leave the gate."[12]

So, he has an Arab name, is traveling alone, bought his ticket with cash at the last minute, is probably quite nervous that someone will stop him at airport security, and no one even questions him. In Israel, we have learned that such people should be stopped for questioning. Israeli security personnel are trained to pick up the slightest twitch or body gesture that would indicate something is suspicious.

Lessons Learned: Athens, Zurich, Berlin, Brussels, Lod

Israel learned its lessons the hard way. Long before the rest of the world woke up to the threat of international terrorism, Israel was already a veteran at battling terrorists. Back in 1968, on December 26, the Popular Front for the Liberation of Palestine struck again. Two of their members attacked an EL AL plane in Athens, killing an Israeli mechanic. Israel responded quickly by attacking the Beirut airport in Lebanon and destroying fourteen planes. In 1969 Arab terrorists attacked EL AL planes and offices in Zurich, Athens, West Berlin, and Brussels.

I recall back in 1972, I was living relatively close to the airport. It was May 31, 1972, to be exact, the day the name "Kozo Okamoto" became embedded in my memory.

Three Japanese terrorists, working on behalf of the Popular Front for the Liberation of Palestine surprised the guards at the Israeli airport. The three terrorists had been trained by the Arab terrorists in Lebanon. Arriving from Paris on Air France, the three conservatively dressed men carrying violin cases did not attract much attention. In the waiting area they opened their violin cases, took out automatic weapons, cut down in size to fit the small case, and opened fire indiscriminately on whoever happened to be there. As they changed magazines in their weapons, they threw hand grenades at the crowd. One of the terrorists, Yasuyuki Yasuda, ran out of ammunition, and was accidentally killed by his comrades (some say he was killed by Israeli counter-fire). A second terrorist, Tsuyoshi Okudaira, committed suicide. The third terrorist, Okamoto, was badly injured, but not before the three terrorists managed to kill twenty-six people, and injure eighty. Those murdered included sixteen Christian pilgrims from Puerto Rico. They had come to tour the Holy Land and pray; instead they experienced what we have to deal as part of our daily life. At the time no one expected Japanese terrorists, today we are wiser. Every guest can expect a close look.

So yes, we do profile. When my non-Jewish students from around the world come to Israel to train with me in Krav Maga, I warn them, "Do not be offended, you will be asked questions at the airport, tell them my name and why you are here. Give them my phone number; they can call me if they want to." Understand that we have learned from bitter experience that we must be careful, even at the risk of offending an innocent tourist.

One of my students was connecting to an EL AL flight in Asia. He is a young, dark, athletic looking man, and was traveling alone. He was spotted in the crowd and pulled aside for extra interrogation. Being a young, happy-go-lucky fellow, he took it all in stride. "Why were you in this country (a certain Asian state)? What were you doing there?" the female officer asked him.

"I have friends there," he responded honestly.

"How do you know these friends? What did you do with these friends?" Extensive questioning, all answered honestly, revealed no nervousness on his part and no contradictions in his answers. His honesty proven, and a thorough body check along with a special test to see if he had come in contact with explosives, cleared him for travel to Israel.

All the above took place outside the borders of Israel, in faraway Hong Kong. As I experienced in Frankfurt, Germany, as soon as you entered "EL AL territory," you felt that you were already in Israel. For me, an Israeli citizen, it is a warm, comfortable feeling, like I am already halfway home. For a terrorist it must be a feeling that the long arm of Israeli security is about to catch him.

Students of mine arriving from the United States also felt they were entering some sort of new reality, a world different from their own. Being young, athletic looking, traveling alone, not Israeli and not Jewish, they naturally aroused some suspicion and warranted extra security measures. One student had his hand luggage taken away for more thorough searching. His music player, cell phone, and other electronic devices were thoroughly examined. His shoes were checked and tested for possible chemical contact. Both he and another student, on different occasions, were escorted from the time of check-in until the moment they boarded the plane. From the moment they checked in until they were on the plane they had an Israeli security guard constantly by their side. One even experienced a "changing of the guard" during the long wait to board. One asked to go to the rest room, his guard at the time was a female officer; she responded, "Wait until you are on the plane." The guards watched my students and did not allow them any contact with anyone from the moment they entered "EL AL territory" until they were seated safely on the plane.

January 2011, I am sitting at Bank Leumi talking about my account when my cell phone rings. I glance at the number of the incoming call, it is a 271 country code; I have no idea where this is coming from. I have never received a phone call from such a number. I answer the call, it is an Israeli on the phone; his accent and perfect Hebrew are unmistakable. But where on earth is he calling from? He is calling from South Africa. He is EL AL security working the South African airport and he has detained a young man for questioning. Clearly the young suspect gave him my phone number, as I instructed him. "Do you know why I am calling you?"

I put two and two together and say, "Yes, you must have detained Alex, he is a student of mine, he is on his way to Israel to train with me. He is a good guy."

"What does he look like, how old is he?" I answer with full details.

"Have you met him before, if so, under what circumstances?" Again, I am able to answer fully, without a hint of hesitation in my voice. "Where will he be staying?"

"In my neighborhood, Mitzpe Nevo, I rented him an apartment at the Cohen's."

"But that is a religious neighborhood?" (Wow, they are good! This is a small neighborhood in a small town, and yet they know the character of the neighborhood; very thorough training.)

"Yes, I know he is not Jewish, but we are very welcoming here."

"You seem to have a bit of an accent, where were you born?"

"I was born in the United States, but moved here many years ago. I have lived in Israel most of my life."

A few more questions and, "Thank you so much for cooperating, we shall let him continue."

"Wow," I thought, "now *that* is serious security!"

Although my student was innocent, there were certain things that caught the attention of our security officers. He had been to Israel just a short time ago; why was he back so soon? In fact, they remembered him from his previous trip. Not only that, but they remembered who he traveled with last time and under what circumstance. Why weren't his previous travel companions with him? Why was he now traveling alone? There were legitimate answers to all these questions, but anything slightly out of the ordinary is noticed and warrants extra questioning. This is Israel, we take no chances.

I always tell my international Krav Maga guests, "As soon as you enter the EL AL terminal, you will already feel the Israeli atmosphere." As the EL AL advertisement says, "EL AL; The most at home in the world. EL AL is Israel."

Rome and Vienna, 1985

Thirteen years after the horrific "Lod Airport Massacre," on December 27, 1985, terrorists simultaneously attacked EL AL ticket counters at the Rome and Vienna airports. In Rome, four terrorists walked up to the EL AL ticket counter and opened fire with assault rifles and grenades. The terrorists killed sixteen people and injured ninety-nine others before three of them were killed and the fourth was captured by the police.

Minutes later in Vienna, Austria, using assault rifles and grenades, three terrorists killed three people and injured thirty-nine others as they were standing in line at the EL AL counter. Years later, on July 4, 2002, I would land at LAX airport in Los Angeles just two hours after a similar attack at the EL AL counter. That attack resulted in the death of two Israelis. A lone terrorist, an Egyptian, opened fire at the EL AL counter, killing the two Israelis, one of whom lived in my brother's community. The terrorist was shot and killed by Israeli security working for EL AL. All these events shocked us and shook our world. Years after the Holocaust in Europe it was clear to us that a Jew and an Israeli must still, always, be on guard.

When I visited Germany in 2010 to teach Krav Maga seminars, I paid close attention to the German airport security. The lines were long and the progress slow, unlike Israel where trained professionals know who to allow through and who to interrogate thus allowing a smooth and rapid check-in process. Again there was an obsession with checking hand luggage and not enough attention to the human element. Even though I was a foreigner, traveling on a foreign passport, not once did anyone ask me so much as a single question. Not once did I sense that anyone was actually looking at me. It seemed they actually made an effort to *avoid* eye contact.

The only exception was, of course, EL AL Israeli security. Upon reaching the EL AL counter I noticed Israeli security at work. The difference was quite obvious to me. I met a young German woman while waiting for the EL AL counter to open. The EL AL female officer, seeing us together, instructed us to go to a certain line. When I inquired in Hebrew why we were being sent to another line, the officer responded, "Oh, you are an Israeli, stay here on this line." She said she thought we were together, perhaps a couple. Seeing that my friend looked typically German, we had been sent to a different line. Now, she questioned me separately while my new friend was sent for more thorough questioning.

"How long have you two been together? Did she pack your bags for you?" I explained that I had known Tamina for about twenty-three minutes; that we met while waiting for the EL AL counter to open, and that, no, she did not pack my bags, she never even saw my bags; I never saw her before. I was passed along quickly and given a certain plastic tag identifying me as a low-risk traveler.

Later, as we went through security, my friend Tamina and another new friend, Claudia, were asked to step into a small room for further questioning and more thorough checking. I went through like I was old buddies with the staff. Clearly everything about me indicated that I was an Israeli very happy to be on my way home. My new friends had to first do some explaining; Tamina said she had friends in Israel, perhaps the officer would ask—Who were they? How does she know them? Claudia would be passing through Israel on the way to another country, spending only a few hours at Ben Gurion airport. Perhaps they would ask—Why only a few hours in Israel? and so forth. In fact their bags were checked carefully, a few key questions were asked and they were allowed to pass. Once again security involved personal interaction, eye contact, studying body language while engaged in conversation, and giving special attention to those who might raise some questions. This is the Israeli way, and it works. So, yes, we do profile, and we stay alive.

Embarrassing Questions

In this day and age, I find that people are often willing to put themselves at risk of personal danger rather than take the chance of offending a total stranger. Clearly tact is important, and respect and courtesy should be valued, but one should not shy away from questions that could uncover important information. In Israel, we learn that one should not be shy or bashful.

In Hebrew, the words for bashful and dehydrate are similar and rhyme, so the saying goes, "He who is bashful will dehydrate." The idea is also that one who is afraid to ask—will suffer the consequences. So we are not shy, we ask questions, even at the risk of offending someone. We are not as sensitive, or as "politically correct" as Americans.

Women are often embarrassed when asked, "Do you have an Arab boyfriend? Have you been spending time with Arabs while you were in Europe?" The questions are personal, embarrassing, intrusive and offensive, and not at all in keeping with today's "politically correct" approach. So what? People's lives are at stake. We know that terrorists will stop at nothing so we have little time for niceties.

On April 17, 1986, a pregnant Irish woman named Anne-Marie Murray made it past Heathrow airport security in London and was about to board an EL AL flight to Israel. Her bag had been checked by British airport security and passed inspection. During standard questioning by Israeli security officers, the Israeli officer became suspicious. "Her answers to our questions just didn't add up," recalled Pini Schiff.[13] She swore she was not given anything to carry on board. When the Israeli team inspected her bag they discovered seven kilos of explosives and a very sophisticated bomb. The detonator was hidden inside a calculator and was set to go off when the plane reached thirty-nine thousand feet. Murray had no idea the explosives were there. During the subsequent interrogation it was revealed that she had an Arab boyfriend, the father of her unborn child. He became her boyfriend only to gain her trust and use her as a human bomb, a martyr for Allah, without her even knowing. He was willing to blow up his "girlfriend" and their unborn baby. Her fiancé, Jordanian Nezar Hindawi, is now serving a forty-five-year sentence in England.

Israeli airport security has four levels. As you approach the entrance to the airport you will see two gates. They are manned by guards armed with M-16 rifles with their fingers on the trigger. These men are not only combat veterans, they are also trained security experts.

You will roll down your window for your first round of interrogation. "*Boker Tov*, Good Morning, where are you coming from?" They will listen to your voice and observe your facial expressions; they will look at your passengers. Any questionable behavior, any hesitation in your response, will warrant a further and more detailed inspection. The idea is to prevent a car carrying explosives or terrorists from entering the airport area.

The second level of security involves profiling the passengers. As you enter the airport terminal there will be some friendly uniformed individual, something like a server outside a nice restaurant. He will observe you as you walk in and might stop and ask you a question or two. He might ask to see your passport. He will write it down in his log book. Again, he is profiling and looking for clues.

Part two of the second level is more direct. Once you enter the line leading to your particular airline you will go through more formal questioning. The young security personnel will ask to see your passport and ask a few simple questions.

For most of us the questions, "Who packed your bags?", "Were your bags with you the entire time?", or "Did anyone give you a package to carry?" seem almost silly. We might ask ourselves, "Would a terrorist admit that someone gave him a package to carry on board the aircraft?" But the questions only seem silly because we do not understand their real intention. The young Israelis asking these questions are looking for clues, for body language, for specific indicators as to who will require further questioning. The body does not lie. They know what they are doing. Just as with Anne Murray in England, certain answers will indicate that more extensive questioning is required, and the Israelis always get their man, or woman.

"People think that profiling is old fashioned and invasive, but it saves the day. The Nigerian terrorist [Umar Farouk Abdulmutallab, who tried to blow up a Northwest Airlines plane over Detroit, December 2009] would have undergone comprehensive inspections at Ben Gurion airport, and without a doubt I can tell you the explosives he was carrying would have been discovered," says Pini Schiff of the airport security division at Ben Gurion Airport.[14] In the United States, it was clearly considered problematic to profile a young African. The result of this misguided policy, this liberal attitude, put all the passengers at risk.

We do not look for weapons first. We look for *terror suspects*, suspicious behavior, and anything out of the ordinary. It is like the difference between a loan officer at the bank who only looks at your financial record as compared to one who looks at you as a person and determines whether you as an individual are a good loan candidate. The Israeli security expert studies human behavior and looks for clues. The expert is constantly asking himself, "Could this person be a possible terrorist? Is it possible that a terrorist is using him?"

As a frequent traveler, and being in the personal security business myself, I have picked up some knowledge of what the experts are looking for. As one officer only half-jokingly said to me, "Don't reveal our secrets!" So I shall not, but I will say this: everything about a person reveals something about that person and his intentions. You can learn a great deal about a person by observing his appearance and his behavior. Anything, anything at all, that reveals potential danger, will be picked up by the Israeli experts and dealt with before the suspect has any clue that they are on to him. In Israel you are protected; someone is looking after you.

Arabs are singled out for extra stringent security, even respectable doctors and lawyers. "Even if he is a perfectly respectable lawyer or businessman, he doesn't know about the Arab taxi driver who handled his bags, and even if he thinks everyone who saw him off is all right, maybe his brother-in-law isn't as all right as he thinks."[15]

Do we profile? Of course! And we don't apologize for it. Our friends will understand while our enemies will be frustrated. A former airport security examiner was quoted in the *Jerusalem Post* saying that the ethnic profiling system, with all the purely personal profiling it entails, is legitimate and necessary because it accurately reflects the demographics of anti-Israel terror. It is an undeniable fact that a hijacker or bomber of an Israeli or Israel bound flight is extremely likely to be an Arab or Muslim, while the chance of his being a Jew is infinitesimal.[16]

Part three of the second level is the level you do not see, but it is there, and deadly. Throughout the airport, inside, outside, and all around, are plain clothed security. You will never guess who they are. They will appear as passengers just like you. But they are watching you, observing you, and should something look out of the ordinary they will arrange for you to be taken away rather swiftly. No one will even notice this. In the unlikely event of an actual attack; they will spring into action with deadly accuracy and eliminate the problem. Their training is based on past incidents, such as the Japanese terrorist attack in the old Lod airport, and an assessment of any possible scenarios that might potentially unfold.

The third level of security is the machines: CT scanners; metal detectors, and explosives detectors add an additional element, but they cannot replace human intelligence. We do not rely on machines. We rely on human judgment and human judgment involves profiling. The former airport security examiner said they were not terribly concerned about accidentally offending people and, "What was important was that the planes left on time and didn't get blown up."

Arabs and Muslims complain about being profiled, but Christian friends of Israel are more understanding. David Parsons of Jerusalem's Christian embassy, and a resident of Israel for a decade says, "I don't blame my government, I blame the terrorists." He and his pilgrims appreciate that they are flying in safety. More and more, as international terrorism spreads, our Christian friends appreciate our attitude toward terrorism.

The fourth level of security is on the plane itself. Armed Israeli agents are seated among the passengers, blending in. They have received special training to thwart hijacking and bombing attempts in mid-flight. Over the years Israel has developed advanced training for these agents using mock planes where agents practice with live fire in realistic scenario training.[17]

Protection of Human Life

Israeli airport security did not simply materialize out of nowhere. It was born out of necessity. El Al is considered by many to be the world's most secure airline, after its security protocols have foiled a number of attempted hijackings and terror attacks. The Israeli method has proven itself in the most important category—the protection of human life.

Airport security reflects the fundamentals of our military training as well. In the Israeli army each member of a unit is trained to be a leader. If a commander can no longer function, there is always another who can assume command. It is a nation of leaders, not followers. As Israeli Prime Minister Golda Meir said to American President Richard Nixon, "It is true that you are president of two hundred million citizens but I am prime minister of four million prime ministers."

Soldiers are taught to improvise, to make do with whatever is available, to adapt to their surroundings and survive. This translates into everyday life where no one is willing to be taken advantage of and no one will take "no" for an answer. Israelis typically try to figure a way out, a way to outsmart the system. That is how they are trained. You can drop Israelis anyplace and they will find a way to survive and thrive, on their own.

That is what happened in 1976, when an Air France flight, with many Israelis on board, was hijacked to faraway

Uganda. Israel had no contacts and no friends in Uganda. Another nation might have given up hope. Not Israel. They found a way to not only land a full commando unit, but passenger planes as well. They came home with nearly all the hijacked passengers. Tragically, one soldier was killed; Yonatan Netanyahu, brother of future Prime Minister Benjamin Netanyahu.

The Bible calls the nation of Israel a stiff-necked people, obstinate to the point of craziness. It can be frustrating and annoying at times, but it serves a purpose. That stubbornness has kept us alive as a people for close to two thousand years while exiled from our land without government or territory, discriminated against everywhere. We refuse to give up, we refuse to trust our enemy, we would rather resist. We have learned that there are few that we can trust, as the rabbis say, "respect him and suspect him." We have learned to take action rather than wait and see what fate has in store for us.

Survival

Israelis are known for their survival skills. Both on a physical and emotional level Israelis seem to have above average survival skills, almost as if it was a genetic adaptation. Whether caught in enemy crossfire, or stranded in a foreign country without documents or money, or facing economic collapse, Israelis seem to have a remarkable ability to remain calm, survive, and come out on top, often thriving. In a classic joke, an Israeli man is captured by wild African tribesman and taken away deep into the jungle. When the rescue team finally arrives, they find him running a successful business staffed by locals who have now learned to speak Hebrew.

Israeli search and rescue teams are known as among the best, if not *the* best, in the world. These teams are sent all over the world to assist in rescue efforts. What accounts for this incredible ability to survive? And how can we learn from it?

Part of the answer can be found in a deep-seated appreciation of human life. This core belief stems from biblical values, is codified in Jewish Rabbinic law, and is embodied in the spirit of the Israeli nation and in the values of the IDF. Unlike other ancient cultures, capital punishment was almost unheard of among the Hebrews. Most such laws "on the books" were meant only as warnings for the purpose of intimidation and deterrence. Everything was done to preserve human life. Nearly all divinely ordained biblical laws were permitted, in fact commanded, to be violated, in cases where necessary to preserve human life. If consuming forbidden products, such as pork, were the only way to survive, then one was commanded to do so rather than forfeit one's life.

A passenger who survived a six-week ordeal as a prisoner of the Popular Front for the Liberation of Palestine when his TWA flight was taken hostage, faced this very situation. After several days he was at the point of starvation and he faced this choice. It was either eat or die, as he wrote, "For the first and only time in my entire life I eat this forbidden food."

Human life transcends nearly all. If a Jew is held hostage and ransom is demanded, our rabbis permit us to sell holy objects, even a Torah scroll or a synagogue, in order to redeem the prisoner. The Rambam, Rabbi Moshe son of Maimon, writes, "There is no greater commandment than that of redeeming the prisoners...as they stand in danger of their lives, and one who turns his eye away transgresses the biblical command of 'Do not stand idly by when your fellow man is in danger,'[18] and 'Love thy neighbor as thyself,'[19] and 'You have no greater commandment than that of redeeming prisoners.'"[20]

Today, we see the same value for human life as Israel routinely exchanges one thousand Arab terrorists for a single Israeli soldier. The value of human life permeates our existence, as individuals and as a nation.

Israel is very reluctant to go to war. War means death. Most militaries have a concept of "acceptable losses," a number of soldiers one can afford to lose to achieve a certain military or political objective. In Israel, even one life is a tragic and unacceptable loss. As the Talmud says, "One who saves one life of Israel it is as if he saved an entire world."

Thus, it took eight years of constant bombardment of towns in southern Israel until Israel finally retaliated and attacked the Hamas terrorists in Gaza. In that conflict, as in all IDF operations, every effort was made to preserve not only the lives of Israeli soldiers, but also the lives of our enemies. As in all conflicts, Israel dropped leaflets in Arabic, warning the civilian population to evacuate before Israel attacked. This humanitarian measure, of course, takes away the essential element of a surprise attack.

Unlike Israel, our enemies do not value human life; they use the civilian population, families, women and children, as human weapons and shields. Their "fighters" hide among the civilian population and in times of trouble shed their military garb and mingle with the general population, putting everyone at risk.

With Israel's advanced modern weapons technology, the IDF was able to pinpoint the homes and families at risk. Israeli soldiers contacted each family and warned them in Arabic of the impending Israeli strike. This move reduces the effectiveness of the strike, taking away the element of surprise, but, it is done out of Jewish respect for human life.

My brother, Ethan, fought against a terrorist stronghold in Israel. From the IDF position, safely outside the Arab town, using advanced electronic maps, they were able to pinpoint the homes where key terrorists were hiding. The safest and easiest approach would have been to simply bomb those apartment buildings from a distance. No risk, no fuss, no mess. However that would cause the death of Arab civilians, noncombatants, the "human shields" of the terrorists. The IDF chose instead to go in on foot and fight house to house. Eleven reserve soldiers, men with families, were killed that day.

In another incident, the IDF had accidentally hit a water pipe, leaving the noncombatant population without running water. Israel sent in repairmen, under enemy fire, to fix the pipe. This deep seated appreciation of human life translates into an appreciation of one's own life. This produces a fierce desire to survive, to preserve one's own life.

International law experts said that the IDF went to "great and noble lengths" to avoid civilian casualties while fighting Hamas terrorists in Gaza in 2014, but warned the IDF is taking "many more precautions than are required." As a result, they feared that the IDF "is setting an unreasonable precedent for other democratic countries of the world who may also be fighting in asymmetric wars against brutal non-state actors who abuse these laws."[21]

Long Term Survival

The Jewish people are survivors. The Jews have a long history of oppression, persecution, and...survival. During the Passover *seder* each year, we say, "In every single generation there arises an enemy who wishes to destroy us, but the Holy One, blessed be He, saves us from their hands."[22]

"The People That Won't Die"
We are the people that won't die.
We've got a vision in our eyes and a mission in our souls,
to return to the days of old,
to our home in Israel.

Two thousand years I wandered, without a place to call my own.
As much as I tried, I could not call it home.

I fought for every nation and I died for every land,
but in my hour of need no one lent a helping hand.

We were burnt, we were gassed, we were shot at
Babi Yar
Numbers on our forearms, covered with scars
and yet we continue to hold our heads up high,
eyes wide open, facing the clear blue sky.

The Jewish people are survivors. The Jews have a long history of oppression, persecution, and...survival. During the Passover *seder* each year, we say, "In every single generation there arises an enemy who wishes to destroy us, but the Holy One, blessed be He, saves us from their hands."[23]

Wandering the world for two thousand years, the Jew has learned to make lemonade out of lemons. At times he has sold his lemonade and made a profit, and has been criticized for doing so. He was denied citizenship, barred from owning land, kept out of professional guilds, denied entry to schools and colleges, deprived of natural rights and privileges, and all too often expelled from lands he called home. And still the Jew adapted and survived.

Without a home or an army, without a government to stand up for his rights, without a church or a pope to plead his case, the Jew survived. The culmination of being hosted in other nations' lands was the Holocaust, the systematic murder of a people: genocide. With this the Jewish people faced the worst nightmare of human history.

And when it was all over, these dry bones, these tattered refugees and survivors, came home to Israel to be greeted by millions of Arabs who sought to finish what the Nazis had begun. Facing a harsh enemy and a harsh, neglected land, these survivors drained the swamps, fought off countless Arab invasions, and made the desert bloom. They created one of the greatest fighting forces on earth, and one of the world's most advanced hi-tech industries. These are the people who make up the nation of Israel. These people know how to survive.

Modern Day Application

There is an old saying, "Tough times never last; tough people do." It is true in life and it is true in combat and in a fight. The attack will eventually tire out; you simply have to outlast it passively, yet actively wait for your moment. For nearly two thousand years the Jewish people waited for their moment to return to Israel. While it may have been passive, it was also active. Hope was actively kept alive through prayer and study; small opportunities were seized and acted upon. Small groups did reach Israel, strengthening old communities.

The same idea applies to fighting. While fighting, I have often found myself in a bad position; an opponent pinning me down or choking me. Most times I did not have the ability to just throw off my opponent. I responded passively/actively. Holding on for dear life, I prevented the choke or arm bar from being applied, thwarting my opponent's efforts and conserving my energy. I bided my time. When my opponent began to tire and his hold on me weakened—I made my move and countered successfully.

The same applies in daily life. We are not always in a position to "counter" our life circumstances, but we can respond passively/actively by doing all we can, hanging tough, knowing that if we just hold on long enough, our moment will come. The rabbis say that in the end of days two angels will be holding a rope, and all of mankind will be holding on to this rope for dear life, for if one lets go he is doomed. "I am telling you this," the rabbi said, "so that you should remember to hold on tight, don't let go."

Minimizing Rather than Overreacting

When I began my Krav Maga training in Israel certain things became clear. There was a lot of full contact fighting, but there was no real dressing room, and for drinking water you had to go to the rest room. Clearly this was a no frills operation.

We were located right next to a hospital. Students joked that this location was chosen to accommodate the many students requiring medical care after getting hit. Our instructor himself was a combat medic and usually handled the injuries on his own, only rarely sending a student to the hospital.

When a student would get hurt, the instructor would look at the wound and say, "*Lo kara shum davar*" (nothing happened, this is no big deal). I figured, well this must be a minor injury. But then I saw some injuries that were clearly more serious and he still said, "Nothing happened, take it easy, it is a minor injury." Much later I figured out what was going on.

It was only when I observed a group of students from abroad, and saw their reaction, that I understood what he was doing. Our teacher, Itay, is a warrior, he has spent his entire life being a warrior. He has served as a combat medic and he knows that the worst possible response is overreaction. If you overreact you cause panic, you make the situation much worse than it is. What a warrior does is minimize the situation. Do not tell an injured man, "Oh my God! This looks terrible!" That alone can kill him. What you need to say is, "Nothing happened, no big deal, you will be fine." This will calm him and help the healing process. A warrior knows that he, and those around him, must remain calm. To overreact is to plant the seeds of disaster. You must always minimize any misfortune, get back on your feet and continue.

In fact, in the Bible it says that even in a most critical war, where all are required by law to serve, the cowardly are sent home, as to not cause their brothers' hearts to melt during combat. "Any man who is fearful and fainthearted let him go and return to his house, lest his brethren's heart melt like his heart."[24]

Attitude

There is a popular Hebrew expression: *yihiyh b'seder*—it will be OK. But *yihiyeh b'seder* is more than just "it will be OK," it is an attitude. It is a feeling that nothing will hold us back, no matter how bad things are, no matter how bleak, *yihiyeh b'seder*, it will be all right, you will see. Sitting on the Suez Canal, being bombarded by the Egyptians, but... *yihiyeh b'seder*, it will be OK, you will see.

And, *yihiyh b'seder* is related directly to *avarnu at Paroh, naavor gam et zeh*—we got through, (survived, outlasted) Pharaoh of Egypt, we will get through this as well. Soldiers sitting in Suez, Egypt, another cup of Turkish coffee, we got through pharaoh once before, we will get through this. It will be OK.

We had the Holocaust, the Spanish/Portuguese/Mexican...Inquisitions, the persecutions of ancient Egypt, the wars of 48, 56, 67, 70, 73, 82, 06, 14. No matter what happens, we survive.

This attitude permeates Israeli society, civilian and military. This attitude is not a simple matter, not just an easy going way of looking at things; it is an attitude of hope, of change. A man's physical body may be shattered, but his soul is intact. Israel may be bleeding, but its spirit strong. This is not the broken Jew of the exile, this is not a Jew who only grieves and hopes. This is the Jew of Israel, the Jew of hope, the Jew of redemption. No matter how bad things may appear we are, in fact, living in the best of times. We have witnessed the miracles return to Zion; we have witnessed the great victories and the revival of the Jewish people. We can cope with anything.

CHAPTER 2

A True People's Army

Biblical Origins

We are a warrior nation out of necessity. We are a small nation and very simply we need everyone, no one is dispensable. This concept goes way back to our earliest days. Long before the modern State of Israel came into being, the ancient people of Israel had already formulated, under God's direction, this warrior nation concept.

The idea was actually born in the Bible, the Torah, in the book of Bamidbar ("In the Desert" or "Numbers"). "From the age of twenty and upwards, all that are able to go forth in war in Israel, you [Moshe] and Aharon shall number them according to their units."[25] Here it is made clear that this is a national obligation, every man who is able to fight must be ready to do so.

Later, in Bamidbar 32, we read how the members of certain tribes were reluctant to serve, they did not want to cross over into Israel and fight, they wanted to stay where the land was good. "Now the children of Re'uven and the children of Gad had a very great multitude of cattle, and when they saw the land of Ya'azer and the land of Gilad, that, behold, the place was a place for cattle, the children of Gad and the children of Re'uven came and spoke to Moshe, and to Elazar the Cohen (Priest) and the presidents of the community, saying, 'thy servants have cattle...let this land be given to us for our cattle.'" They did not want to cross over the Jordan River, they wanted to stay put and not participate in the battles against the inhabitants of the land of Cana'an.

Moshe's answer is relevant even today, "And Moshe said...Shall your brethren go to war, and you shall sit here?" This answer echoes through the generations, "**Shall your brethren go forth to battle and you shall sit here!!**" We can still hear Moshe, Moses, today; this is a national effort and no one is exempt. Your personal philosophy is of no interest to us, all must serve; all have a responsibility to protect the nation.

Moshe further explains that the act of sitting out the war has a disheartening effect upon the warriors. Not only are you not serving, but you are causing harm to those who do. "And why do you dishearten the children of Yisrael from going over into the land which God has given them?"

Moshe refers to the unfaithful spies who told the people of Israel that the land was too heavily defended and would be impossible to conquer. He compares the current draft dodgers to those spies and refers to them as "a brood of sinful men" who "augmented the fierce anger of God." Upon hearing these powerful words from the great leader, the men of Re'uven and Gad change their attitude. The women and children and cattle will stay behind in the fertile land, but the men will go and fight alongside their brethren. "But we ourselves will go ready armed before the children of Yisrael until we have brought them to their place....We will not return to our houses until the children of Yisrael have inherited every man his inheritance."

"And Moshe said to them, 'If you will do this thing, if you will go armed before God to war, and will go all of you armed over the Jordan before God, until He has driven out His enemies before Him, and the land be subdued before God, then afterwards you shall return and be guiltless before God, and the land shall be your possession before God. But if you will not do so, behold, you have **transgressed against God**.'" The answer of the men of Re'uven and Gad was crystal clear. "We will pass over armed into the land of Cana'an."

War in Gaza with Hamas

A Nation of Warriors – Another Definition

As our ground forces entered Gaza during the war with Hamas, the idea of a "nation of warriors" once again emerged, reflected in the emotion-filled voice of the Minister of Defense and in the look of concern on the faces of the citizens of Israel. For us, deploying the military is not just a matter of "sending in the troops." The word *troops* sounds too impersonal, the word *troops* has no personality.

What we are really sending in are our children, nephews, neighbors, friends, husbands, colleagues, and students. For us it is not "the troops," it is Moshe, and David, Abraham and Jonathan; it is *real* people with names and personalities. We know their faces, their smiles, and their laughter.

There is not a home that is unaffected. If it is not your child that is sent in, then it is "all my friends' kids." It is the son of the guy at the desk next to you at work. It is the older brother of the boy whose *bar mitzvah* you just attended. It is the young man whose wedding is scheduled for next month. It is very close and personal.

Every single life is an entire world to us. Every single life is precious. As such, decisions to go to war are not taken lightly. We are not trigger happy. And still, we are a nation of warriors; us, our fathers and our mothers, our sons and our daughters. We do not have "acceptable losses," each loss is a major tragedy. We cry over each and every soldier, we pray for each and every soldier. Each one is an entire world to us. We want to know as much as we can about each one, each one is an individual, a precious gift.

A Japanese friend commented on how I always say "our army" even though I am no longer in the army. The comment surprised me. She explained that Japanese people do not identify as such with the army; it is not "their" army. For us, yes, it is very much "our" army. We speak in terms of *we* are going in, or, *we* are pulling out, *we* suffered no losses.

One of the most beautiful phrases, music to our ears, is when we hear on the radio, *"Kol kohotainu hazru be'shalom."* (All our forces have come home safely, in peace). I nearly get tears in my eyes just thinking these words. When we hear those words, all our emotions come out, and we say...Thank God!!! Thank God everyone is home safe, today no mothers will cry, today no wives will mourn, today no children will become orphans, today no fathers will recite the prayer for the dead, Today we have peace...if only for a day.

A recent first time visitor from Eastern Europe commented to me how surprised he was to be constantly surrounded by guns and soldiers; in the streets of Jerusalem, on the bus, in restaurants, everywhere. He was not prepared for it, but this is *our* reality.

A People's Army From the Start

The Israeli army has been a people's army from the very beginning. There was no draft, just a bunch of people who said, "If no one fought, everyone would die."[26]

One retired professor who fought in 1948 recently said that despite his preference for books, he chose to fight, "It was natural, it was necessary."[27] Two generations later, that professor's grandson is about to be drafted. Now as then, he points out, "There is no questioning military obligations."

The IDF is composed of three groups: a small number of professional career soldiers and officers, young men and women serving their compulsory military service, and the reserves. The uniqueness of a people's army is expressed and manifested in Israeli society in three ways.

1. Compulsory Military Service

Every man or woman who turns eighteen years old receives a draft notice, and by law, must report to the draft board. Beginning in 2015, men will serve for thirty-two months, women for twenty four months. At the conclusion of their service some will be offered jobs in the standing army, known as *Tzva Keva*. The rest will be discharged and will be part of the reserves.

2. Obligatory Reserve Duty

Israel is a small country, always in great danger. Our economy cannot afford to sustain a large standing army even though it needs one. The unique solution is the reserve system where nearly the entire nation takes part in its defense, a true people's army as envisioned by the American founding fathers in the 1770s. At the time, Americans feared a large standing army. They were concerned that it would lead to centralized power and tyranny. They had fought the British to escape just such a system. They wanted the power to remain with the people, and, in times of need, the people would defend democracy and freedom.

There were problems with the people's army from the beginning. Although at the time many Americans owned guns and knew how to use them, serving as part of an army was a whole different ball game. General Washington was constantly frustrated by the different mentalities—the New Englanders were very different from the Virginians, the mountain people were different from the city folk. He had a rough time disciplining them to work as a single force. It is an indication of his brilliance, and fervent patriotism, that he succeeded. When the war ended the men went home, back to their farms. There was no reserve system and no follow-up training.

In the period following the Revolutionary War of Independence there was a great debate in America—some favored maintaining a large standing army to protect the newfound freedom while others feared it would become an instrument of tyranny. For the first hundred years or so of American history, the peacetime army remained very small—just big enough to fight the Indians and enforce laws.

In times of war, men were drafted and trained. However once the conflict was over, a familiar pattern developed—the great army that had saved the nation was rapidly demobilized. The people were tired of war and the soldiers went home, leaving only a skeleton force.

When the South seceded in 1861, the United States army consisted of sixteen thousand soldiers. It was a tiny regular army backed up by local militias. There was no reserve force. With the outbreak of the war, men were recruited and trained. Three million men fought in the Civil War, but once the war was over the army and navy were demobilized. The army was left with only twenty-five thousand soldiers while the navy was reduced from nearly seven hundred ships to forty-eight. Once the conflict was over, the great army that had saved the nation was rapidly demobilized, again leaving only a skeleton force.

Eventually the standing army theory prevailed. The United States realized it could not depend on untrained militia; it was simply impractical to expect ordinary citizens to fill the role of professional soldiers. Israel has accomplished just that.

Ordinary Israeli citizens are trained warriors. The standing army is small, but in times of danger it quickly expands, by the rapid mobilization of the reserves, to more than a million and a half well-trained fighting men. Wars in Israel are generally short; they begin suddenly and are over in a matter of weeks. These are not conflicts like the Civil War or the World Wars that last for years and allow time to build up an army. Our army has to be ready for action at all times. In times of war, reserve soldiers make up eighty percent of the ranks.

In 1967, Israel was attacked in the south by Egypt, in the east by Jordan, and in the north by Syria. Other Arab armies sent units to help with the attack. These were professional armies trained and equipped by the Soviet Union. In response, Israel called up the reserves. Universities emptied. Men and women left their jobs. Six days later—it was all over. Israel defeated the combined Arab armies and was on its way to capture all the Arab capital cities when a ceasefire was arranged.

The battle for Jerusalem was particularly difficult. The Israeli forces avoided using heavy artillery in order to spare the ancient holy sites. They avoided harming sites holy not only to Jews, but also sites of historical and religious significance to Christians and Muslims. This made the soldiers' advance very precarious. The Jordanian Legion, Jordan's crack troops, defended the ancient walled city. Shimon Cahaner was the commander of a paratroopers unit that was among the first group of soldiers to break into the Old City of Jerusalem. He recalls, "The Jordanians fought hard. The fighting in the narrow alleyways there is etched on my mind. We lost twenty-eight of our battalion in the first two days. They were all reservists with families. It was a mixture of euphoria and sadness."[28] Once again the heroes were ordinary people. Cahaner himself is something of a legend, but balks at the idea that he is a hero.

In the Second Lebanon War, the IDF reported one hundred percent enlistment among the reserve soldiers. The secret is in a nation of reserve soldiers who are trained, motivated, and instantly available.

Upon completion of compulsory service, discharged soldiers automatically join the reserves and can be called up for active duty anywhere from thirty to forty-five days each year—longer in cases of war or emergency. Most will be part of the reserves until their forty-fifth birthday. In most cases, they will serve in the same unit as they did during their compulsory service, and, with the same people. Serving with the same group of guys for so many years creates a special bond. Women with specialized training, such as doctors or technicians, now also serve in the reserves.

3. The Universality of Service

The military becomes a common experience that bonds and connects people from different walks of life and diverse cultural backgrounds. Just as in the martial arts, a high priced lawyer might train and become friends with a construction worker. Due to the military, nearly any two people will automatically have a shared experience and starting point for conversation. Military service is considered essential for anyone who wants to integrate into Israeli society. I know this first hand.

My first day at the base, I arrived early and was told to wait in the dining room. I bumped into an old friend, Tzviyedka. She was born in Russia, moved to the United States as a teenager and now was here in Israel serving with the paratroopers. She had moved up the ranks and, in fact, was in charge of our group. Her diverse background, fluency in three languages, and fervent desire to serve, were typical of the people I would meet.

Soon the rest of my group arrived, one hundred eighty-three men in all. We were all "late joiners," immigrants well past the age of eighteen. There were seven of us from the United States and Canada, about six Spanish speakers from South America, a bunch of Ethiopians, a truckload of Russian speakers, one guy from Turkey, two guys from India, and one fellow from the Republic of Ghana! Our commanders were nineteen-year-old Israelis. Somehow we would have to coalesce into one coherent unit. I thought to myself, "This would not be easy." And yet, this was the story of Israeli society. I did not envy our commanders. Younger recruits are easier to mold. In any event, at least their commanders are a full year or two older than the recruits and have a sense of authority.

But age is really not a factor, nor is social or economic standing. They say Israel is the only country in the world where reservists are bossed around and commanded by officers, male and female, younger than their own children. Sometimes they are bossed around by people who had served with their children.

This is an accepted part of life. Whatever you are in your civilian life changes as soon as you put on your uniform, you are back to taking orders, cleaning a tank or the latrines, you are back to a different reality, a reality where we all must contribute to our national safety and nothing is more important.

In a sense it is a returning to your true self, the self you were before you became the CEO of a hi-tech company. Your childhood friend who served with you in a tank unit, and is now running a falafel stand, is once again your equal, he might drive the tank as you load it up. Your life might very well depend on him.

The army tries to break up existing cliques. To be effective, a combat unit must be like a family; brothers, regardless of background or native language. In the case of older recruits, like my group, this proved difficult. Each group kept to itself, spoke its own language, and shared newspapers and magazines in that language. The cultural difference between the Russians and the Ethiopians was particularly difficult to bridge.

Coming in speaking a dozen different languages, we were told that on base we were only to speak Hebrew. Nonetheless, I was often accidentally spoken to in semi-Russian. "*Kakdila shmira*?" (How was guard duty?) *Kakdila* is Russian for "how was," *shmira* is guard duty in Hebrew.

"Sorry, I don't speak Russian," I answered.

"Not at all?" asked Yivgeny.

The common goal of defending the country must unite us despite our vast differences in culture. The lack of knowledge of Hebrew proved to be a real obstacle in our training and led to many comical situations. On one occasion a Russian speaker demanded "*kavod*" (honor, in Hebrew), when he really meant to say "*kova*" (hat, in Hebrew). The commander gave him a whole lecture on how *kavod*, honor, respect, must be earned; you cannot just demand respect; you must earn it over time. The poor soldier, of course, had no idea what the commander was talking about. All he knew was that it was terribly hot and he still did not have a *kova* to protect him from the blistering heat.

On another occasion, when the latrines were being cleaned and were thus temporarily unavailable, our commander, Riki, told one of the Ethiopian guys to use the "*etz*" (Hebrew for tree) instead. The poor fellow thought she meant "*et*" (Hebrew for pen). He took his pen out from his pocket and asked, "But how?"

In the army, you will see people from all sorts of backgrounds, in every sense of the word. Not only is nearly every ethnic and skin color represented, but every type of person as well. You will see Olympic athletes and top scholars alongside the special needs individuals as well as "troubled youth."

Special Needs

For an Israeli, service in the IDF is part of one's self-esteem, a feeling that you are contributing to society, you are part of society and you are "just like everybody else." You have served—where and how long is secondary. In March 2009, for the first time, five men and women with special needs, two of them with Down Syndrome, were accepted into the army. For them it was the "fulfillment of a dream." Until then many special needs individuals had volunteered, but being a real soldier brought them great pride.

"I feel very happy about my enlistment," one new soldier explained just before beginning the enlistment process. "I want to see my uniform already." He can hardly hide his excitement, which is evident even in his clothing choice—army style camouflage pants and a shirt that features the Border Police logo. "Now I finally change from a volunteer into a soldier. Since I was eighteen, I've been dreaming of enlisting, and now my dream is finally coming true," he boasts.

During the emotional event at the Induction Center, the enlistees were accompanied by their friends from the unit who worked with them throughout the past year. "They came to the unit before I got drafted, and at the beginning I was very surprised to meet them," remembers Private Karin Lovkovski, "but we connected very fast—we have a lot of fun with them and they are amazing people. We all work at similar tasks, and apart from the fact that until now they did not have soldier ID cards and identification tags, they have been soldiers just like us."[29]

The army finds each person a job they can handle and perform with dignity. Uri, an autistic young man, also wanted to serve in the army. He served for over a year working in the laundry department and other jobs. He had the honor of wearing the uniform of the armed forces of Israel, and like others his age, he could feel the pride of serving his country. Truly this is an army of *all* of its people.

Troubled Youth

For some, the military experience will be the first time in years that they are in a structured framework. For others, it will be their last chance for a future in society.

An Israeli documentary, "Yes, Miss Commander," brought to attention the amazing work being done by a group of young women at the *Havat HaShomer* (Ranch of the Protector) military base in Northern Israel. We see here the kind of youth one normally tries to avoid, an issue we prefer not to deal with. But these people are also part of our society. "I won't put on the uniform. It's my father's grave," shouts one angry young man. Others fought, swore, and disobeyed the commander's orders. But the patient commanders do not give up.

These boys are called "Raful's boys" in honor of former IDF Chief of General Staff, Lt-Gen. Rafael Eitan, known affectionately as Raful. He founded this program thirty years ago. His mission was to bring young soldiers who cannot seem to survive in society, into the army. The military training and discipline will hopefully turn them into productive citizens. These youths all come from disadvantaged homes, difficult backgrounds, and usually have a criminal record. Most have little hope of fitting in with society. Often this is their last chance before a life of crime.

Havat HaShomer has more than four hundred young men. They are divided into groups of one hundred, each led by a female commander. Many of the youth have no parents, or have parents in prison. Most of these young men have dropped out of school long ago, at an early age. Base commander, Raz Karny, said, "I hear stories from these soldiers, where I sometimes have to pinch myself to recognize they are real. I do not believe they are bad people. These are people who do bad things. You cannot blame a boy who is hit by his father from the age of five, or a boy who searches for food in the garbage."[30]

This is their chance, their opportunity to reform, to change the way they lead their lives. A recent graduate of the program went on to become a paratrooper. At the paratrooper graduation ceremony he stood with another young man, who just happened to be the son of Israeli politician, Tzipi Livini. This is Israel, where two young men from such different backgrounds can stand side by side at a graduation ceremony.

The female commanders show a deep concern for all "their" soldiers. "These strong women are the best found in Israel." They are with the soldiers every day and they are committed to helping them. "You don't understand how intense it is until you get here," says Commander Noa Levitt, twenty-one years old. "Your soldiers become a real part of your life, they become you—you become them"[31]

Some people wonder how wise it is to invest in these young men, but the guiding principle is embodied in the words of Israel's first Prime Minister, David Ben-Gurion, "The army is not just to guard our country's walls; it is also for the continuity of future generations."

The *Hesder Yeshiva*, Scholars and Warriors

What is a *yeshiva*? The word *yeshiva* is Hebrew for "sit." The institution known throughout Jewish history as *yeshiva* is a place where Jews sit and study the book. Which book? The book they study is the Bible (Torah) and its commentaries, in particular the Talmud.

The Talmud is a commentary on the Bible, but it is more than that, it is five hundred years of passionate Jewish debate, discussion, and argument on every possible topic of relevance to the Jewish people. It is law, folklore, magic, stories, and mind sharpening dialogue about every topic from the meaning of existence to the details of a marriage contract. It is Jewish life. It is from the Talmud that a Jew learns how to live as a Jew; it is from these ancient teachings that we derive our strength and inspiration.

With the establishment of the State of Israel in 1948, many new voices were heard; they felt it was time for the Jewish people to put down "The Book" and pick up the gun. Others felt that only through prayer and study would our ultimate salvation be achieved. We must abandon all such nonsense, they said, forget politics and guns, and patiently wait for the Messiah. Along came a third approach—combine obligatory military service with traditional religious studies.

This arrangement became known as *hesder*, Hebrew for "arrangement." Instead of serving three years, ages eighteen to twenty-one, in the IDF, the boys would join the *yeshiva* and study for five years. During that time, they would also serve in the IDF. After about a year and a half of study, the young men, as a group, join the IDF and serve for about nine months. During the next few years, they alternate between military training and religious studies.

The result has proven very successful. The *hesder* soldiers are among the most motivated in the country. Their religious beliefs and training, the idealist nature of these institutions, and their group cohesiveness, produce a highly motivated soldier willing to go to the greatest lengths to protect and defend his people.

Many commanders hope to be assigned to such groups, as the groups' reputations precede them as the most motivated and self-sacrificing. My nephew's commander said he had never seen anything like it; everyone was volunteering for extra tasks, each was willing to take the burden off the other, each saw the service as fulfilling a divine commandment. He himself had come from a very non-religious background and was unfamiliar with the sense of duty and commitment exhibited by these young men. His service with them deeply moved him. Sadly, this young commander was killed during the Second Lebanon War.

The *hesder* boys, as they are known, also take time for community involvement—collecting food for the needy and distributing it, tutoring disadvantaged students, and adding to the quality of life in the community. In my community of Maaleh Adumim, on the holiday known as *Simhat Torah*, a most joyous holiday marking the completion of the reading of the five books of Moses, the *hesder* boys go from synagogue to synagogue, dancing with the Torah and adding joy to each and every congregation.

Nearly all *hesder* students serve in combat units. There are about forty *hesder yeshiva* institutions in Israel, with about thirteen hundred student/soldiers at any given time. At the end of the five years of the *hesder* program, some soldiers choose to continue their military service. Many have become high ranking officers. As a result, we have rabbis who are also top military commanders—very reminiscent of biblical days. Like Moses, Joshua, and David, these men are steeped in faith and in the art of warfare. They lead their troops in combat and in prayer. I am proud that my three nephews all serve in *hesder* units.

Religious Observance

Many of Israel's top combat troops are devoutly religious Jews. Much preparation and attention is devoted to how to observe Jewish law and tradition in difficult combat and military situations. Some students devote a full year of their pre-army time to prepare for their service. They attend special institutions that deal with how to observe Jewish law in combat, and how to cope with morally challenging issues.

My nephew, Arie, and his unit had to deal with the question of how to carry their *teffilin* into the combat zone in Lebanon. *Teffilin*, or phylacteries, are the square boxes containing scripture passages that Jewish men wear during weekday prayers, as prescribed in the Bible—but these cannot be carried on *Shabbat* (the Sabbath). The soldiers had to consult with their rabbis as to how to handle this situation.

Just think about how different this is from combat units in other countries. They were going into battle, going to engage the notorious Hizbullah terrorists, their lives were on the line, and they were concerned with the minutiae of religious observance. They were concerned with serving God with purity. God is part of every daily action.

During Operation Cast Lead in the Gaza Strip, another religious question came up. According to biblical law, a newly wedded man is exempt from military service for one year, to celebrate life with his new wife and make her happy, unless it is a war of survival. "When a man takes a woman in marriage, he will be exempt from military service for one year...so that he may rejoice in his house with his wife whom he married."[32] The Talmud clarifies this exemption and limits it, "In a war which is a *mitzvah* (commandment, that is to say this war is a matter of survival) all go out to fight, even a groom." The great scholar Maimonides writes, "Let him lean on the God of Israel...let him risk his life and not fear or be scared, and let him not think of his wife... but wipe them from his memory and focus only on war."[33]

Such a case arose during the Gaza war. Lt. Aharon Karov, twenty-two years old and son of Rabbi Ze'ev Karov, married his "heart's desire." Aharon Karov served as commander in the elite paratroopers unit. The day after his wedding he was called into action. He had been enjoying his first breakfast with his new wife when his commander called. "We planned to have a relaxed breakfast together and to open the wedding gifts, when Aharon's commander called," his wife said. "I was naïve enough to think that he called to congratulate him. In my worst dreams I could not imagine he would be called up for reserve service a day after our wedding, but I am trying to be strong. Ultimately we are at war and the people of Israel need us now, so we must sacrifice our personal life for now."[34] Much religious debate went on; the commandment of making your wife happy was considered versus the commandment to fight for the country, all factors were carefully weighed. It was a religious matter.

The Yom Kippur War of 1973 stretched into the holiday of *Sukkoth*, the Feast of Tabernacles. Yoel Bin Nun, the future Rabbi Yoel Bin Nun, found himself in the Sinai desert, but without a *sukkah*. A *sukkah* is the small hut that Jews erect for the holiday of *Sukkoth* (plural of *sukkah*, hut). These *Sukkoth* huts, are to mark the period of the exodus from Egypt, God's watching over the nation of Israel during its wanderings in the desert. It is also to symbolize how all life is fragile, thus we leave our strong homes for the fragile huts.

To be in the Sinai desert, where this holiday originated, and not to erect a *sukkah*, was too much for the young soldier. He was in a foxhole, but decided he could turn that into a *sukkah*. He knew the exact laws, found some makeshift materials and turned his foxhole into a *sukkah*, symbolizing God's watching over Israel. Once it was complete he recited the traditional blessing, "Blessed are You our God, king of the universe who has sanctified us with His commandments and commanded us to dwell in the *sukkah*."

National Security Comes Before Personal Happiness

After consulting with the rabbis and the holy texts, Karov returned to his unit. He and his troops were among the first to enter Gaza, an operation essential for the defense of Israel. His wife supported his decision to go into combat one hundred percent. She told the press that national security comes before personal happiness. One week later she sent him a note, "I am with you from afar; I strengthen, support and pray for you. I believe in your decision to go to the battle for the sake of the people of Israel, a day after our wedding. Take care of yourself and your soldiers."

A week later, Karov was critically wounded by an explosion in a booby-trapped house. He was flown in a military helicopter from the battlefield directly to the hospital. At first look, the doctors did not know how he would ever recover as he suffered severe wounds to the head. Against all odds, Karov regained consciousness after a few days. A few weeks later he was walking. Doctors consider it a miracle, although he still had a long way to go. When his trainees finished their course and were awarded their pins (of their unit), Karov was there to participate in the ceremony. For Aharon Karov and others like him, ancient religious texts and rabbinic rulings are as relevant to the battlefield as are the latest advances in military hardware.

At any military camp, you will see soldiers draped in their prayer shawls, their *tallith*, and holding a prayer book in their hands. These are not hired killers or Spartan warriors, they are religious men fulfilling the word of God and fighting for a worthy cause, a cause they believe in with complete and total faith. Military service is a religious duty, dating back to the days of Moses and Aharon.[35]

Special Protection, Prayer and Ritual Observance

They say there are no atheists in foxholes. That is particularly true in Israel. During one of the wars in Gaza, religious faith was integral to many soldiers' morale. A special hotline was started where soldiers called in and gave their names. They were matched up with a noncombatant who prayed for them on an individual basis. There were many thousands of requests, both from religiously observant soldiers and from "secular" soldiers. "Just the other day an entire battalion of soldiers, just about to enter Gaza, gave us all of their names.

They passed the phone from one to the other, secular and religious—not one of them refused."[36]

During the fighting, an IDF rabbi noticed there was a tremendous thirst for "anything spiritual." The rabbi also said that more than fifteen hundred sets of *tzitzit*, the four-cornered fringed garment worn by religious men under their shirts, had been distributed to soldiers "who want the spiritual protection of being wrapped in holiness. *Tzitzit* are a heavenly 'flak jacket,'" the rabbi commented.[37] The obligation for Jewish men to wear the fringed garment dates back to biblical days. "And God spoke to Moshe saying, 'Speak to the children of Israel, and bid them that they make them fringes in the corners of their garments throughout their generations...'"[38]

Many soldiers also carry small copies of the book of Psalms, written by King David and viewed as providing special protection in times of danger. Rabbis regularly visit the front lines to provide spiritual guidance and inspiration.

Civilians and Warriors

In most societies, there are civilians and there are professional warriors. The two groups are very different, have different views of society, war, and lifestyle. If you were to ask a Vietnam veteran and some other "ordinary" citizen to describe the Vietnam War, it would probably sound like two totally different wars; each one's interpretation might be unacceptable, even incomprehensible, to the other. One might describe "a just, moral, patriotic war that we nearly won. We were over there fighting for democracy, assisting our allies and fulfilling America's role in the world." The other group might describe "a disaster, a place we had no right to be, violations of human rights, and horrific war crimes."

The two classes would have different historical memories, read different books, and in many ways speak a different language. Even their physical appearances would often be different; a muscular fellow, short hair, tattoo, standing erect, and answering with a loud and clear "Sir!" He would speak of "service and devotion, the good old USA, and our role in the world."

Some civilians, the non-warriors, might lack the military bearing of the warriors, have a more casual attitude about them, and might speak of "corrupt governments duping the public into pointless wars." There may be a distinct lack of respect for those who serve the nation. Mostly, they seem to lack an understanding and appreciation of what it takes to be a warrior and why without warriors we would all be doomed.

In Israel, these distinctions hardly exist, if at all—almost everyone serves. If you have not been in combat then your brother, father, cousin, neighbor or friend was, and you have lived it through them. During your military service you would have been taught "combat legacy," the history of Israeli wars, stories of individual bravery, and how one person can make a significant difference.

It is a very small country and the enemy and the threat are real and close by. There are still some who manage to hide from the truth, but few can claim ignorance of the precarious reality of our situation. As one expert said, "I don't think we have two groups, the uninitiated civilians, nor the professional warrior class; we only have the citizen warrior class."

Appreciation of Service

The universality of service leads to an understanding of what others have gone through, and an appreciation for their sacrifice and experience. It is said that more than wealth or power a person wants recognition; to be appreciated. No money can buy that, but service to your people can.

It is difficult indeed to appreciate another man's pain or sacrifice. I like to use the boxing analogy.

A few buddies are sitting on the couch watching a professional boxing match on TV. It could be the heavyweight championship. By the tenth round, the fighters look like a swift wind could knock them off their feet. The buddies are relaxing on the couch, eating pizza and guzzling beer and shouting at the fighters on TV, "You bum, stand up and fight, my grandmother fights better than that!" Of course, our beer drinking fan has never been in such a fight. If he had, he would not be shouting those rude insults. He does not seem to realize that he is watching top athletes who have trained long and hard for this bout, that they are giving their all.

Having fought myself, I can testify that after a few rounds of fighting, and of getting hit hard, it takes superhuman will power just to stand and continue. The urge to stop is overwhelming. Like the song, "Burning Heart" in the Rocky films, "Though his body says stop, His spirit cries—never!"[39]

Our pizza-eating fans on the couch have no clue what these fighters are going through. They do not have the background to understand and appreciate what fighting at this level is like. They have not earned the *right* to criticize.

When I test students for rank, and I watch them get punched, kicked, flipped, and bent, I say to them, "The only reason I can stand here and judge you is because I have experienced every one of those blows myself. I can *feel* your pain. I can appreciate what you are going through."

In the United States, when the boys came home from Vietnam, after living through the fires of hell and watching their buddies die, they were greeted with a clear lack of appreciation by the American public. The "fans" back home, did not understand what the soldiers had endured. They did not understand how in war sometimes civilians must die. They did not understand how when fighting in hell sometimes you have to make split second decisions or else you and your men might die.

They did not put themselves in these warriors' boots—tired, fatigued, scarred and scared, living from day to day never knowing if you or the guy next to you will see the morrow—and yet they criticized. The privilege to criticize must be earned. In a warrior society it is earned.

When my nephew, Arie, came home from the war in Lebanon, the one thing that hurt him was when some people questioned the need for certain battles. It is the right of the citizen to question, but it is his obligation to show respect for those who put their lives on the line to protect him. To question—yes! But first show respect; honor the dead, help the wounded, comfort the mourners, rehabilitate the veterans. This is our obligation.

In Israel, the situation is somewhat different. Almost everyone has served, many have seen combat. Almost everyone knows someone who sacrificed his life. We are more sensitive and respectful.

In the United States, Memorial Day is a day off; a vacation day for most of the population, barbecue and fun. Only a relatively small percentage of the population mourns and visits the graves of their loved ones who died in combat. In Israel, this would be unthinkable, a complete social disgrace. The TV and radio programs are totally devoted to mourning and memorials, only sad songs are played, only memorial programs are broadcasted; the national mood is somber. It is a national pain. We appreciate our warriors; they are the backbone of our society. We stop our cars to give them a ride, we stop at roadblocks to offer them a drink or a snack; we include them in our thoughts and in our prayers.

I was on my way home for my first weekend of leave from the IDF. I got off at the Central Bus Station in Jerusalem. The place was crowded as it always is on Fridays. A young girl approached me, *"Chayal,"* (soldier) she said, and she handed me a flower. This is Israel.

Vietnam Memorial in Washington, D.C.

Chayal – Soldier

Every Hebrew word consists of a three letter source. Whether the word is long or short, it always stems from three "root" letters that will determine all the variations and conjugations of the word. From these three letters, one can compose many related words. This academic linguistic study can shed some light on the true, oftentimes hidden, meaning of a word.

The Hebrew word for soldier is *chayal* (ha-yal) and consists of the root letters of *chet* (het), *yod* (y), and *lamed* (l). These letters can also form the word *chail* which means "military force," as in *chail Par'o*, "the military force of pharaoh." Today this word is used for military branches as in *chail raglim* (infantry) or *chail avir* (air force). Pronounced slightly differently, these three letters are a different word, *cha-yil*, which means "valor," as in "A woman of valor, who shall find"[40] or, "Choose ye men of valor."[41]

If one has done a super act, an act of great altruism, both the biblical and modern Hebrew expression is "he has done *chayil*" (he has done a great and noble act), in other words he has truly outdone himself for the benefit of others.

The single word "soldier" (*chayal*) combines and includes all these various meanings. A *chayal* is a force, both physically and morally. A *chayal* represents self-sacrifice, valor, and altruism. The word is deep in spiritual and historical meaning, as is the nation of Israel itself.

I will never forget the first time someone called me *chayal*. It was my first day in the IDF, we had just been issued our uniforms, but still had to go through a battery of medical procedures, X rays, and inoculations. I was standing in a crowd when a female soldier called out to me, "*Chayal*!" Strange, but somehow I knew she was referring to me even though with that "title" she could have been referring to any individual on the entire base. With that one word I felt I had just been awarded the greatest title, the greatest honor of my life. I already had earned several college degrees and martial arts ranks, yet with that one word, *chayal*, I felt the greatest honor. I felt I had joined the ranks of the long line of Hebrew warriors dating back to Abraham, Joshua, Samson, and King David. With that one word, I felt I was truly part of Israel.

The young girl came up to me at the bus station, handed me a single flower, smiled, and finished her sentence, "*Chayal, todah*," (Soldier, thank you). This girl and her friends spent their free time handing out flowers to soldiers—flowers and smiles. In the United States, in the 1960s, hippies also handed out flowers to soldiers—they put them in the barrels of their guns, but not in gratitude. That was a sign of protest, of disapproval, a way of saying, "you shame us; we protest your violent actions in Vietnam."

In Jerusalem, these young, sweet girls greet soldiers at the bus station with a single flower. "This single flower is my sign of appreciation to you. Thank you for protecting me; I want you to know that every single one of us appreciates every single one of you. From my heart to yours, here is a single flower." One smile produces another. A single flower, on a busy Friday afternoon as the Sabbath was approaching, expressed all the beauty of Israeli society.

Mount Herzl, Jerusalem

Perhaps no place tells Israel's story better than Mount Herzl, for it is those who rest there that have paid the highest price for our independence. It is a national cemetery, divided into two sections which are interconnected. One section is for key political figures in Israel's history; Dr. Theodor Herzl, Ze'ev Jabotinsky, Golda Meir, and many others. The other section is a military cemetery; soldiers killed in combat and in the line of duty, but there is more, much more.

Interspersed among the many graves are monuments. There is a huge monument to the two hundred fifty thousand Jewish soldiers who died in combat fighting for the Soviet Red Army against the Nazis. Of course they are not buried there, next to this monument there is not a single grave, but they are remembered. They died abroad, fighting for a foreign army, but yet they are given recognition here, in Jerusalem. They are recognized because some say that the Jews did not fight for themselves, but only waited to be rescued by others. In fact, over one and a half million Jews fought as part of the allied armies, with many casualties and many POWs. About five hundred thousand Soviet Jews fought the Nazis and close to two hundred fifty thousand fell in combat. In Jerusalem, at Mount Herzl, these warriors are remembered and honored. Their heroism and sacrifice is part of the story of Israel. Here they shall not be forgotten. To be a Jew is to remember.

There is also a monument honoring the many thousands of Jews from the Land of Israel who volunteered for World War Two in Europe. They joined the British army, left the security of the Land of Israel and fought on European soil, defeating the Nazis in several key battles and contributing to the war effort. They had their own unit, a unit from the Land of Israel with a Star of David. When the downtrodden and victimized Jews of Europe saw these Israeli soldiers they could hardly believe their eyes; Jewish soldiers from the Land of Israel fighting the Nazis! In Israel these brave soldiers are remembered.

Israel honors those warriors who fell before the official establishment of the state; none are forgotten. Among those buried are members of Nili, a pro-British spy network that operated during World War One. These were Israelis under Turkish rule providing information to the British. Their contribution was significant to the British conquest of Israel, ending four hundred years of Turkish rule and helping turn the tide against the Muslim empire. Most of the members of Nili were caught and killed by the Turks. They now lie in Mount Herzl with full military honors. They are remembered.

Here too are members of the pre-state militias; the *Haganah*, *Etzel* (*Irgun*) and *Lehi*. All these warriors are interned and honored as equal members of the Israeli fighting forces. They are remembered.

During World War Two, a group of Israelis parachuted into Eastern Europe to try to save the remnants of the Jewish community. They were all caught and murdered. Some of their bodies were never found; they are marked here with tombstones. Here they are recognized as soldiers of Israel, as freedom fighters and warriors. They too are remembered.

Mount Herzl also honors and remembers others who are part of the story of Israel. Many Jews tried to escape

Europe, but all they could find were old, unseaworthy ships. Some of those sank with their passengers. The names of the passengers are engraved in stone at Mount Herzl, though their bodies disintegrated at the bottom of the ocean. Alone at sea, escaping a horrible past, they yearned for Israel and dreamed of "being a free people in our own land." Instead they found tragedy at sea as families, communities, drowned together. Their names live on, each one carved individually in stone. Their names and their heroic efforts to join the community in Israel are remembered and honored.

Grave of Chana Szenes, born in Hungary, immigrated to Israel, parachuted back into Europe to try to save the Jews. She was caught and executed. She is buried at Mount Herzl.

Mount Herzl added a new monument, a stone wall on which hundreds of names are engraved. These are the victims of modern Arab terrorism. When Israel was established, the Arab nations put aside their differences and united to put an end to Jewish independence. Despite their overwhelming numerical superiority, unlimited resources, and international support; they lost every war. Yet their efforts continue to this day as they terrorize the population of Israel. The stones and the names engraved on them are the innocent civilians killed by suicide bombers, stabbings, drive-by shootings, kidnappings, and torture. They too are remembered and honored. They too are part of the struggle for the Land of Israel. For in Israel, just living is an act of defiance.

Tombstone of Daniel (Danny) Hass, American born, moved to Israel, killed during the First Lebanon War. Danny attended Bar Ilan University shortly before I did. His sister lives in my community and is distantly related to me. The stone reads, "Daniel (Danny) Hass son of Shoshana and Meir, born in the United States, moved to Israel in 1980, fell during the battle in Lebanon in Operation 'Peace for the Galilee'"

Walking around Mount Herzl you can learn the full history of the struggle for Jewish independence and the modern State of Israel, from the thinkers to the builders to the fighters, they all are there. There are sections devoted to each war; the War of Independence, Yom Kippur War, Six Day War, War of Attrition, Lebanon wars, and the Gaza wars.

At the request of bereaved parents, Israel's Defense Ministry agreed to recognize the 2014 Operation Protective Edge in Gaza as a full-scale war. Eli Ben-Shem, chairman of Yad Lebanim, an organization that supports bereaved families in cooperation with the Defense Ministry, said, "Because both the state and the army now officially recognize Protective Edge as a military campaign, an official memorial ceremony will be held each year on Mount Herzl, as is done for all Israeli military campaigns."[42]

Each grave is cared for; some have grass, some have flowers, some have photos and personal mementos of the fallen, rank, favorite objects, or items left by family and friends who deeply miss them. The tombstones are simple; military insignia, name, name by which the person was called, names of parents, country of birth, date of birth and death, place where the soldier fell. Their countries of birth include Israel, Poland, Yemen, Germany, Tunisia, Romania, Egypt, Holland, South Africa, Iraq, Russia, and the United States.

Kavod HaMet – **Respect for the Dead**

Jewish tradition and law place a great deal of emphasis on respect for the dead, for the human body. After every terrorist attack, teams of volunteers collect all possible human remains of the bodies. The goal is always to bring the body to a "Jewish burial." It is a great source of pain for a Jewish family to know that a loved one did not merit a proper Jewish burial. We go to great lengths to insure a proper burial. Israel has been known to trade prisoners of war, as well as terrorists, in exchange for bodies of Israeli soldiers. Everything is done to "bring the boys home," even if it is only their physical remains.

Israeli soldiers have been known to take risks to retrieve the bodies of fallen comrades, even under fire. One such story is told by former Knesset Member, Yoni Shtabon. Lebanon, Hell, July 26, 2006. The battle of Bint Jebil. Three revered commanders had already fallen in the terrible battle. Commanders Roei Klein, Alex Schwartzman and Amichai Merhavya were lying dead. The area they were in was what is called *tofet* (a living hell). Yoni Shtabon was in a safe position, a brick house, well protected. The bodies lay five hundred meters away under heavy enemy crossfire. "It was the most difficult decision of my entire life." He recalled that six years earlier, in another battle, Klein had saved his life. Something inside of him, an inner voice, told him he must retrieve the bodies. Shtabon took six soldiers and began to move toward the olive grove where the bodies of five soldiers lay. One of the soldiers took a bullet in the leg and could not continue. Shtabon sent the injured soldier back, along with another soldier to accompany him. Shtabon continued with four men. When he reached the area near the bodies, he met Itamar Katz, who told him that the body of Klein and four other soldiers were in the olive grove.

Israeli soldiers were on the roof of the house firing at Hizbullah in an attempt to keep them away from the bodies. Despite the incredible odds, Shtabon was determined to enter the grove and make sure that all the bodies were brought to a proper Jewish burial. "I signal to our helicopters to give me air support and to start firing." As soon as there was an opportunity and Shatbon had proper cover, he decided to go in. He took two soldiers and ran toward the olive grove. "The first body I run into is Schwartzman, near the wall I find Merhavya and Klein, and next to them First Sergeant Asaf Namer and First Sergeant Shimon Dahan. At that moment you don't think of anything other than the assignment."[43]

Carrying the bodies was very difficult so Shtabon and the two soldiers with him could only take one body at a time. One man would carry a body and the other two would cover him. They brought each body to the house, and then came back for another. Such they did five times, covering eighty meters each time while the enemy fire did not let up for a minute

Shtabon received an award for bravery from the IDF Chief of Staff. He and his men did not suffer any injuries. After many hours the fighting subsided and Hizbullah retreated. Shatabon was able to bring the boys back to Israel. He took great comfort in that five families could at least give a proper burial to their sons and not have them remain in enemy hands. Since that time, Shtabon spends every Memorial Day with the families of his friends who were killed in that battle.

A Commitment to the Fallen

Young soldiers are brought to Mount Herzl as part of their military education. They will learn the history of those who walked before them, of those who created the army to which these young soldiers now belong, of those who made life in Israel possible. They will learn their names, hear their stories, and feel a bond, the bond of one generation of warriors to another. By the time they leave, Memorial Day will be a personal day, a day they can relate to and understand.

1948

There is a song that was popular when I was a child growing up in Israel, *"At Va'Ani Noladnu BeTasha"CH"* ("You and I Were Born in 1948").[44] In many ways the people of Israel were reborn during that fateful year. 1948 was clearly a turning point, for the first time since the days of General Bar Kochba back in 135 CE, the nation of Israel was living as a free people in its own land. The "hope of two thousand years" had come true. Jews and Christians around the world saw this as a miracle of biblical proportions. (Muslims saw this as an unparalleled, inexplicable tragedy.) Once again the few and the pure had defeated the many and the evil.

Since the days of Muhammad and the birth of Islam thirteen hundred years ago, Jews and Christians had been relegated to the humiliating status of *dhimmi*, or "protected" people. Muslim persecution of Jews began as soon as Muhammad realized that the Jews did not see him as a prophet along the lines of Moses. The Jews of Arabia did not accept Muhammad's claims of divine revelation. This rejection would cost them dearly in lives and property.

One after another, the followers of Muhammad laid siege to Jewish areas, each time the terms of surrender were worse. In one case, that of the Jews of Qurayza, all nine hundred Jewish males were decapitated, their wives and children taken as slaves, and their property divided among the "faithful" Muslims.

Under Muslim rule, no Jewish or Christian house of worship could stand at the same height as that of a Muslim mosque, no Jew or Christian could be equal to a Muslim. The *dhimmi* rules, or all those referred to as "*ahl al dimmahh*" (the people of the contract), date back to the defeat of the Jews by the Muslims in the year 628 CE. The Jews had fought valiantly, but were defeated after a captured Jewish spy revealed crucial strategic information.

During this dark period, the fortunes of the Jews in this region fluctuated with the times and the rulers, but the Jew was always reminded of his lowly status. Massacres and humiliation were common. When the opportunity arose for the Jews to have a small state of their own, the entire Arab world united against them. Jewish independence was something they had put an end to back in Saudi Arabia. The idea of Jewish independence was something antithetical to the Muslim world-view. Islam rejects the idea of equality among religions.

Thus, David Ben-Gurion understood that the declaration of independence by Jews anywhere in the *Dar al Islam*, Land of the Muslims, as the Muslims saw it, would provoke a powerful response. Ben-Gurion knew that a terrible attack would be forthcoming and the consequences could be dire.

Arieh Handler, a witness to the signing of the Israeli Declaration of Independence, recalled the difficult deliberations that led to this declaration of freedom. The United States, more specifically President Harry Truman, had approved and backed the idea of Jewish statehood. However, as usual, the State Department objected. They claimed that backing Israel would undermine America's position with the oil rich Arab countries, and that the people of Israel would be incapable of winning such a war. "On the basis of the *Haganah's* limited skirmishes thus far, secretary of state George Marshall and other officials were dubious about the ability of the Jews to repel the regular Arab armies. They warned against the overstretched American army being drawn into the conflict. Some senior officials in Washington argued that a state formed in good part from immigrants from Eastern Europe would inevitably go communist."[45]

The United States was pushing for a delay and the leaders of Israel had to decide whether to accept the American position. The position of the nation of Israel was difficult; surrounded by enemies whose population was forty times the population of the Jewish community in Israel, possessing regular armies with an abundance of weapons, and being actively assisted by the British. "The Arabs were quite strong and the British didn't like us," said Handler.[46] Some delegates felt there was no option but to accept the American position and not declare independence.

The Talmud teaches us that some people earn their place in the "World to Come" in a single instant. For David Green (Grüen), by then David Ben-Gurion, that moment was about to come; it was his passionate speech that decided the issue. He was the man of the hour.

What defines a nation of warriors? What makes a people worthy of such a title? Despite overwhelming odds, without the support of any superpowers, without a real army to speak of, this tiny nation agreed to follow their leader and defy the odds. Handler recalls, "Ben Gurion was almost the only person who didn't care what the US or Britain said. Or Russia."[47]

A people long considered unworthy of a fight were taking on the greatest odds. Once again, it was David against Goliath. Once again, it was the spirit of King David, the Maccabees, Samson, and Bar Kochba. An entire nation would fight; women and men, teenagers and the elderly, intellectuals, farmers and rabbis. Ben-Gurion told Golda Meir, herself a future Prime Minister, that it was vital to prepare the population for the inevitability of heavy losses. Indeed Israel would lose one percent of its population in the war, but the State of Israel would be reborn.

1967

During Israel Independence Day celebrations at one of the leading rabbinical academies in Jerusalem, Mercaz HaRav Kook, Rabbi Tzvi Yehuda Kook gave a rousing talk to his students. Those who were there recall his emotion packed words, "Nineteen years ago, on the night when news of the United Nations decision in favor of the re-establishment of the State of Israel reached us, when the people streamed into the streets to celebrate and rejoice, I could not go out and join in the jubilation. I sat alone and silent; a burden lay upon me. During those first hours I could not resign myself to what had been done. I could not accept the fact that indeed '**they have...divided My land!**'[48] Yes [and now after nineteen years] where is our Hebron—have we forgotten her?! Where is our Shehem, our Jericho—where?! Have we forgotten them?! And all that lies beyond the Jordan—each and every clod of earth, every region, hill, valley, every plot of land, that is part of Eretz Israel [the Land of Israel]—have we the right to give up even one grain of the Land of God?! On that night, nineteen years ago, during those hours, as I sat trembling in every limb of my body, wounded, cut, torn to pieces—I could not then rejoice."

On the very same day, at the national song competition, a new song was heard. "Sing to God a new song, the entire land."[49] The song was "Jerusalem of Gold" written by Naomi Shemer and sung by Shuli Natan, a nineteen-year-old Israeli soldier.[50] Her voice longed for Jerusalem, from which we were banned by the Arabs. With a voice strong, but sweet, she cried out, "The city that sits in solitude, and its heart a Wall (from the Holy Temple)." As the verse said...the nation sang along. "How the cisterns have dried up, as have the market and the city square, and no one visits the Temple Mount, in the Old City." Sadness, pain, longing, for a Temple destroyed nearly two thousand years ago.

Three weeks later, as if by prophecy, those words came true. The Six Day War of June 1967 brought many of these regions under the control of the people of Israel. The Temple Mount, the ruins of the Holy Temple, were in Jewish hands. For the first time in nearly two thousand years Jewish soldiers stood at the location of the Temple. It was said, "The Western Wall has seen many things, but it has never seen paratroopers cry."

Battle hardened soldiers, who had just lost some of their best friends, stood at the Wall. Secular Jews said, "I am not a religious man but standing at the Wall, my emotions are overwhelming. I am at the Wall!"

Rabbi Goren, chief rabbi of the IDF, appeared with a *shofar*, the ram's horn, to proclaim the freedom of the Temple. "As God has returned His people to Zion we were as dreamers."[51] Rabbi Tzvi Yehuda Kook and his friend Rabbi David Cohen, called "the *nazir*" (the monk), with long flowing white beards, came to the Wall as well. Religious soldiers thought it was the Messiah and his assistant. With such miracles, anything could be true! Commander Motta Gur reported, "The Temple Mount is in our hands." Holy words had been spoken.

Naomi Shemer, author of "Jerusalem of Gold," heard the news. She was in the Sinai desert singing for the troops. She grabbed pen and paper, and used a soldier's back as a desk. She wrote the final verse of the song. "We have returned to the water cisterns, the market and the city square, a *shofar*—ram's horn, calls out at the Temple Mount, in the Old City. Jerusalem of Gold, and of bronze and of light, for all your songs I shall be a violin."

I am six years old, walking through the courtyard at the Savyon school, I hear kids singing this song, "We have returned..." The song runs through me, "for all your songs I shall be a violin." We live for Jerusalem.

Jerusalem, Shechem, Jericho, and Hebron came under control of the descendants of those who lived there thousands of years earlier. The people felt the prophesies of the Bible being fulfilled in their own times. The warriors of 1967 fought with a bravery reminiscent of biblical days. Into the ancient corridors of Jerusalem they streamed, up the Golan Heights, and into the Sinai desert. Truly they had fought as lions. And as the Bible said, "Behold this is a nation that dwells alone, and among the nations is not recognized."[52]

Israel had promises, guarantees, allies, but in the moment of truth, again Israel stood alone. Again, as in the Holocaust, the Jewish nation felt isolated. Israel's foreign minister, British born Abba Eban, sought out help around the world, but none responded. France, a close ally at the time, turned against the Jewish state. The United States was busy with other matters, and the United Nations was silent.

"We can only depend upon ourselves," the young reserve soldiers said over coffee. Nervousness spread across the land. Would it be the destruction of the State of Israel? Could this be happening again to the Jewish people?

The euphoria that was experienced after the war can only be understood in the context of the fear and isolation that was felt before the war. I arrived in Israel only two months after the war. Signs still warned us, "Caution, minefields ahead."

Jews who had lost their faith, along with their families, during the Holocaust, were reborn with new faith; there was hope. "Our hope is not yet lost" ("*Hatikva*" – "The Hope").[53]

Some Israelis thought that we would never be attacked again...

1973

The Yom Kippur War of 1973 was perhaps the greatest victory of all. Unlike the Six Day War of 1967 Israel did not take a preemptive strike. In fact, many key generals were convinced that the Arabs would not, could not, launch a major war—but they did. Israel was caught off guard.

The early days of the war were marked by unprecedented losses. The soldiers fought heroically, many a story is told of a handful of men holding off major enemy attacks and fighting to nearly the last bullet. Yet the numbers were simply impossible to overcome.

"Along the Suez Canal, 450 IDF soldiers with 50 artillery pieces tried in vain to stop 100,000 Egyptian troops crossing the waterway under the covering fire of 2,000 artillery pieces and under the shield of one of the most extensive anti-aircraft ASM missile umbrellas in the world. Within a few days, two whole Egyptian armies had occupied the entire Israeli held east bank of the Suez Canal. Simultaneously, on the Golan Heights, 1,400 Syrian tanks hurled themselves against Israel's 160. Its defenders fought ferociously at point-blank range, lurching and roaring and dying in an unequal entanglement of tanks and armored personnel carriers and howitzers and other lethal paraphernalia that culminated in a contest of wills which left the IDF hemorrhaging."[54]

The men in the field did not know what the politicians knew, that Israel was low on equipment (some claim this is not entirely accurate) and that Golda Meir was desperately seeking an American airlift. Richard Nixon came through with the airlift, but there was a price; not allowing Israel the full victory that it was able to achieve, and political concessions as soon as the war was over, i.e., being pressured into territorial retreat. Once the supplies arrived, the soldiers fought back and turned the situation around completely.

There were many heroes, but the key was the officers in the field. The turnaround was due mostly to the initiative taken by the field officers, this is how they had been trained; to think on their feet and take decisive action. Individual soldiers took action as well. Survivors of units that had been decimated found each other and formed new units. They returned to the battle. They returned to the hell and inferno of Sinai—burning tanks and hopeless odds. This is Israel. This is the land I call home.

The years pass, but the memories remain...I can still recall my neighbors and my dad walking out of their houses in their IDF uniforms, casually going off to once again fight back the Arab invaders. Unlike the battles in Saudi Arabia thirteen hundred years ago, this time we would prevail. The nation of warriors came alive; our mailman, gardener, teachers, friends, and neighbors were all off to war.

"Reenergized and re-equipped, the IDF decisively moved over to the offensive. What had begun three weeks earlier as an ignoble retreat ended in an almost total rout of the Egyptians and the Syrians, and the humiliation of their patrons – the Soviet Union. Israeli forces advanced to a mere

40 kilometers from the gates of Damascus, battled their way along the highway to Cairo, smashed two Egyptian armies, surrounded a third and were poised to strike a knockout blow when Nixon and Kissinger put the squeeze on."[55]

The war had ended, but the soldiers remained on the front lines for a long time. It seemed like there was no end to this war. Many soldiers remained in the Sinai Peninsula, where one of the bloodiest tank battles in history took place, where so many soldiers fell. But Sinai, to us, means something else as well. The word Sinai to any Jew means the place where God gave us the Ten Commandments, where Moshe went up to Mount Sinai to meet with God, face to face. It was said that when the nation of Israel stood at the footsteps of Mount Sinai they were as a single being, "One nation with one heart," and now again our people were united. Religious and secular, "hawk" and "dove" sat together in Egypt, in Sinai, for long days and nights. With all the fire and hell there was a unity of brother with brother.

The rabbis teach us that destruction comes from the lack of unity among our people; that God does not like to see us disunited. Perhaps this costly war had brought us together, to some degree. It is said the redemption comes through unity. This war had it all; unity, sacrifice, pain, and heroism. And the singer sang, "May this war be the last war." ("*Hamilchama Ha'achrona*" – "The Last War").[56] But it was not to be...

A Nation of Reservists

Israel is a nation of reserve soldiers. Wherever you are, you are among the reserve soldiers. As in the Second Lebanon conflict, the reserves are the backbone of the army. They have the experience and the training. This is a remarkable system—an army of civilians, going about their daily business, students, family men, people in all walks of life receiving yearly military training and refresher courses. The transition from civilian life to military life can be sudden and abrupt. For this transition to be possible, yearly training must take place.

As the reservists enter camp, they must make a quick mental adjustment. Soon, they will be carrying jerry cans (water containers), stretchers, military equipment, guns and ammunition, tens of kilograms of equipment. They will head out for long marches in the heat of the day or in pouring rain. These heavy military demands might take their toll, but the men will keep on going. They have to train to deal with the conditions they will face when they face the enemy—bunkers, tunnels, and possible ambush.

These are just "ordinary guys" doing their reserve training, in preparation for their worst nightmare; Lebanon, Gaza, or the refugee camps. They must face an enemy that is not afraid of death and has no regard for human life. This is our reality; welcome to our nightmare. Anyone can be plucked from his daily routine, taken away from a business negotiation, and within hours find himself on the Lebanese border or in the Gaza strip chasing terrorists or dodging bullets.

This is what happened with our two reserve soldiers whose capture led to the Second Lebanon War. Eldad Regev had just completed his tests to be accepted to the law school at Bar Ilan University. By the time his letter of acceptance arrived, he was already in Hizbullah captivity. His fellow reservist, Ehud Goldwasser, was recently married. They were called from their daily life and sent to the border. Shortly afterward, they were hit with overwhelming enemy fire.

As the war progressed, many more reservists would be called up, putting an abrupt end to anything else they were doing. "August 6, 2006. Things are heating up in Lebanon – it is past midnight, the phone rings. An automated female voice asks me to punch in my service number, and a split second before the voice goes on I understand: 'The emergency procedure has been activated. You are to report to your unit's emergency gathering point at 8 am.'[57]

On that day, Sunday, August 6th, in the early afternoon, a tragedy, a terrible loss, took place. As the sky was becoming covered with smoke, twelve Israeli men, twelve bodies of the soldiers of reserve unit 9255, lay on the ground. Only two days earlier, they were going about their daily business when they received their call-up. Now, under a rain of Katyusha rockets, twelve soldiers lay dead and eighteen injured. None of them had hesitated to answer the call. As soon as they were called up, they dropped everything and reported for duty, despite being well aware of the grave dangers at the front.

Some people will serve in the military in a similar position as in civilian life. A public relations expert might be a military spokesman when called up, a doctor will serve as a medic. Dr. David Shashar was an obstetrician at Sheba hospital; he also served in the infantry reserves as a doctor. During the Second Lebanon War, he was busy delivering babies when he received the call to join his reserve unit. He was sent to southern Lebanon. On August 9, 2006, Hizbullah fired antitank missiles at the building where he was taking cover. Nine of his fellow soldiers were killed and he was badly injured, his arm nearly torn off. Ten days later he woke up, back in the same hospital where he was delivering babies, only now he was a patient. His arm was reattached, but no one knew if it would ever function again or if the doctor would ever be able to work again in his field. He knew this was a risk, yet when he was called up, he responded immediately.

Many things go through the mind of the civilian about to become a soldier again. You have to inform your family and your employer or business associates, cancel all your appointments, arrange your military kit, and make sure you have everything. Are you in shape? Perhaps you put on a few pounds, and of course, the idea that you are going into war...

"You meet up with your unit: 'Have you heard anything? Do you know where we are going?' We move up north – rockets are landing everywhere; we hear news that the previous reserve unit was bombed before they reached their destination. Twelve reservists are dead. Twelve reserve soldiers just like us – called up last night. 10:15 pm – the battalion commander assembles us. 'Thank you all for coming,' he says quietly. 'We don't take it for granted that less than 24 hours ago you were all civilians and you dropped everything to come here, knowing the risk.'"[58]

Another soldier, a friend of mine, recalled, "A week after the war began, on July 20, the 401st brigade was ordered to the eastern sector of the Lebanese border. It was a Friday when we were called up to the North; people were home on leave, but everybody rushed in and we had 100 percent reporting for duty. They grew up overnight. I never heard a word of complaint from a single soldier during that time. Not a single argument. It was as if they, 19- and 20-year-olds, suddenly rose up to meet the responsibility that had been placed upon them. They fought among themselves to 'go in' and join the operations in Lebanon." The battalion engaged in close combat operations until the second week of August.

Moshe, a reservist with the paratroopers, is going abroad for a year, but says, "If they call me up to go to war next year, I'll be on the plane. That's the way I was educated in this country."[59]

One of the most difficult times for the reserve army was in October 1973. It was *Yom Kippur*, the Day of Atonement, a sacred day in the Jewish religious calendar. Most men were in the synagogue praying.

*Israeli forces attack Hizbullah terrorists in
Lebanon, summer 2007. Photo: Arie Katz*

The Egyptians attacked on the Southern front, men had
to put away their prayer shawls and pick up their military
gear and travel long distances to get to the front. It is a day
of fasting and no one had eaten. Professor Stuart Cohen of
Bar Ilan University writes, "They deserve great credit for
having performed at all." The synagogue, the house of prayer,
emptied out as all the young, and not so young, men, were
called to the front lines.

I was only in seventh grade, but I could see and feel the
change that was taking place. Kids had older brothers who
were serving in the army, most had dads in the army; no one
knew what would happen. Our education was interrupted as
all young teachers were called up for action. I recall reading
the postcards our teachers sent us; they were posted on the
bulletin board. One of our teachers never returned. I can
still picture his last postcard from the front, encouraging
us kids to be strong and not to worry. I listened to the radio
and heard strange things like "Black Snake, Gray Wolf,

report to the den." The reserve units were being called up for action.

A Mark of Respect

One's reserve unit, as with compulsory service, is a mark of respect. Being a paratrooper is like being a member of the Harvard Rowing Club, only far more important; you put your sticker on your car, you meet periodically with the members of the club; you take pride in being an active member.

I met a commander who said he told his soldiers, "This battalion was in the *Palmach* (pre-state underground army) and in every war since 1948 it has been in the vanguard. At Mitla Pass, at the canal in '73, on the Coastal Road in 1982. And now our turn has come to make history."

Our turn; a soldier views it as his turn to defend his people and be part of history. It is with joy that they go out to battle, performing the sacred duty of defending the people of Israel. It is a *mitzvah*, a religious obligation.

It was 1982, the country had been suffering from terrorist attacks from Lebanon for some time. The boys in the *yeshiva* were waiting for their turn. The news arrived, "Our unit is going in! We were so excited," said my neighbor, Avigdor, "it was our chance to finally do something. We never thought of all the friends who would not come back."

Among those who would not come home were Yehuda Katz, Zacharia Baumel, and Tzvi Feldman. To this very day they are considered missing in action. The names of the MIA's are recited each week in the synagogue and the congregation prays for their safe return. Other MIA's included Sgt. Yosef Fink and Sgt. Rahamim Alsheikh who were taken prisoner on 18 February 1986. The two were part of a *Givati* brigade escort convoy in South Lebanon. Near the town of Beit Yahoun, Lebanon, the convoy was attacked by Hizbullah terrorists in a surprise ambush. Yossi Fink (my sister-in-law's cousin) and Rachamim Elshaich were taken prisoner. For years their fate was unknown. In 1991 the chief military rabbi declared them officially dead. After many years the bodies of Fink and Elshaich would come home. The others are still missing.

Despite the danger, there is no sign of hesitation, only eagerness to serve with pride. During the Second Lebanon War, men in the gym teased each other with, "Have you received your call-up yet? No? Well then, that just shows what the army thinks of your unit. I got my call-up today, off to Lebanon soon."

In Israel, most businesses, even small ones, will be partnerships, enabling one partner to keep the business alive when the other is called up. The reserve service also serves as a motivation to keep in shape. You can go directly from a sedentary desk job to hiking across the Golan Heights carrying an M-16 rifle and heavy supplies. The change is abrupt and you must be prepared.

My friend, Menachem, who I trained when he was an elite security guard, was in the process of moving into his new home when he received his orders. He was a young man with a wife and baby and had recently opened his own business selling fabrics. He was finally preparing to move into his new home. Without warning, he had to drop everything. He spent the next three weeks in Lebanon. "The fighting was fierce," he said, visibly shaken as he spoke to me. "We lost three men in my unit, we bore the brunt of the fighting in our area," he relayed to me as we stood in line at the checkout counter of our local supermarket. "They were good guys, good friends, the fighting was very tough."

Do you see the contrast? Here we were, doing ordinary Friday shopping in preparation for the Sabbath, and he was speaking of house-to-house fighting and watching friends die. Menachem picks up a newspaper, looks at a story about soldiers taking food from people's homes and says, "Yeah, that's right, we did take food from Lebanese stores and homes, we had no choice, the trucks bringing our food supplies were fired on with antitank missiles, we were starving, no one was willing to risk driving up to bring us food." Some soldiers brought US dollars with them and left money in the homes where they had eaten.

The front-page news and the guy standing next to you at the checkout counter are one and the same, a people's army—ordinary people. "I am going back in [to Lebanon] on Sunday," he says, with a look of concern taking over his face. I do not know what to say to him. Today he is comparing grocery prices; tomorrow he may be facing armed terrorists and antitank missiles.

In the United States, when you meet a soldier, it is usually obvious. He looks like a soldier, stands like a soldier, and talks like a soldier. He is a professional soldier. In Israel, the warriors do not stand out. You could never guess who they are. They are just ordinary guys who fight because they have to. The words on a soldier's lips are, "It's my responsibility, but it's also my privilege." The heroes do not act special because they know that so many others are heroes as well. You may have just liquidated a terrorist cell, but the old guy sitting next to you at the bus stop may have defended your hometown back in 1948 using only an M-1 rifle and a couple of hand grenades.

A Mark of Identification

I was asked by one of my American students if Israelis identify with their colleges the way Americans do. In the United States people retain ties with their college for life. They will have bumper stickers on their cars, even thirty or more years after graduation. They might still come to the "big games" and support the school in other ways. Identification with one's college is a major aspect of the culture.

In Israel, I have never noticed anything of the sort; the identification is with your military unit. Again, years later, people will have bumper stickers proudly declaring their affiliation with their unit. They will take pride in their son serving in the same unit, keeping the "family tradition" much as an American will be proud that his son attends the same college.

Israelis must serve in the military before they go off to college; so their studies rarely begin before the age of twenty-one. For Israelis, college is more of a practical step and not so much a life-changing experience. It is not their first experience away from home and the roof of their parents. They have served at least three years in the military, many have faced life and death situations; they are older and more mature than their American counterparts. College is a training ground for the work force; many students have part time jobs and live off campus. The military will always remain their dominant identification.

Balancing Civilian and Military Life

It is not only emotionally difficult to balance the transitions between job and combat, university studies and tracking down terrorists, it is also difficult on a practical level. You have to maintain a job, a family, perhaps a business. Today, with laptop computers and cell phones it is a bit easier.

Major A.G. is on a break. He is on his base, sitting outside the firing range, in the shade, working on a business proposal. His cell phone is ringing. He picks it up—it is a business associate from overseas. "What is that noise in the background?" asks his European caller, "Oh, that's firing, I am doing reserve duty."

A.G. is an officer in a reserves brigade, a father of four, and a marketing vice president in a hi-tech firm. He has been in the reserves for sixteen years. Why? "I will be honest, there are certain cases where work clashes with reserve duty." Nonetheless he feels a need to serve; it makes him feel he is contributing something to his country. And then when Holocaust Memorial Day comes around, and he thinks back to what life was like for Jews before the State of Israel, his resolve to serve is reinforced. "A country as small as ours and surrounded by enemies is dependent on us; the army and its reserve soldiers."

Devotion to the Cause

Immediately following the Second Lebanon War cease-fire and the demobilization of some of the reserve forces, something unusual took place. It started with a petition and continued with an active protest; the reserve soldiers were protesting against the government. They felt they were not given the proper chance to fight; they believed they were pulled back too soon before they had a chance to "complete the job." They said the political and military leadership was not aggressive enough during the war; that the cease-fire left Israel still vulnerable to Hizbullah attacks; that the leadership did not let the IDF win. The petition said the leadership had "cold feet" that led to "inaction," and that the soldiers wanted "to engage in combat." The protesters camped outside the government buildings in Jerusalem and would not budge.

Think about it! Rather than running home to their jobs, businesses, and families, these idealistic reserve soldiers were complaining that they were not given the chance to engage the enemy and properly neutralize the threat to our country. There are no words to describe this sense of idealism and patriotism.

"We have doctors, lawyers, company owners and government officials in our unit, and we leave our families and our jobs every year to serve our country, we drop everything and go where the army tells us, to risk our lives."[60]

These are soldiers who served at least three years

of compulsory service and for years have been fighting terrorists during their reserve duty. In most countries, people get time off from work to go on vacation and sit on the beach and then complain about going back to work. In Israel, people get time off for reserve duty during which they chase terrorists, put themselves at risk, and push themselves to their mental and physical limits, and their only complaint is, "We need to engage the enemy in combat, just give us the chance."

Personal Responsibility

This is a small country where the feeling is that every man counts. The Chinese say a single grain of rice can tip the balance. In Israel, many battles have been decided by the heroic actions of one man. Each individual soldier feels important. One soldier writes, "Before the war, I thought the IDF could get along without me, but now I see more clearly that the army depends on everyone taking individual responsibility for it."[61]

Other soldiers feel it is their responsibility to better prepare themselves personally for combat. Lior, a paratrooper, says that he and the other paratroopers in his unit have begun taking more personal responsibility—way beyond the call of duty—for their preparedness to fight. With a nation of warriors, each individual feels a sense of responsibility to the national cause. It is every man's cause.

Rich Man, Poor Man

In some countries, during some wars, a cry came forward, "rich man's war, poor man's fight." During the American Civil War, many Southerners felt that way; the war was being fought to protect the economic interests of the rich southern plantation owners, but the boys dying on the front lines owned neither land nor slaves. Many wars have been fought for economic reasons yet the rich have been able to buy their way out while the poor fought and died for the economic benefit of others. The wars benefited the rich industrialists, but the bodies in the field belonged to poor boys. In Israel this is not the case.

There is no such thing as "rich man's war." The wars are not fought for ideology or for economic gain or political influence; they are fought for survival, nothing more. The Second Lebanon War was fought because for the previous six years Hizbullah had been kidnapping soldiers, bombing civilian homes, and sponsoring terror. Israel fought back because it is the basic obligation of a state to protect its citizens. Thus the war was every man's war. War is also every man's fight. No one is exempt; you cannot buy your way out of military service. The draft is universal; it is the law. Not to serve is to be shamed for life.

Giving Everything

Bnaya, a gifted tank commander, was killed in the Second Lebanon War. His last words to his mother were, "You raised us to give everything, and sometimes everything means everything." Despite this tragic loss, his younger brother enlisted in a combat unit.

Uri, killed during the Lebanon war back in 1997, left a note behind. It was found folded up in his wallet, a little motivational thing, it read, "Give your utmost for the nation."

Lt. Ofer had his left arm shattered when his armored personnel carrier was hit by a roadside bomb in Gaza. He told his commanders that he was coming back—after surgery. "I think about my friends and my country and I realize that I am needed back in the army." He was given an award for heroism which he played down, saying, "I was only doing my job. I feel like I am on a mission and that I need to return to service. I am concerned about my soldiers and friends and believe that my country needs me."[62]

Roy was hit five times by terrorists in Lebanon. His right femur was shattered, as was his jaw. For two weeks he could not speak, he lay in the hospital and wrote his mother a note telling her he didn't regret anything for a minute. "If I could go back three and half years to when I was drafted, I would make all the same choices, even if I got hit again, because I'm proud to serve my country. I'm proud to defend it."[63]

Grave, Roei Klein, died a hero. "This is how you raised me, to give everything."

Roei Klein, a thirty-one-year-old father of two, a saxophone player and an engineer, ran to help a group of soldiers caught by a Hizbullah ambush. Klein rushed through a hail of fire to the platoon commander's side, firing as he ran. He prepared to move the wounded officer to cover. Suddenly a grenade landed close to the group. Without hesitation Klein jumped on the grenade, absorbing the blast with his body. Mortally wounded, he uttered the words of the *Shma*, the affirmation of faith Jews recite when they believe they are about to die: "*Shma Yisrael*, Hear Israel, the Lord our God, the Lord is one." He wired his last report, gave his second in command the code to his encrypted transmission device, and passed away. Klein was such an amazing soldier that he even reported his own death. Yoni Shtabon, now a member of the Israeli Knesset (Parliament) recalls, "The moment I heard over the communication device Roei's voice shouting 'Klein dead, Klein dead,' I understood that he was actually reporting his own death."[64]

August 2006, the Second Lebanon War, the Last Few Days

Nimrod Segev, reservist, family man, two children, hi-tech worker. Nimrod is called up. Turns out there was some mistake and he is not needed just yet. He can go home. Nimrod decides to stay until everything is straightened out. Later, his father is notified that Nimrod is in the hospital, he is suffering from dehydration. "He looked as pale as a ghost," his father recalls.

"Father, I am afraid," said Nimrod.

"And then I heard for the first time his dream," says the father.

Nimrod: "From this war I shall not return, I have seen my own death. I will die and in my coffin there will be nothing to bury, they will put bags of sand for weight. We will stumble upon a land mine and we will not be able to proceed. We will take a direct hit. I have seen the tank consumed by fire and explode and we are all burnt alive. I know, I will not return from this war. Father, Abba, I am afraid." The father shuddered and tried to talk his son out of returning to the front, but he knew it was of no use. Nimrod had this look on his face, with a smile, and with complete peace of mind. He said: "Father, that is not how you raised us. I must be there for my state, for my friends and for my family. I cannot turn my back on the values with which I was raised."[65]

"Who is like your nation Israel."[66]

Four days later, Nimrod's tank drove over a land mine and then took a direct hit in the battle of *Ayta al Shaab.* The announcement came at 11:30 pm, twelve hours after the incident. The father recalls, "I heard the knock on the door, I opened the door and saw the military officer and the doctor. I ran inside the house, I collapsed on my knees and I begged that they would tell me he was injured, that he is alive and not dead. I asked mercy from the heavens, but it did not help. They informed me that Nimrod is dead and that there are no remains."

Just at that moment the younger brother, Ehud, who was known to have telepathic ability, and who was in Mexico, called home and asked, "I see on the news that Israeli soldiers were killed but they are not giving out all the names yet. Isn't it true that Nimrod was killed but they are not saying the names since I was not informed yet?"

The father asked the IDF officers what to say. They asked him to say nothing because representatives from the Israeli embassy were on their way to the brother. When the ambassador reached Ehud with the bitter news, he responded; "I know. I have been waiting for you for two days."

Later, the commander told the father that Nimrod's death was exactly as Nimrod had seen it four days earlier in his dream. The family established Mitzpe Nimrod, a beautiful park, a peaceful place, to perpetuate the name and memory of Nimrod; a soldier who saw his own death and yet would not abandon his assignment. He was raised to give his all to his people. He is now at peace.

The Reservists Prove Themselves in Gaza

After the difficult war in Lebanon only two years earlier, one might expect a lack of motivation for a very similar war in the South. This time the war was with Hamas in the hellhole known as the Gaza Strip.

The headlines of the local papers read, "Reservists Answer the Call En Masse, Ready to Take on Hamas." The reservists, as always, dropped everything—work, school, and family—picked up their M-16s and headed for the front with complete and total dedication. As soon as the call went out, tens of thousands of citizens put on their uniforms and headed down to Gaza, ready to give 'em hell. I recall many saying, "We will make the south safe again. The children of southern Israel deserve to sleep in their beds, not in bomb shelters."

"One reservist showed up a week after his wife gave birth to their firstborn son. Another is scheduled to get married next week."[67]

"Everybody showed up for duty" confirmed Major Ido of the Negev brigade. "There are concerns, but it's only natural and despite the concerns, everybody answered the emergency orders."[68]

Chaim Elbaum of Jerusalem, a father of three young children, spoke on behalf of his friends when he said, "We have been preparing for this for three years. We are motivated and ready."[69]

Yehuda Broyner, a thirty-eight-year-old teacher and father of four, fought in "Defensive Shield" back in 2002. He came back again, this time to fight in Gaza, "In situations like this I don't think about myself. We are here to protect all of Israel and to bring security to the South."[70]

This is the feeling that is echoed again and again; self-sacrifice, selflessness, devotion to the nation. Personal concerns come second. Their sacrifices, in turn, motivate the non-combatants to do their utmost as well; arranging packages, bringing hot meals to the soldiers, donating warm clothing, and praying for their welfare and success.

Volunteerism

Another unique aspect of this people's army is volunteerism. Many people are discharged for various reasons—age, health, family situations such as having many children, or severe financial difficulties. In the Second Lebanon War, as in previous wars, many of these discharged soldiers showed up anyway, uninvited, at the military bases. Despite having no obligation to serve, thousands showed up, eager to volunteer for combat. Men who suffered severe injuries, men too old to serve—they came. It is an unparalleled phenomenon in the modern world. I have seen men in their 70s insisting that they still can serve; "I can still fight! You should have seen me in the Sinai campaign in '56—I am a fighter!"

One handicapped soldier, Avshalom Erez, lost an eye in the battle of *Ayta al Shaab*. He was part of the 101st battalion of paratroopers. He no longer had to serve, but said, "Even though I don't have to do reserve duty now, I think I'll volunteer. But I can't fight in a war anymore...that's the worst part of it all. It's unbearable to think there could be another war and my friends will fight and risk their lives, and I won't be there with them."[71]

Volunteers come from all over. Israelis vacationing abroad will often cut their vacations short, take a flight home, and report for active combat in Gaza. Israelis who have emigrated to other countries will often contact their unit and find out if the unit is being called up. If the unit is being activated, these foreign residents will fly home to fight, at their own expense, leaving behind jobs and families. Sadly, there have been stories of Israeli students in American universities flying home only to be killed in combat and never return to complete their degrees.

One such case occurred in the Second Lebanon War. Perhaps this is the highest demonstration of self-sacrifice and patriotism—you are at your desk in Boston or New York, concerned with completing a term paper. You are safe. No one expects you to return and fight, and yet, you drop everything to be with your fellow soldiers dodging enemy bullets. You are part of this people, and being part of this people makes you part of the people's army. They are your brothers-in-arms for life.

There are also special volunteer programs for non-Israelis. A unique aspect of this people's army is the presence of foreign volunteers. People of all ages come to Israel on various programs and serve, as non-citizens, in the Israeli army. Speaking English, French, Spanish, German and Dutch, they arrive at the airport and are taken straight to military bases where they change into military fatigues and begin serving. Some do menial tasks, which frees up regular soldiers for more active duty; others use their specific training in medicine or engineering. On some bases, you can find grandmothers cleaning weapons, older men fixing military vehicles. They are all smiles, from ear to ear; they are serving the people of Israel. They are making a difference. Younger men will often be trained for guard duty, again, freeing regular soldiers for more active duty. The motivation level among all soldiers—regulars, reserves, and volunteers, is remarkably high.

These volunteer programs began with the underground freedom fighters before the State of Israel was established. In 1948, the program became official when approximately thirty-five hundred overseas volunteers came from forty-four countries to defend the newborn state. Most were World War Two veterans and their experience was of decisive importance in the War of Independence. They brought with them military experience, knowledge of equipment and arms, and understanding of military frameworks.

They contributed a great deal to the newly-formed IDF. In fact, the bulk of the pilots in the first Israeli air force were foreigners. About half of the pilots were Christians.

During the War of Independence, one hundred twenty-one of the volunteers would lose their lives. Over the years, thousands more came and today the program is still going strong. As part of the program, the volunteers learn Hebrew, some live on a *kibbutz* for a while. During the Second Lebanon War, one unit had one hundred twenty foreign volunteers who flew to Israel to enlist.

Civilian Volunteers

There is a great deal of support from the non-military civilian population. There are organizations that arrange "enlistment parties" for all members of a community being drafted that month. Their photos appear in the paper; they are honored in the synagogue. Gifts are purchased for new recruits. Some units are short on supplies such as warm winter clothing. It can take many months of bureaucratic paper shuffling until the clothing is purchased—in the meantime, private donors will often buy the necessary clothing.

My nephew, Ari, arranged for a donation to purchase winter coats for the members of his combat unit. Volunteer groups arrange special food packages for soldiers on the front, offering some treats as well as a feeling that the people back home appreciate their sacrifice. In the Second Lebanon War, one hundred forty thousand packages were sent up in three weeks—each package was celebrated by the soldiers far from home.

A Package from Home

One of those organizations is called A Package from Home. It began back in 2001 with a grandmother's personal reaction to the second Intifada (Arab terrorist uprising). Barbara Silverman, Chicago native, long-term resident of Jerusalem, was "aghast at the intensity of the Arab campaign against Israelis." Her reaction? Bake cookies. As a grandmother, she explained, she had few options. She was not going to start training with an M-16 rifle, but she sure knew how to bake cookies. Together with some of her friends, many of them with sons or grandsons in the army, she began to bake. Soon the packages grew to include many important items such as fleece jackets, fleece blankets, ski hats, extra underwear and toiletries in addition to the cookies and chocolates. Help came from the Association of Americans and Canadians in Israel (AACI), as well as donations from the United States. More volunteers came to help pack and the word spread. Vendors provided products at just above cost. They too had been soldiers and wanted to help in any way they could.

IDF soldiers in Lebanon enjoy a snack

The project is still going strong. During the Second Lebanon War, A Package from Home sent twenty-two thousand packages to the front in thirty-three days. In the first week of the war in Gaza they sent over three thousand packages. Today, the organization focuses on "lone soldiers" as well as soldiers in the hospital.

Packages also come directly from the United States. In an amazing story, my brother, Ethan, who lives in New Jersey (and is a former combat soldier in the IDF), had a neighbor who told him he had just contributed money to have a package sent to the boys on the Lebanon front. Later, my nephew, Arie, serving in Lebanon with the paratroopers said he had, in fact, received a package with a note that it was contributed by that very family in New Jersey. Small world and one filled with much caring.

To Build and To Be Built

Israel is built on the spirit of volunteerism. From its earliest days, volunteers, both local and foreign, have played a crucial role in the formation of the spirit and landscape of this society.

One such volunteer program is called *Livnot U'Lehibanot* "To Build and To Be Built." Young American volunteers, led by Israeli guides, come to explore their heritage through volunteering, hiking, and seminars. The major focus of this program is community service. Activities range from cutting vegetables at soup kitchens to rebuilding dilapidated homes for the needy who cannot afford the repairs.

My niece, Mindy Katz, chose to volunteer in the *Livnot U'Lehibanot* program. She led a group of young American volunteers who came to spend three weeks exploring Israel. They were on a daylong hike in the North when the Second Lebanon War broke out. When they returned to their base, in the holy city of Safed, parents from the United States called frantically, urging their children to come home to safety. With only one exception, the entire group of volunteers stayed in Israel, to serve, and to share the fate of the people of Israel.

When the group awoke the next morning, they could see that the beautiful forests of Mount Meron, the mountain right across from Safed, were ablaze. These forests were planted by an earlier generation of volunteers who came to this barren, neglected land and made it bloom. The group was able to see the Katyusha rockets, fired by Hizbullah terrorists, landing nearby.

Mindy and the other group leaders gathered the volunteers and spirited them off to the town of Tiberius. In this town, centuries earlier, Jewish scholars set down the codes and cantillations of the Torah, preserving the ancient traditions for future generations. With the destruction of the Temple in Jerusalem, Tiberius evolved into a major Jewish center. By the 3rd century, Tiberius boasted many synagogues and houses of study. When Tiberius came under Hizbullah fire, the group made its way south to the safety of Jerusalem, too far for the rockets of the terrorists.

For the rest of their three week program they set out to do what they could for the war effort. They prepared care packages containing toothpaste, toothbrushes, food, whatever the soldiers needed. When the army announced a blood shortage was approaching, the volunteers made their way to donate blood that would be sent to the wounded soldiers up north. The Hizbullah rockets could not crush the spirit of volunteerism.

Volunteerism is built into Israeli society. Young women of eighteen who choose not to serve in the armed forces for reasons of religious modesty, will volunteer for two years in a program called, *Sherut Leumi*; National Service.

Near Gaza, 2014

In Operation Protective Edge, Or Shachar, 18, volunteered with security forces and medical emergency teams. Yam Pozner, 17, helped run activities for children. Gan Yavne mayor: "If our future is going to be shaped by this generation, we are going to fare extremely well." In Gan Yavne, near the Gaza Strip, where residents had to run for cover several times a day, dozens of teenagers ran day camps for children, took them on excursions during lulls, patrolled the area with local security forces, took care of elderly and immigrant families, and responded to medical emergencies with first responders.

Amit Malul, 17, has just graduated from high school and will spend the next year volunteering with various projects ahead of her army service. During the operation, she helped collect donations for Givati brigade troops. She also helped run day camps for new immigrants. Most of the activities were held in bomb shelters.[72]

Appreciation

Appreciation on the part of the general population, and their desire to help, is perhaps the most remarkable aspect of the people's army; the feeling that you are fighting for your people and they fully appreciate you.

I recall a cartoon showing a young Israeli boy. James Bond walks by, the boy yawns. Superman walks by, the boy yawns. An Israeli soldier walks by and the boy's face lights up. They are the *real* superheroes.

Special Needs

As a nation of warriors, Israel embraces all its soldiers. Soldiers lacking in basic education will be provided with one, soldiers with special needs will be accommodated. Because serving in the military is considered so important sociologically, every attempt is made to include everyone who wants to serve.

Many handicapped individuals serve in the military; there are many jobs that they can handle. Autistic and mentally disadvantaged people also serve. They will wear a uniform, do some task, and feel that they are a part of the army and are serving the country. Israel recognizes that as much as the soldiers do for the army, the army does for them. The army makes you part of the family and the family takes care of all its members, including those who have physical or mental handicaps.

The "Lonesome" Soldier

Many young people come from abroad to serve in the Israeli armed forces. They come alone—without family. The army takes care of them. Israel's Lonesome Soldier law gives special benefits to soldiers whose parents left the country, soldiers without the support of a family such as orphans, soldiers who have no contact with their families, and soldiers from very poor families who cannot assist financially.

Lone soldiers receive a monthly stipend in addition to their standard military pay. This is double the amount other soldiers receive. On the holidays they will receive special gift certificates, and, once during their military service, they will receive financial assistance to visit their parents abroad, in cases where the parents are abroad. In addition, if the soldier needs housing, he will receive either a place to live or financial assistance to rent a place. This will be his home during his vacations. There are also *kibbutzim* (plural of *kibbutz*) that will adopt soldiers and provide a home for them during their military service. Many soldiers will remain close with their *kibbutz* family for many years to come.

The people of Israel have reached out to their lone soldiers to let them know they are never truly alone, that their sacrifice is very much appreciated. One such example is *Beit Richman LaHayal,* the Richman Home for Soldiers. An Israeli-American couple was watching a TV program about the lack of affordable housing for lone soldiers. They decided to turn a villa they owned into a home base for these soldiers. Today, it provides a warm and welcoming atmosphere for many soldiers. With fresh cooked meals and all the comforts of home, the lone soldier is not quite so alone anymore.

In 2006, Allen Garfel of New York came to Israel for a year abroad program. During that time he decided to enlist in the IDF. He served in the paratroopers unit and was injured in Lebanon in the battle of *Ayta al Shaab.*

During the Second Lebanon War, three lonesome soldiers were killed; Michael Levin of the United States, Yonatan Vasliuk of the Ukraine, and Asaf Namer of Australia. The lonesome soldiers are known as being particularly idealistic and motivated. Today, there are about twenty-four hundred "lonesome" soldiers serving in the IDF.

Search and Rescue Volunteers

Yahtza

One of the best known and unique Israeli volunteer organizations is *Yahtza*, the National Search and Rescue reserve unit. The unit is made up entirely of volunteers. These are men and women who are veterans of the IDF and possess special skills in areas such as the medical field, construction, use of power tools, and other skills that are useful in disaster zones. Volunteers sign a contract allowing the army to call them up whenever they are needed and for as long as they are needed. Due to the nature of the work, there is usually no notice at all. The volunteers simply must drop everything and go, for however long it takes.

The unit operates both in Israel and abroad. It was developed for our local needs, but soon it became apparent that the unit was needed around the world. The unit has seen action in many countries. One such country was Haiti.

The *Jerusalem Post* reported on the story of one of the volunteers. "Captain (res.) Nir Hazut is a lawyer who, after having been wounded in Lebanon while serving in the combat engineering corps, had to fight the system in order to be allowed to do reserve duty. When he found out about the unit he did everything he could to be a part of it. His first time on a mission was in 2010, when he was part of the delegation sent to Haiti following the country's overwhelming earthquake."[73]

Hazut and his team arrived at the scene; it was already the fourth day after the earthquake and the local rescue workers had given up. There was a man outside who said he knew his cousin was still alive, but no one was willing to risk going into the collapsed building. Hazut and his team went in. Seven and a half hours later they emerged with the cousin who had been buried alive.

In Turkey, a similar situation took place. The locals had given orders to stop the rescue operations because of the risk of aftershocks, but the Israeli team refused and ended up saving the life of a young girl. The girl was eventually brought to Israel for advanced medical treatment.

Even in cases where there are only bodies to recover, the unit operates in a special way and tries not to damage the bodies. It is part of Jewish tradition to bring the body to the grave in as complete a state as possible. The value and respect for human life, whether in Israel or abroad, is what motivates the unit to go to extraordinary lengths to save a single life.

ZAKA

One of the most famous and noble organizations in Israel is *Zihuy Korbanot Ason* (ZAKA), "Disaster Victim Identification." Whenever there is a terror attack, a suicide bombing, an explosion, a shooting—the men of ZAKA are on the scene. Tragically, they have become all too familiar to the Israeli public.

It all started in 1989 when an Israeli bus was attacked by an Arab terrorist and fell down a hill, killing many people. Members of the nearby town, all religious Jews, swarmed down and tried to help. They tried to save the living, provide medical care to the injured, and carefully collect the body parts of those no longer alive—in keeping with the Jewish value to try to bring a person to the grave with as much dignity as possible. As such, there is an attempt to collect as much of the body as possible. Over the years, this spontaneous group action turned into one of the most celebrated volunteer organizations in Israel. Their members carry beepers and are on call 24/7. Today, ZAKA has over fifteen hundred volunteers throughout the country.

CHAPTER 3

Secret Ingredient of Israeli Defense

In the old story of the fox chasing the rabbit, a wise man is asked, "Who will prevail?" He answers "The rabbit. The fox is fighting for his dinner while the rabbit is fighting for his life."

"It is a fight for the home"
נלחמים על הבית

"It is a war of existence"
מלחמת קיום

I wrote the following words on August 8, 2006, in the midst of the Second Lebanon War, which was really just a continuation of our enemies' unsuccessful attempts to destroy us.

The Israeli army, Israeli self-defense, is fierce. We are surrounded by enemies who day and night seek our destruction; we have no choice but to be better fighters. Our secret ingredient is our motivation, spirit, and necessity. We are a peace seeking nation. Every war this nation has fought was forced upon us. Each war is a war for existence and survival. We fight, therefore, we still exist.

Two boys were killed in combat this morning; Philip and Noam. One came from Russia, the other from the United States, both reclaiming their national heritage, both descendants of those exiled by our enemies of many years ago.

Philip Moscow (left) medic, paratrooper, with captured Hizbullah flag. Photo: Arie Katz

Philip lived in my town, Maaleh Adumim. My mother is close to his mother. We were in the car when we heard the 11 am news, "The news from the front... killed in action this morning...and Philip Moscow of Maaleh Adumim." My mother shouted, "That's Luba's boy! Oh my God, poor Luba!" We pulled over to the side of the road to digest the tragic news. Living is a game of Russian roulette.

You ask why we fight, and why we fight so well; because if Philip and Noam, and all the other boys, were not up there fighting, then the enemy would be at the gates of our towns as they were before, before we had an army. The enemy would be in our homes, as they were in Hebron in 1929, slicing open pregnant women, slitting the throats of old rabbis and young students, raping women, smashing the heads of babies against the wall, massacring entire families as their shrieks cry out to heaven. We have seen the enemy.

So we fight because we must. And Noam and Philip are holding strong, knowing the extreme danger they face, because they are fighting for their families and friends, they are fighting so little children do not have to spend their childhoods in bomb shelters, so old people can finally enjoy some peace, so our weary people can enjoy a moment of rest. They are fighting to fulfill the words of the prophet Zechariah who wrote, "And it will still come to pass that old men and old women will sit in the streets of Jerusalem, and a man will lean on his cane for he has reached a ripe old age, and the streets will be filled with little children playing in her streets."[74]

And today, their time ran out. As I write these very words, Philip, of blessed memory, a young man of twenty-one, is being buried in the military cemetery in Jerusalem. Today they returned their souls to heaven and left grieving families who will never recover.

But their spirits will not die. Another soldier will pick up the rifle or the medical kit of Philip, the combat medic, and continue. He will continue; running into battle without fear. He will continue as the defender of Israel. The torch will be passed on and the request of the dying soldier fulfilled:

"I fought as long as I could; I gave my life, now it is your turn to protect our people. Carry on."

Philip has returned home.

Thousands of years ago our people were exiled from our land by overwhelming enemy forces. In the exile, our people were persecuted and massacred, yet we survived. In Russia, an evil government arose that tried to estrange us from our age-old religion. For years, they did not allow our people to return home to Israel.

Finally, Philip returned home. He was overweight and was rejected for military service, but this did not stop him. Although he volunteered with the Civil Guard and the emergency medical services, he wanted to serve his people in the army. Nothing would stand in his way. He lost an enormous amount of weight and qualified for combat service. He served in the combat zone of Lebanon, treating injured soldiers, until an antitank missile hit his armored personnel carrier. Less than a year later his younger sister would join the IDF. We all serve.

Close to four thousand years ago, the pharaohs of Egypt were determined to wipe us out. Many have tried since. But we are a stubborn, stiff-necked people, motivated and spirited. The people of Israel, despite all odds, lives.

Leadership, Independent Thinking

1973, the Yom Kippur War, the October War. Despite a surprise attack by a well-prepared, Soviet-trained army, the IDF managed to thoroughly defeat and rout the Egyptian army.

One of the keys to the outcome was the leadership factor. With some armies, when the commander is killed or disabled, there is no one who can really step into his shoes and take charge effectively. In Israel, each member of the unit is trained as a commander. If the commander is no longer able to function, the next in command immediately fills his shoes, even down to the last soldier.

Each soldier is trained to use what he has available. They know that the situation in the field may not be ideal, so they train to adapt to whatever the situation may be. The saying is, "Tough in training, easy in battle." Regardless of the number of soldiers, the type or amount of equipment, the position of the forces, the terrain, or the weather, the soldiers will know how to adapt. Leadership and independent creative thinking helped the soldiers continue with effective combat even after key commanders were no longer able to function.

In the 1973 war, the Egyptians initially took several Israeli positions. Israeli Prime Minister Golda Meir had decided against a preemptive strike, such as the one Israel used successfully in 1967. She was concerned about world reaction to "Israeli aggression."

Overwhelming Egyptian forces crossed the border with Israel. When the Egyptians finally managed to conquer a small post, using hundreds of soldiers and dozens of tanks, they were amazed to find the Israeli defenders had held out so long. They found a dozen soldiers, half of them injured, using a few semiautomatic weapons. The surprised Egyptians looked fruitlessly for the "hidden" weapons used to hold them off for so long. They could not find the weapons since these "weapons" were in the hearts of men.

This type of training manifests itself in everyday Israeli life and in Israeli self-defense. Success in self-defense does not depend upon any particular technique or weapon, but on responding to whatever the circumstances may be, just as in military combat. The situation is unlikely to match the ideal training environment, so the training environment must match the chaos and uncertainty of real life. An Israeli self-defense practitioner is trained to think on his feet and, as Bruce Lee said, "To respond as an echo." We learn to thrive in chaos.

Idealism and Patriotism

Interviews with soldiers from around the world reveal a low level of idealism. They were sent to fight wars they did not understand. Even heroes will often say, "I was just trying to save my buddies and get home alive."

In the American Revolutionary War, soldiers truly felt they were doing God's work. They were building a new nation and fighting for freedom. They were protecting their fellow citizens from tyranny. They were true patriots and often served without adequate food or pay. Letters reveal that these early Americans were true patriots; fighting for a cause they understood and believed in.

In Israel, that spirit still exists. Soldiers interviewed during the battles in Lebanon knew they were risking their lives. They were pulled out of university or taken from their jobs; they left businesses and families behind, some even flew home from overseas vacations and reported to their units. The interviews reveal the same answers again and again, "We are fighting for our homes. The people back home depend on us; we will stay here as long as it takes." "This is a war for survival; this is a war for the home."

Ordinary people, thrust into battle, find themselves acting as the saviors of the nation, protectors of the people. This develops in them a feeling of patriotism and self-sacrifice that will permeate their lives and affect their future. It will also develop a unique bond with their nation, and a feeling of trust between the soldiers.

Trust

When your life depends upon your fellow soldiers, you learn to trust them, you have no choice. You rely upon them and they are counting upon you. The self-sacrifice to save a fellow soldier manifests itself in superhuman courage and bravery. Running under enemy fire to rescue a soldier caught in cross fire, leaping into a burning tank to pull out a friend, even risking one's life just to return a soldier's body home to give it a proper burial, all these and more took place in the Second Lebanon War and in all the wars of Israel. The trust formed in such challenging times lasts a lifetime.

A Privilege to Serve

For about two thousand years the Jewish people did not have an army of their own. They used their economic leverage, persuasive skills, and whatever means they had to secure the temporary security and protection provided by their current host country. They were powerless to return to their own homeland, they were powerless to establish their own army. They could only dream.

The dream, the hope; to return home, to be a free people once again. The Jews of Europe had a poem called the *Yidishe Medina* (*The Jewish State*, in Yiddish), Dr.

Theodor Herzl wrote a book, *Der Judenstaat* (The State of the Jews, in German), the Jews dreamed of someday being masters of their own domain, free to defend themselves. When an Israeli soldier fights he may think of those days, not so long ago, when a Jew could *not* fight, when a Jew could *not* hold a military weapon, when only our oppressors had such weapons and they were pointed at us.

When I met with the families of our POWs, Yehuda Katz and Tzvi Feldman, I discovered that both boys were named for grandfathers who were murdered during the Holocaust. The grandsons went into battle carrying the legacy of their martyred grandfathers. They may have been feeling, "You were taken away, pushed into a ghetto, perhaps gassed, or shot, or suffered some other cruel death, your body may have been burnt in an oven, but I, your grandson, your namesake, am fighting proudly as a free member of the State of Israel, I am the fulfillment of your greatest dream."

My brother, Ethan, served in a combat unit. Having a strong sense of Jewish history, he felt this message in a powerful way. He wrote, "I remember in basic training, we were on a long hike and my back was killing me and my arms were aching. I just wanted to throw down the gun and the heavy gear. Then I started thinking of what the previous generations of our people would have given to be in my boots, to carry an Israeli made assault rifle (a Galil) with close to three hundred bullets and a couple of hand grenades. I was thinking what would this have meant to Ze'ev Jabotinsky (legendary Zionist leader who wrote, "Jews! Learn to Shoot!") and to Dov Gruner (Jewish martyr who fought to liberate Israel from the British who occupied this land) and the rest, and how much more this would have meant to the previous generation; what would this have meant to the warriors of the Warsaw Ghetto. I realized that in reality I was living the dream of thousands of years of Jewish fighters; how dare I complain about some aches and pains."[75]

My nephew, Arie, the paratrooper, was named for his great-grandfather, Aryeh Yehuda Landau of Poland. When his grandmother Rachel was four years old, the Nazis came to their home and took her parents away. She never saw them again and to this day has never learned their fate.

Rachel survived the worst of the concentration camps, made it to Israel, served in the IDF, and raised a family. When Arie visited Poland with his high school, as part of the March of the Living program, he recited the Jewish mourners' prayer, the *Kaddish*, in honor of his great grandparents. I believe that when he enlisted in the Israeli army he elevated their souls and fulfilled their dreams. He is the embodiment of all they could hope for. He brought them the greatest comfort and pride. When we fight, we fight not only for ourselves, but for all those generations *who could not*, and for all those future generations who should not.

POW – Prisoners of War

Israel is known for going to great lengths to retrieve prisoners of war. So much so that it is seen as a weak point by our enemies. Often Israel will exchange thousands of Arab terrorists for one Israeli soldier, and in many cases it will turn out that the soldier is already dead. Israel places such an emphasis on human life, even after death, that it weakens our bargaining position. Often dozens of live terrorists have been exchanged for the body parts of an Israeli soldier. Even this is considered part of our policy of "bringing the boys home."

In my community of Maaleh Adumim, an unprecedented act of nationalism took place. The town is known for producing many elite combat troops, devoted body and soul to the cause of Israel. In May 2011, a group of pre-army teens came out with a signed declaration, "If we fall captive to the enemy do not release terrorists with blood on their hands in order to free us." This took place during the great national debate over the negotiations for the release of Israeli soldier Gilad Shalit, who was held hostage by Arab terrorists. The debate centered around the question, "How many do we release for one soldier?" If we release terrorists with blood on their hands, i.e., those convicted of murdering Israelis, these terrorists will return to active duty, today, and will try to kill again. So as much as we want to free one soldier we must be aware of the cost; the likely death of many more Israelis. These pre-army teens in Maaleh Adumim felt it was in the national interest that if, God forbid, they fell into enemy captivity, Israel should not release convicted terrorist murderers to secure their release. Imagine—these boys were saying they were willing to stay in captivity indefinitely rather than cause harm to the citizens of Israel! Can there be a greater sacrifice than this! Tomer Mendel, one of the organizers of this act, and a Krav Maga student of mine, stated, "I do not believe that releasing a thousand terrorists is the way to free Gilad Shalit. The State of Israel should have pride, and I am not prepared, if I were to fall captive or taken hostage, that the State should hurt its national interests in order to release me."[76]

CHAPTER 4

Warriors from Childhood

I was having some trouble with the neighbor's kid. I asked my dad to take care of it for me. After all, he was my dad and that is what dads do. He said, "Son, you have to learn to fight your own battles." That was many years ago, but I have never forgotten that lesson. Truly we must all learn to fight our own battles.

We are not just a nation at war. We are involved in a special kind of war. Some call it "The War against the Jews." This war has been going on for a long time and has seen many enemies—the ancient Egyptians, Philistines, Babylonians, Romans, Crusaders, Cossacks, Nazis, the modern Egyptians, and all the other Arab nations. We not only have enemies at our borders, we have enemies within our borders, and beyond our borders—hard core terrorists.

The opponents change, but the war remains. This is not an easy concept to grow up with—the idea that you are hated. But we learn early on that we must be prepared to fight or we will suffer as previous generations of our people have suffered, for in every generation "An enemy rises to destroy us."[77]

We must never be unprepared. From the time a boy is very young, he knows that when he turns eighteen he will be a soldier. To get out of the draft is considered a mark of shame that follows one for the rest of one's life. When I was interviewing for a job, every interview began with the question, "Where did you serve?" At least in my circles, a courtship and a friendship involve that question. Everyone knows where their friends served. People define you by where you served. Were you in a combat unit? Did you serve in intelligence? Were you in the air force or the navy?

For many it will be the pride of their lives. They may work many years in meaningless unfulfilling jobs, but they will think back with pride to their days in the military, to the days when they led brave men into battle.

Friendships formed in the army will create a bond that lasts a lifetime. A warrior will always be there for his brother warrior. He may turn old and gray, but to his brother warriors he will always be eighteen. They will remember him as a young warrior—they will reminisce about the days when they stopped the Syrians in the North or the Egyptians in the South.

Speak to just about any sixteen or seventeen-year-old Israeli boy or girl and they will already be experts on the different units and what it takes to qualify for each one. They will know how long and how difficult basic training is and which units have the best reputation. They will be able to identify each unit's symbol and tag.

Most high school students are involved in some sort of pre-military training to prepare them for military service. This is not mandatory—it is done on a private basis outside the framework of the IDF. Gyms are filled with seventeen-year-old boys. You will find them lifting weights, hitting the heavy bag, and doing push-ups. Late at night you will see teenagers running up hills, sprinting—they are getting ready for Lebanon and Gaza. They want to be the best. They dream of being in the top, most elite combat units, but some are placed in support roles such as logistics, ammunition, or repairing weapons. Sometimes, in Hebrew, this is referred to with the rhyme "*ha moach me'achorei ha koach*" or "the brains behind the brawn."

Follow Me

There are many organizations and programs, like college prep courses, that promise to train the boys and help them get into the best units. There are also programs run for free by veterans who just want to help. One organization is called Aharai! Follow me! This slogan is used by Israeli officers who lead their troops into battle. Israeli officers lead from the front, not from some far-off post or in the back of the troops. Israel has a high rate of officer casualty because officers are the first to face the enemy.

The Aharai! Follow me! organization started more than ten years ago when a discharged combat officer was walking through a poor neighborhood. He saw a group of high school students training on their own to prepare for combat units. He offered to train them, for free. Over the years, this group has grown and now has branches in more than one hundred locations throughout Israel (a state smaller than New Jersey). The group prepares high school students for military training, tours the country, teaches the history of this ancient land, and volunteers by helping needy communities. At the end of the course, the participants sign a declaration to serve faithfully in the army and continue as community leaders after completion of their service.

In the various youth movements a great deal of time will be devoted to hiking and getting to know the land. The nation's history will be learned and will become part of their individual psyche. They will walk where the biblical Abraham walked, they will stand where Joshua stood before attacking Jericho, they will see where King David fought, they will relive the battles of Israel from biblical times to our own and they will hear the stories of heroism. They will learn how to use a compass and "read" the land. They will hike on difficult terrain and cook their food outdoors. It is all fun, but it is also pre-military training. They will feel the thread that weaves from ancient history to modern challenges, they will live Jewish history.

After regular service is completed, many will sign on for a few more years or for a career in the military. All will continue to serve in the reserves. They are a people's army; plumbers and farmers, accountants and teachers, ready to be called up at any moment, change into their uniform and become the saviors of their people. There is a code of honor, an unwritten pact: when you need me—I will be there.

During my college years, a former soldier came to speak to us, something about him stood out—he had only one arm. He said words I will never forget, "When my people needed me I dropped everything and reported for duty. Now I am no longer able to fight, my arm was shot off; I can no longer defend my young children. It is now your turn, you owe it to me."

Soldiers Remain United

Soldiers will meet in the reserves over the years; their families will meet. And tragically, those many families who have lost a father, a son, a brother, will mourn forever, keeping the photos and awards of the fallen soldier proudly displayed for all to see. When a young member of the family comes home for his first vacation from the army, the older members will compare notes about everything from the type of weapon used to the food served in the kitchen. Stories will be exchanged. The military is a thread woven into all aspects of life. Military expressions are a part of everyday life; to "return equipment" means that something has come to an end. Military time (using 1400 instead of 2 pm) is in standard use. One of the frustrating aspects of this society is that you can come to pick up your laptop from the repair shop and find a note "Owner has been called to the reserves, back in three weeks. Sorry."

Alertness

Every mall and restaurant in Israel has security guards and most are armed with a handgun or a short rifle. The larger establishments have metal detectors. Customers are searched and bags are checked. Roadblocks line the highways; cars are stopped, trunks are opened, and identification papers are requested.

From a young age, we are taught not to pick up a cigarette box or button from the floor. As a child, I recall we had a poster on the wall with pictures of boxes, buttons, and various toys. The caption read, "Suspicious objects: don't touch, it might explode." From time, to time a security expert would come and talk to us kids about the dangers in the world. Caution became part of who we are. Even now, I will never pick up a box of cigarettes or a matchbox from the floor, despite my tendency to clean up and to be a good citizen.

A bag must never be left unattended, if it is, it is assumed to be a bomb and the bomb squad will be called. You will not be reimbursed for any damage done to your personal possessions; *you* are to blame for your careless negligence. An American tourist showed up at a bank to cash his traveler's checks. The only problem was the checks were filled with holes. "What happened here?" the teller asked. The tourist said he put down his backpack for a few minutes and went to get a drink. When he returned, the entire area was roped off and the bomb squad was detonating his bag. His checks were damaged in the controlled explosion.

Blowing up abandoned articles is standard. One often hears the expression "suspicious object." You can be walking along King George Street in Jerusalem when you find a crowd gathered and no one proceeding. "What's going on?" you ask. The answer comes in the expression that all understand, "suspicious object." No further explanation is necessary. We are used to this kind of alertness and security; it becomes second nature.

To complain about delays is practically unheard of; people understand that national security is more important that anything you may have to do. Suddenly life takes on a different perspective. Your personal errands no longer seem so crucial. Employers readily accept "suspicious object" as a valid excuse for being late.

I recall when I came to train at Karate College in the United States—we were all lined up for registration. I had my heavy duffle bag on my back and my carry-on bag in my hand because "one never leaves a bag unattended." Then I noticed something strange—I was the only one doing that. Everyone else had piled up their bags next to a wall and proceeded "bag free" during the long registration process. I could not understand this lapse in security. How could martial artists leave their bags unattended? How could they be so careless? For us, any bag unwatched for a few minutes can no longer be assumed to be safe—it must be examined by an expert.

Children here in Israel enjoy watching the robot that bomb squads use to pick up a suspicious object. They watch it place the suspicious object in the "security hole" and then detonate it. We understand what is going on. This has the effect of creating a nation of very alert and careful people.

Many stories have been told of Israelis spotting suspicious activities while on vacation abroad and alerting others. Like trained detectives, they are looking out for something that is a bit out of the ordinary, a sign of trouble. We learn to listen to things that "go bump in the night." By the time an Israeli begins his military service, he has already had significant training in gathering intelligence, basic detective work, and spotting suspicious objects and characters.

An Orthodox Jerusalem man was walking along in his neighborhood of Mea She'arim when he noticed something odd inside a garbage can. He alerted the police. It turned out to be a large explosive, placed just a few feet away from a school where hundreds of children were studying.

When my brother was a newlywed, his English wife was shocked to learn that he slept with a handgun under his pillow. This comes as no surprise to an Israeli as we all do this in the army. We learn that a weapon is never, ever, to be left unattended; it must be kept under a double lock, never handed to anyone without a license. Carelessness with weapons will lead to long jail terms.

Before we enter a cab we try to verify the identity of the driver, Israeli or Arab. An unknown driver can be a terrorist looking for a victim. We check before we buzz someone into a building, we look in the peephole before opening the door. We have learned to be careful, the hard way.

A young man and his wife, new immigrants from England slept with their window open. We have an expression in Israel; "an open window invites a terrorist." The inexperienced young man heard a sound and went to look. A knife-wielding terrorist climbed in. The man was killed that night. Another widow was created.

A student of Greek origin came to train with me in Krav Maga; he was only nineteen years old, but had the wisdom and knowledge of a much older man. There was something about him that struck a chord with me, like we had some deep connection. I finally understood that there was something very "Jewish" about him; carried Greek history in his soul, he felt the pain of Greek land occupied by foreigners, he bore the scars of massacres and expulsions that took place years before he was born. He was a serious person, as are Israelis.

This is a serious people. It is commonly said, "Israel is the only country in the world where 'small talk' consists of loud, angry debate over politics and religion." Israelis tend to think less of some tourists, or some new immigrants, as being somewhat shallow and preoccupied with matters of insignificance. They talk about topics of little significance, debate matters of no importance. In Israel, even children have an opinion on politics; children know their history. Israelis get loud and angry when discussing politics, religion, and history because they care passionately about these topics. These are issues that truly matter in their daily lives; they are not indifferent about them.

National issues affect everyone. You care about national policies because it is you who will be sent to the border to defend them, you or your kids, or you and your kids. In many wars, fathers and sons are fighting at the same time, each with his unit. National policy affects us all, and we have an opinion we want to share; we feel we understand the issue at least as well as the prime minister and we should be heard. This is a democracy of warriors. We fight and we want a say in the decisions that affect our lives. So if you are going to argue with an Israeli, make sure you know your facts first, otherwise, as we say over here, "the women will eat you for breakfast."

Young Warriors

Foreign Krav Maga students who come to Israel to train often remark about the toughness of Israeli kids; the way they train, the way they fight. It is as if they are indeed warriors in training, their mental fortitude, their attitude, is already being prepared for combat. Perhaps it is seeing fathers, uncles, cousins, and older siblings preparing for military service. Perhaps it is the news, the ceremonies at school honoring the fallen, and stories about heroes. Or is it seeing guns everywhere; M-16 rifles, grenade launchers, and a variety of handguns? Perhaps it is learning our history, how we defied the odds and managed to survive war after war.

There is something in the air that makes kids grow up differently over here, they are not like their counterparts in Europe or America, you can sense it in their look, in their eyes. These are battle hardened kids. Somehow they know that at eighteen years of age they will not be trying to choose a major at college, they will be chasing down terrorists or protecting the citizens of Israel from a foreign invader. This knowledge permeates their childhood and changes their outlook. Like an animal in the wild, they are aware of danger and conditioned to respond, their survival instincts are honed. They develop an ability to take charge and respond, an ability that will serve them well in the military and throughout their lives.

Some people hope that "when my child reaches eighteen there will be no more wars, there will be no draft." But we know this is not true, we know that another generation must be trained and prepared to fight.

CHAPTER 5

Everyday Heroes

Fighting off terrorists and other bad guys; stories of heroism, self-defense, and self-sacrifice.

Jacob the Bus Driver

Jacob, now in his mid-fifties, woke up that morning as any other morning, bright and early. He had the morning route for the bus company and could not be late. The route began as it always had—familiar faces, smiles, and greetings of *shalom* (hello); people on their way to work or school. This was before the days where most bus stops had armed security guards; the driver was alone with his precious cargo—his passengers.

Suddenly a passenger pulled out a knife and began stabbing. It was a terrorist who tried to take over the bus. Jacob pulled the bus to a halt and was upon the terrorist in no time. He sustained cuts, but disarmed the assailant.

TV crews interviewed the "hero for a day" and asked what went through his mind when he attacked the armed terrorist, wasn't he afraid? "My military training just kicked in," he said. "You know I was a fighter! I served in a combat unit. I came to the rescue of my passengers just as I would on the battlefield. I did not think of myself, I just reacted." This self-sacrifice is not a conscious thought process. It is an instinct that is developed through military training and carried over into civilian life. One may take off his uniform, but his military spirit remains.

Imagine sending your child to school knowing that the bus driver is a trained soldier with combat experience. Once he drove a tank, now he drives a school bus. As your child walks into school, he walks past the school security guard, a recently released soldier from the *Golani* or *Givati* brigades. When your child enters the classroom, he is greeted by his teacher, formerly a member of an elite combat unit. The school nurse served in Lebanon and she completed basic military training and can take apart an M-16 rifle in minutes. The janitor is a special forces veteran; the principal was a tank commander. These are the people that make up your child's day—this is Israel.

The story is so common that one cannot possibly remember how often it has occurred. Nearly anyone can be a hero for a day; nearly everyone has some training and experience. It is as if secret agents are hidden all over the country, dressed as ordinary people, waiting to be activated by a secret signal.

You could be sitting on a bus, surrounded by ordinary-looking people, some old, some young, some male, some female, some Israeli born, some with foreign accents. You do not know who they are, but I can assure you of this—each one has a story to tell. One young fellow has a plastic leg; he lost his leg while fighting terrorists in Gaza. Another fellow was among the first to cross the Suez

Canal back in '73 under Egyptian artillery fire. Most of his unit was hit, but he survived and is still traumatized. An old gray-haired woman was a messenger for the French resistance against the Nazi occupiers. An old man fought at the Battle of Stalingrad in Russia and has many medals for valor and courage. His Hebrew may be weak, but he carries himself with an air of dignity, he is a warrior. Yet another survived the ghettos of Nazi occupied Europe, escaped to the forest where he joined the partisans and fought the Nazis, joined the illegal immigration movement, challenged the British blockade, came to Israel to fight for independence, defended his kibbutz against Arab raiders, and lost a son in the 1967 Six Day War. Another fellow, young and "wet behind the ears" recently led his troops into Gaza and liquidated a terrorist cell. You show respect to all, because, despite their humble appearances, you are among true heroes.

This is a nation that has fought on countless different fronts, speaking numerous different languages. There are Polish-speaking Jews who fought the Nazis and held out for longer than the entire Polish army. There are French-speaking Jews who sabotaged Nazi war efforts and blew up their trains and railroads. There are English speakers, veterans of World War Two, who came to Israel to volunteer and helped form the Israeli air force. There are Russian speakers who served for years in the Russian military. There are Amharic speakers from Ethiopia, serving in elite combat units.

An eighteen-year-old girl, serving with a combat unit, put the "makeup" on "her boys" before they went out for their big nighttime operation against terrorists, and cried out to them, "Every one of you is coming home, you understand! Do you hear me? You are all coming home!"

You show respect because any of the people you bump into could be a hero. You show respect because it is these people who allow us to lead normal lives as a free and independent people.

The Flight Attendant

During a flight to Turkey, a knife-wielding terrorist attacked a flight attendant. His goal was to use her to get into the cockpit, take over the plane, and fly it into a tall building in Israel.

The flight attendant surprised him by using evasive movements to avoid his slashing attempts. She later admitted she was terrified. Her delaying tactics gave the armed security guards the opportunity to subdue the terrorist. No one was hurt. Passengers remarked that during the episode the flight attendants were "very cool, they calmed us down." The crew consisted entirely of former soldiers.

The female flight attendant used evasive movements, as taught in Krav Maga, to avoid the knife and buy some time. Disarming a knife attacker is very difficult, it is better to use body movements and just get out of the way. The idea behind evasive movements is to move that part of the body most imminently threatened, e.g., if it is to the head, pull your head back, to the stomach, pull your stomach in, to the leg, jump back. While doing this, keep your forearms in front of you as a barrier. The forearms can take a potential cut, but much better than your wrist, neck or stomach. Her quick movements saved herself and possibly all those on board and many more on the ground.

The University Student

Following obligatory military service, three years minimum for men, many begin their university studies. As a result, nearly all university students are in the reserves and can be called up at a moment's notice. Naturally, this causes disruptions in their studies. Due to this situation there are always three different dates for final exams in order to accommodate students called up for reserve duty. A student can be in the lecture hall one day listening to a professor and taking notes and then within forty-eight hours be on the battlefield listening to his commander and loading his tank. Walking to the mailbox to pick up his mail, the university student is always aware that finding a brown envelope with a military stamp means, "I've been called up again!"

Recently, the IDF pulled off a daring raid and in a bloody operation eliminated a dangerous terror cell that had cost us many lives. The leader of the operation was praised for his bravery and professional undertaking of the operation. "What are your plans now?" the press asked him.

"Well, I was immersed in my biology studies before I got this call-up. I was studying for a major exam and the pressure was really getting to me. This has been a welcome break and now I feel I am ready to return to my studies. I just hope my professor accepts my excuse for missing the midterm." Within a few days, he was just another student in the classroom. In Israel, you can be sitting in a lecture hall, never realizing that the young man sitting next to you is a real-life Rambo.

The Waiter

After military service, many young men take a "light" job, something that does not involve too much thinking, something to ease their way back to civilian life and make a few dollars (actually shekels) so they can afford a trip abroad. One such man was working as the main waiter at Caffit; a popular coffee house in Jerusalem.

One day, one of the customers trying to get in aroused his suspicion. Based on the art of profiling—judging his accent, body mannerisms, a touch of nervousness—the waiter decided to jump him. Single-handedly and without warning, the waiter immobilized the man, who turned out to be a terrorist. He had several pounds of explosives in a "suicide bomber belt" around his waist. The lives of the coffee house patrons were saved.

If you are tackling a suicide bomber on your own, you must grab one of his arms, swing around the back and grab his other arm. Speed and the element of surprise are crucial. Pull his arms up and lock them from behind. Actually, the most important ingredient is courage.

The next day the waiter returned to work as if nothing had happened. To his surprise, he opened the mail one day to find a check for five thousand dollars. It was sent by an American supporter of Israel who wanted to reward the "everyday, soon to be forgotten, heroes."

The Security Guard

Eli was interested in martial arts. After his compulsory military service he traveled to Thailand and trained in Thai boxing. He returned to Israel and hoped to open a gym, but did not have the finances to do so. He got a job as a security guard at a Tel Aviv nightclub, Zigota. The job of a security guard is not easy, standing long hours for little pay, closely eyeing hundreds of people, wondering who might be a terrorist. One night he saw a vehicle driving toward the club. By the nature of the speed and angle of the driving, Eli evaluated the approach as a suicide attack. Dozens of club goers were outside the club waiting to get in. Eli reacted quickly and opened fire on the driver, killing him on the spot. An explosion went off in the car. After examining the vehicle, police discovered large quantities of explosives. The driver, an Arab terrorist, planned to crash his vehicle into the partygoers and set off the explosives, causing massive damage. Eli's quick thinking and rapid fire saved countless lives.

The Cook

During basic training, one learns many essential skills, such as taking apart and cleaning various types of weapons, and how to clean the latrine. Equally important are the lessons on attitude, *moreshet krav*, (fighting heritage). We are taught that regardless of your official position, tank driver, cook, intelligence officer, you are first of all a soldier and you must always behave as one. You might be a military doctor or a computer expert, but you are first a soldier and you must possess the attitude, training, and the fighting spirit, of a soldier. You must possess the initiative and "take charge" attitude of a soldier. You must be able to lead when leadership is required. To illustrate this point, we were told of an incident where terrorists managed to infiltrate a base. It was the early hours of the morning and the cook was busy in the kitchen when he heard something. The career cook grabbed his M-16 rifle, went outside carefully, took cover, and opened fire. He eliminated both terrorists.

In the army, it is ingrained in us—your rifle must always be within arm's reach: you sleep with it, eat with it, go to the bathroom with it, and shower with it. At all times, you are a warrior. This attitude translates into everyday life, as civilians, all soldiers in the reserves, are alert to potential danger and suspicious behavior.

The Post Office

"It is Not the Age, it is the Attitude," read the morning papers. A young thug tried to rob a post office. Two customers waiting in line—a retired schoolteacher and a retired plumber—thwarted his efforts. The plumber, a man in his seventies, jumped the young thug from behind while the retired school teacher, a woman in her sixties, joined in and grabbed his legs. Together the two subdued the attacker. Later, when they were interviewed, they said, "This is my branch, I like the people here, I could not stand to see some kid come in and rob this place. I just reacted without thinking of my personal welfare."

The Insurance Agent

Israelis are used to the sudden sound of terrorist activity and react quickly. Case in point: Eli, an insurance agent working in his third floor office in downtown Jerusalem. Eli heard an explosion. He immediately raced down the three flights and out to the street. He spotted two terrorists and drew his personal handgun that he always carried. He opened fire and hit one of the terrorists. He chased the other one and fired, but his gun jammed. Eli caught up with the terrorist, smashed him over the head with the butt of his gun, knocking him to the ground.

Eli was not just a mild-mannered insurance salesman. He was a commando soldier in the reserves. In an instant, he was able to make the mental switch from businessman back to commando soldier. Whether it was the Sinai desert where he fought during the 1973 Yom Kippur War or downtown Jerusalem, the same mental training and attitude guided him.

In another incident in Jerusalem, two friends, both members of the military border police, were casually strolling down the street when they spotted terrorists. They drew their sidearms and opened fire. What followed was a classic Wild West style shootout in a modern urban center. At the end of the exchange one terrorist was dead and the other injured and taken into custody.

The Lawyer, the Hero

I was in a lawyer's office to sign some documents. I tend to look at the walls while waiting, and read the diplomas. I noticed several diplomas that did not fit in with your standard law office. These spoke of "bravery in the service of mankind," "saving lives during terrorist attacks," and "excellent emergency care under fire." I asked Dror, the lawyer, about these diplomas. He smiled, ever so modestly, and said that although he had a busy law practice, one day a week he was an emergency paramedic. As such, he was often called to a scene seconds after a bomb went off, or as a shooting was taking place.

He said he felt like he was continuing his military service, his national service; he was helping his people in a real hands-on kind of way. I looked at the walls of his office and saw photos of his family, a wife, and six children. Surely this man needed to make a good living to support his large family, surely it cost a great deal to put six children through private religious schools. And yet, he found the time to leave a successful law practice and run to the scenes of suicide bombings and other attacks. Just to view such scenes is horrific, and yet he did it. He was, to me, one of the unsung heroes of Israel, and there are countless others. They go through life nearly undetected, giving of their time, putting themselves in the line of fire, seeking no reward. It gives one hope for mankind.

The Emptying Synagogue

It was October 1973, *Yom Kippur*, the Day of Atonement, the most solemn day in the Jewish religious calendar. I was, of course, in our local synagogue, praying with my father and brothers. It is a difficult day; no food or drink allowed, just endless praying.

The Egyptians must have thought of that when they decided on a surprise attack on that special day. We sat in the synagogue, in prayer, totally unaware. Gradually the synagogue began to empty. Men walked out in the middle of prayer and didn't return. Rumors began to circulate.

By the afternoon break, we knew what was happening. Once again our enemies initiated a war, violating our holy day. Details were still blurry, but the flow of men from the synagogue told us everything we needed to know. Once again, the men were leaving the house of prayer and heading for war, a war that would cost us nearly three thousand lives.

Most of my teachers would not return for many months. One popular teacher would write us postcards that were posted on the school bulletin board. I remember the day the postcards stopped coming and we heard the sad news; he would not be returning; he had been killed in a battle on the Egyptian front.

Most of us students used our free time to volunteer and fill in for men who were called up. We picked crops in the *kibbutz* fields, painted car headlights (so enemy bombers would not spot them at night during the blackouts) and I delivered the mail for a while. All the regular workers were on the front lines.

Gradually, school resumed. Our substitute teachers were mostly older men who were over military age. It was a somber year. Kids canceled their customary *bar mitzvah* celebrations. Our whole attitude toward life changed. Everyone had a father, an uncle, an older brother, in the service.

My father, although over the age for combat duty, was called up. He served in connection with the home front. Nearly everyone served in some way. Over the radio we would hear code commands such as "black crow report to base," and "mother bear return to den." We knew this meant more reserve soldiers were being called up. Air raids would send us running to the nearby bomb shelters.

The thing I remember most was that first day—when men had to put away their prayer books and pick up their rifles. These were the everyday heroes—the men at the local synagogue, our schoolteachers and our mailmen—who pushed back the Egyptians and the Syrians and kept us safe.

The Fighting High School

A knife-wielding terrorist broke into a Jerusalem high school. He did not know that this was a school for "challenged" kids with discipline issues. These troubled kids had dropped out of most regular schools. Before the terrorist knew what was happening, a bunch of eager teenage boys were all over him. The terrorist realized he had just attacked a hornet's nest and tried to escape, but was pursued by the students. The principal—it takes a tough guy to run this kind of school—grabbed a stick and joined the enthusiastic students. He too wanted a piece of the action. The battered terrorist was taken into custody. The headlines the next morning read, "Terrorist Picks Wrong School."

Fighting off a Rapist

Rona had mistakenly allowed a "nice boy" into her dorm room, to "watch a video." She had taken some Krav Maga classes, "As a precaution, since I had heard there are a lot of rape attempts on campus." She learned a few basic techniques and practiced them occasionally.

When Rona's date started making advances, she made it clear she was not interested. The rejected lover did not take no for an answer. He pinned her down and grabbed her throat. Rona saw the writing on the wall and reacted as she had been trained. She pulled his hands a bit to the side, to allow enough air in so she could breathe, and grabbed his throat and squeezed as tight as she could. As he recoiled from the pain she kneed him in the groin, pushing him off. She got up and ran out the nearest door. It turned out he had tried this before on a friend of hers, but the friend "did not want to ruin his reputation" so she kept it a secret. Rona was wiser; she reported him at once.

Unwelcome Approach in Turkey

Samantha was sitting alone at a café while vacationing in Turkey. A local man saw this as an invitation. When she stood up and told him to take a hike, the unwelcome intruder grabbed her for a forced hug. She held on to his shoulders and thrust a powerful knee kick directly to his groin. He keeled over and walked away in shame. Samantha learned this technique from watching a movie on TV. In the movie, an abused woman used Krav Maga to defend herself and regain her self-respect.

Off Duty but Always on Duty

Yaakov and Uri were off duty. They had finished their shift as security guards for a private company in the Old City of Jerusalem and were casually walking home when they noticed a group of somewhat drunk Arabs harassing a *yeshiva* student. They walked up and advised the aggressors to take a hike.

Instantly, the five Arab youths jumped on the two guards. One was knocked to the ground while two of the Arabs were kicking him and trying to get to his gun side. He knew there was a danger of them trying to grab his handgun. He rolled on the side of his handgun, thus protecting it from being taken away and used against him. Although he was getting severely kicked, he knew he must never leave the handgun exposed. His friend, using a spare magazine, managed to slash the face of the one of the assailants. The sight of blood freaked them out and they all ran. The *yeshiva* student and the guards were unharmed. Elite security guards are taught to conceal their weapon as much as possible while still being able to access it as quickly as possible. A shirt or jacket should always cover the gun; this makes it harder for someone to grab it from you.

Deranged Man Disarmed

A distraught man was holding a gun, pointing it directly at his family. He was unemployed and desperate and wanted someone from the government to come and speak with him. A security guard approached him and said he was, in fact, sent by the government. He signaled to another guard to come from behind and disarm the unfortunate fellow.

Walking his Dog

Vladimir was walking his dog in the valley of the Judean desert one evening when he spotted two unfamiliar men. They were Arabs. One extended his hand; the other was suddenly out of view. Vladimir responded by extending his hand in friendship. The Arab pulled him forward and stabbed him with his free hand. The second Arab reappeared and both stabbed Vladimir repeatedly. Vladimir managed to fight back and kick the knife out of one of the Arab's hands. Both Arabs fled. Vladimir was stabbed thirteen times and nearly bled to death. Fortunately he survived.

Vladimir was caught off guard. What he should have done, despite the risk of appearing rude, was offer only a slight nod instead of a handshake. A handshake can prove very dangerous. Just because someone extends his hand does not mean you *must* take it. If someone does have a grip on your hand, there are many options open to you; you can strike the person with your free hand and then, using your entire body, twist out of the grip. You could strike him under his radar with a knee kick to the groin; this will loosen his grip right away.

Girls Hitchhiking

I advise against hitchhiking, period. However, there are many places in Israel where public transportation is limited, and many young people do hitchhike. Israeli youth are fearless and believe this is their land, as God said to Abraham, "Arise, and walk through the land, the length and breadth of it, for to you I will give it."[78] As such, they are everywhere, despite the dangers.

Two teenage girls from a religious academy near one of the settlements were waiting for a ride. A car pulled right up to the curb, the girls had been trained to be careful. As they took a look to see if the driver was a Jew or an Arab, the two Arab passengers in the back seat got out and tried to grab the girls and pull them into the car. The girls fought them off and managed to get away. Their alertness and fighting spirit made the difference.

Security Guard

At the entrance to the supermarket in the Beit HaKerem neighborhood in Jerusalem worked a trustworthy security guard, an older man trying to make a living. He noticed something odd, a young Arab girl, only sixteen years old walked over to an old Arab woman selling figs outside the supermarket. Very quickly the old Arab woman rose up, grabbed her bags of figs and left. The young girl then tried to enter the supermarket. The security guard stopped her and blocked her entry with his body. She detonated her bomb, killing herself and the security guard. He paid the ultimate price. No one in the supermarket was hurt.

The Professor, the Olympic Team, and the *Yeshiva* Student

Heroism by everyday heroes is not limited to Israeli soil. The unique spirit of this nation shows itself outside the borders of Israel as well. In the 2007 massacre at Virginia Tech in the United States where thirty-two students and faculty were killed by a student, Professor Liviu Librescu died fighting, as a hero, as a warrior.

A student in the French class described how the gunman walked into the class, went up and down the aisles just shooting people. He said, "Nobody tried to be a hero." The teacher and many of the students were killed. (There is some speculation that the teacher attempted to barricade the door and stop the gunman, but she did not succeed, only seven students in the French class survived).

The story was quite different in Professor Liviu Librescu's, engineering class. By blocking the door, he used himself as a shield to stop the shooter and give his students time. He had the clarity of mind to give his final lesson: jump out the windows, save your lives! All but one of his students made it to safety. Who was this man? He was a Jew, an Israeli, and a survivor of the Holocaust. His behavior reminds me of two similar incidents.

In Munich, Germany, 1972, the world's finest athletes gathered to compete in the Olympics. It had been only twenty-seven years since the Nazi Holocaust and the memories, for the Jewish people, were still fresh. Many of the members of the Israeli team had lost relatives in the Holocaust, but those interviewed prior to the event looked on the Olympic games as a way of making a statement of defiance to the Nazi murderers of the past by showing the resilience of the Jewish people.

The day before the games began, the Israeli team visited the nearby concentration camp where Jews had been murdered.

Fencing coach, Andre Spitzer, laid a wreath. He himself would soon join the list of victims of anti-Jewish hatred.

The Israeli team enjoyed a night out on the town, watching the play *Fiddler on the Roof*, starring a fellow Israeli. All seemed brotherly in the Olympic village.

The Arabs sent a team of their own; armed terrorists. With AK-47 assault rifles, handguns, and grenades, they entered the sleepy, peaceful village. As they tried to enter the Israeli athletes' room Yosef Gutfreund, a wrestling referee, was awakened by the faint noise at the door, which housed the Israeli coaches and officials. He investigated and discovered masked men with guns. He shouted a warning to his sleeping roommates and threw his nearly three hundred pounds of weight against the door in a futile attempt to stop the intruders from forcing their way in. Gutfreund's actions gave his roommate, weightlifting coach Tuvia Sokolovsky, enough time to smash a window and escape.

Wrestling coach, Moshe Weinberg, fought back against the intruders, who shot him through his cheek and then forced him to help them find more hostages. Leading the kidnappers past the apartment with more Israeli athletes, Weinberg lied to the kidnappers by telling them that the residents of the apartment were not Israelis. He risked his life to save his fellow Israelis. The wounded Weinberg again attacked the kidnappers, allowing one of his wrestlers, Gad Tsobari, to escape via the underground parking garage. Weinberg, a powerful man, knocked one of the terrorists unconscious and slashed another terrorist with a fruit knife. Another terrorist shot him to death. Moshe Weinberg died a hero's death, fighting back and saving the lives of others. He died a warrior. Inside the apartment, weightlifter Yosef Romano, a veteran of the 1967 Six Day War, attacked the intruders, slashing terrorist, Afif Ahmed Hamid, in the face with a paring knife and grabbing his AK-47 away from him before being shot to death by another terrorist. Romano's bloodied corpse was left at the feet of his teammates all day as a warning. Yosef Romano died a hero.

Other Israeli members were awakened by the screams and warnings and managed to escape. The two women on the team were housed in a separate part of the Olympic Village inaccessible to the terrorists. Two Israelis died hero's deaths while nine more were taken hostage. In the failed West German rescue attempt, several terrorists would be killed, but so would all the Israeli hostages. Most of the bodies were found riddled with multiple gunshots. The world had been waiting to see how Germany would protect these Jews.

Jim McKay of ABC News reported, "When I was a kid, my father used to say 'Our greatest hopes and our worst fears are seldom realized.' Our worst fears have been realized tonight. They've now said that there were eleven hostages. Two were killed in their rooms yesterday morning, nine were killed at the airport tonight. They're all gone."

They are all gone! Words like these shake your world. I was just a child at the time, but the "Munich Massacre" became part of my childhood, part of my vocabulary, part of who I am, part of our history as the Jewish people, as the people of Israel. We came as athletes, we came in peace, and the world failed us again. Back home in Israel we were all stunned, shell shocked, devastated. The wound was deep.

Five terrorists were killed during the botched rescue attempt and one German police officer was killed by the terrorists. The remaining terrorists, with only one exception, and many other leading terrorists who were involved in the planning of the massacre, were eventually tracked down by the Israelis and eliminated. One reporter wrote that the Israeli revenge operations continued for more than twenty years. He detailed the assassination in Paris in 1992 of the Palestine Liberation Organization's head of intelligence and said that an Israeli general confirmed there was a link back to Munich.

The Olympic Games continued, but the Israeli team went home. The bravery and heroism of the Israeli athletes would not be forgotten. Yet, forty years later, despite pressure and fervent requests, the Olympic Committee refused to honor the dead with one single solitary minute of silence.

In a *yeshiva* in Jerusalem, once again Arab terrorists broke in with the intention of gunning down students. They broke through to the kitchen, but two of the boys blocked the door to the main dining room with their bodies, again, dying as heroes while allowing others to escape. They gave their lives to delay the terrorists long enough for the others to escape and for help to arrive.

So what was Professor Librescu at Virginia Tech thinking? What was going through his mind? He was living the lesson of Jewish history.

We will never know for sure what the professor was thinking, but I have a theory. I recall the story about the American Nazi's planned march in Skokie, Illinois; home to many Holocaust survivors. When the leaders of the community spoke and advised people to "stay inside, lock the doors, close the shutters, don't pay them any attention, don't look," a survivor rose up and said, "As I sat here listening to you I was reminded of a similar event, with similar speakers, men in suits who came from the big city to tell us what to do. But it was not in America, and it was a long time ago. It was when I was a boy in Germany, with my parents. The Nazis there too wanted to march, and the Jewish leaders there too urged restraint, 'Don't make trouble. Don't give them attention.' Those people were all killed. So don't tell me to stay home, don't tell me to be quiet, I will not listen this time, I will be out there with a baseball bat or a hammer, I will fight them with whatever I have, but I will no longer be silent. Never again."

Professor Librescu was born in Romania. When Romania joined forces with Nazi Germany in World War Two, the young Librescu was interned in a labor camp, and then sent along with his family and thousands of other Jews to a central ghetto in the city of Focsani. Hundreds of thousands of Romanian Jews were killed by the collaborationist regime during the war.

Perhaps Professor Librescu remembered all those who were massacred back in his native Romania, perhaps he remembered killers like "the Butcher of Bucharest," perhaps he learned that a nation of warriors fights back, that ordinary people *do* try to be heroes. The attack took place on "Holocaust Memorial Day," and he gave the greatest memorial to the victims of those massacres and killings, he fought back.

The *Yeshiva*: Eight Holy Victims

As a young man, I was a student at the *Mercaz HaRav* rabbinical college, or *yeshiva*, in Jerusalem. This is an elite rabbinical institute, the crown of the religious Zionist academies, where young scholars study the Talmud and biblical texts. I recall my days there as days of purity; from morning until night our entire beings were immersed in holy pursuits. Our days were filled with the words of God, the prophets of old, ethical teachings of the rabbis, and lessons on how to conduct ourselves.

While I was in the United States in 2008 on a Krav Maga seminar tour, my rabbi called me with the terrible news; an Arab terrorist infiltrated the *yeshiva* and opened fire with an automatic weapon. He murdered eight holy students who were busily engaged in studying the word of God.

A nearby resident, David S., heard the shots. Like many, he was a young man home on leave from his basic military service. He grabbed his army issue rifle and without concern for his own safety ran to the scene of the slaughter. He chased the terrorist up to the roof where he shot him dead. Soon his brother-in-law would also have the opportunity to be the hero. One hero inspires another.

The Bicycle Rider and the Bulldozer

In 2008, while riding his bicycle down the main street of Jerusalem, Moshe P. notices a commotion. An Arab terrorist has come up with yet another original idea, he is driving his bulldozer into people on their lunch break, he is turning over cars, he runs his bulldozer into a commercial bus filled with people. The bus is overturned and several passengers are already dead as the ruthless terrorist continues to crush them with his bulldozer. Moshe leaps off this bike and runs toward the terrorist. He grabs a gun from a passerby, climbs on the tractor, and shoots and kills the terrorist. Several other passersby had also jumped on the tractor and wrestled with the terrorist before Moshe shot him. Later when interviewed, Moshe said, "I did what is expected of any civilian or soldier."

Moshe was a member of the *Golani* brigade and was home on vacation. He was a resident of Jerusalem and a graduate of a *yeshiva* high school. Like many religious Israelis, he chose the challenging five-year *hesder* program, combining military service with religious studies.

After his heroic spontaneous action, Moshe received an award from General Eizenkot of the Northern command. The general said, "What is special in his actions is we are dealing here with a soldier at the start of his military path, who during a vacation happened upon an incident, displayed initiative, clear thinking and calmness, made contact with the enemy (a central teaching of Israeli military doctrine) and as such saved human lives. Sergeant P. set an example of how an IDF soldier should behave." Present at the ceremony were friends and family, including his brother-in-law, David S., who killed the terrorist at the *Mercaz HaRav Yeshiva*. The General added, "The same values came into play in both incidents and should serve as an example to all of us."

The Second Bulldozer Attack

Not three weeks later, another chance passerby had an opportunity to be a hero. Just before 2 pm, Ghassan Abu Tir, a twenty-two-year-old Jerusalem Arab, a construction worker working on a project near the King David Hotel in downtown Jerusalem, crashed his bulldozer into a local Jerusalem bus. He then continued to ram into five cars before he was shot dead by a driver. In this attack no civilians were killed, but several were injured and one lost a leg.

The terrorist succeeded in inflicting terror on the drivers. "I was driving on the main road when suddenly the tractor hit me in the rear on the right-hand side," said Avi Levy, the bus driver. At first the bus driver thought it was a traffic accident, but the terrorist kept striking the bus again and again. Pandemonium broke out, passengers shouted, "God save us" and "escape, escape." "He made a U-turn and rammed the windows twice with the shovel. The third time he aimed for my head—he came up to my window and death was staring me in the eyes. Fortunately, I was able to swerve to the right onto a small side street; otherwise I would have gone to meet my maker," said Levy.

"There was panic on the street as people were running away from the bus," said Yohanan Levine, an eye witness.[79]

The carnage came to a quick end due to the sharp reactions of another driver, Yaki Asa-El, a fifty-three-year-old grandfather of eleven. Asa-El lived in the town of Sussiya in the Southern Hebron Hills. This was an area prone to Arab violence and the residents there needed to be tough to survive. Many violent attacks had taken place around there. Asa-El was on speaker phone when he drove near the attack. A former company commander in the armored corps, Asa-El jumped out of his car and shot the terrorist, Abu Tir, through the window of his bulldozer. "He behaved the way the army trained him," testified his younger brother.[80]

The Gas Station Manager

In my town, the local gas station is managed by a friendly man and his two sons. Gadi is severely handicapped. He walks very slowly, limping along, trying to balance himself. He speaks with great difficulty and his speech is difficult to comprehend, yet he manages. He goes up and down the stairs by himself, speaks with clients, and runs a successful business.

One of my visiting Krav Maga students took notice and commented to me, "A stroke, right?"

"No," I answered. "You missed the obvious choice—war!" I asked the man's son, who happened to walk by, to tell the story to my students.

The son explained that back in 1967, during the Six Day War, his father had been a leading commander of the *Golani* unit. His father was asked to lead a group of soldiers to defend against an attack in the northern Golan Heights. This became one of the most famous battles in the history of Israeli warfare; the Battle of Tel Faher.

His father did not have his regular *Golani* troops; they were active elsewhere. His father was given a group of less well-trained reserve soldiers. He was told, "You must take this Syrian position; there is no alternative." Gadi took these men and did the impossible. On foot, they stormed with a frontal attack; several of the commanders were hurt. They took the Syrian position, although there were many Israeli casualties. It was during this battle that Gadi was hit and became semi-paralyzed for life. Despite this, he married, established a business, and contributes to our local community.

Just in Case—Precaution

Sometimes it turns out that a suspected terrorist is not actually a terrorist. But in Israel one cannot take chances. Apprehending these individuals also involves risk.

Zion Square

An Arab in Zion Square in Jerusalem pulled out a gun. In the blink of an eye, a former commando disarmed him. An angry and frightened crowd stormed toward the Arab. The former commando managed to block the crowd and pull the Arab to safety. As it turned out, it was only a toy gun. The former commando saved the Arab from an angry crowd.

Now, in Israel, it is not wise to pull out a toy gun. The days when kids could play with certain toys is long since over. Toy guns must be treated as real guns. In this case, a tragedy was averted due to the professionalism of a trained commando who happened to be out on the town on that Saturday night.

The Bus

My friend, Eva, had trained with me years earlier in Krav Maga. Most importantly, she had learned to be constantly aware, a very good citizen indeed. One day on the bus, she saw an Arab woman acting suspiciously and carrying a large suitcase. There were no police officers or guards around. She felt she must do something. Eva pulled out her monthly bus pass, which was in a leather case, and flashed it quickly at the women. "Police!" she shouted, "I must check you!" The Arab woman protested and asked to see the "badge" again. Eva was adamant, "I am a police officer, I have no time for this; I must proceed immediately with my search." Eva is actually not a police officer, but a cosmetics salesperson.

Eva opened and searched the suitcase—it was totally empty, very odd. She was very thorough. She searched the pockets, linings, any place that could contain a bomb, but nothing showed up. Mentally, she prepared herself for a possible attack by the suspect. She reviewed in her head the Krav Maga techniques she had been taught. Next, she checked the woman herself; this felt awkward, but she felt she must do it.

In the end, nothing turned up and she released her suspect. She had been terrified the entire time, but she felt it was her responsibility. This is the type of brave action on the part of ordinary citizens that helps keep Israel safe. Yes, sometimes it is not a terrorist, but we must always be on the alert.

CHAPTER 6

A Gun Packing Nation

In most other countries, one hardly ever sees a soldier carrying a rifle or even a handgun in public. In Israel, it is the norm—we are armed and dangerous. It is the norm to serve in the military and become proficient in handling weapons. Most towns have a shooting range. People come to practice, to renew their licenses, for sport shooting competitions, or just to let off some steam.

Guns are everywhere, not only M-16 rifles, but various grenade-launching rifles and other high-caliber weapons. Uzis, Tavor, the Galil, and other short rifles are carried by soldiers and security guards.

Women also carry guns. On Saturday night, you can walk around town and see teenage girls in civilian clothing, lots of makeup, beautiful hair, and M-16 rifles slung over their shoulders; they are soldiers home for the weekend.

Many civilians carry handguns as well. You do not need special circumstances to qualify for a permit. Living, working, or traveling in a dangerous area (almost any part of the country) qualifies you. One often hears casual talk comparing the qualities of a Glock to a Jericho, or an FN to a CZ. People know their guns and their ammo.

We have a well-armed, well-trained population, ready to respond to any suspicious sound. A bus blew a tire in Jerusalem. Before anyone knew for sure what caused the loud sound, several people had drawn their weapons and began to search for escaping terrorists. Ambulances were on the way when word was passed that it was simply a blown tire.

On *Purim*, the Israeli dress-up holiday (like Halloween), the police warn kids not to use toy guns that look or sound like real guns; the consequences could be tragic. Sadly, two young men dressed as Arabs were stopped on their way to a costume party. They ignored police officers who told them to stop, and were shot in the legs. When questioned in the hospital about their behavior, they explained; "We thought they were dressed up as cops and were on their way to the same costume party as we were. We thought they were kidding around."

Guns are so common that they do not arouse suspicion. As a former bank employee, I went to visit my old co-workers. They greeted me warmly and invited me to join them for a cup of coffee at their desks behind the counter. An American tourist pointed out what seemed odd to him. "Only in Israel can a man armed with a handgun walk into a bank, go behind the teller's desk where cash is being counted and arouse no suspicion whatsoever."

Once, when making a quick stop at our local mall, I left my handgun at home. The guard stopped me, as is usual practice, waved his metal detector around me, and asked if I had a weapon. "Nope, I left it at home today."

His reaction surprised me. "What's the matter with you?! You should never leave home without it."

When I would visit my parents, my mother would ask before I left, "Do you have your wallet? Your keys? Your gun?"

Guns are so common and so frequently seen at restaurants and cafés that sometimes we have to remind ourselves just how deadly they are. Israel has far more guns per capita than other countries. Many civilians carry handguns, while soldiers and security personnel often have fully automatic weapons. Yet the crime rate involving firearms is minuscule compared to the United States. Why?

As one gun owner said, "We are all soldiers; we know what guns can do, and we have seen the damage firsthand. We don't learn about guns from video games—we learn in the army, where we also learn safety precautions."

The saying "Guns don't kill, people do." is true, and our nation of warriors carry their guns with caution and responsibility in order to defend themselves and others, just as the American founding fathers envisioned more than two hundred years ago.

First Response

The United States has suffered tragically from rampage shooting incidents at schools, malls, and places of worship. A deranged killer gets a firearm and keeps shooting—killing people until he runs out of ammo. Statistics show that the average arrival time for SWAT teams is fifty minutes. By then, the damage is done. The problem is there is simply no way to have SWAT teams everywhere, all the time. Americans need to learn some basic gun disarm techniques, as they are taught in Israel. If a trained practitioner can at least get within arm's reach of an assailant, he might be able to talk and distract the person long enough to do a gun disarm technique.

In Israel, the situation is different. Incidents usually end much sooner as some off-duty policeman, soldier, reserve soldier, or ordinary armed citizen becomes the first responder and takes out the shooter. In nearly every instance in recent history, it was such a response that ended the incident. Several cases come to mind.

A terrorist opens fire in downtown Jerusalem. Two off-duty border policemen chase him down, engage him in a shootout, and kill him—no casualties.

Two knife-wielding terrorists break into a school and attack students. The students fight back, two dorm counselors come in and shoot the terrorists dead—no casualties. When I say "no casualties," I mean no casualties of ours; there are no innocent victims. Perhaps this is not "politically correct," but I do not count the terrorists among the casualties; they brought their death upon themselves.

In a tragic incident, an armed terrorist sneaks into a major Jerusalem *yeshiva*. Opening with automatic fire, he kills seven. He is chased and shot by a student armed with a handgun, and an off-duty soldier who chases him to a roof and guns him down. The quick response prevented the incident from being even more tragic.

On two occasions, Arabs grab hold of a tractor and start rampaging through the streets of Jerusalem. In both cases, civilians using private handguns ended the incidents long before the official police teams arrived on the scene.

November 18, 2014 – as men were praying at the Kehilat Bnei Torah synagogue in Jerusalem, two armed Arabs ran into the synagogue. The worshippers were caught off guard during their silent devotion. Nonetheless, they fought back as best as they could, trying to physically grab the terrorists, hit them over the head with furniture or whatever they could find.

Two traffic policemen heard the shooting. They did not hesitate, they ran in with guns drawn and opened fire on the terrorists. Later, I was able to confirm that these brave men responded exactly as they should, on par with an elite counterterrorist team, even though they were "only" traffic cops.

One of the police officers, an Israeli Druze named Zidan Saif, died a hero's death as he took a bullet to the head. For his funeral, an entire busload of Orthodox Jews came to honor him, traveling to his village and final resting place in the north of Israel. Four members of the synagogue, all rabbis, were killed that day, and seven were wounded. One of the wounded is still in a coma. Had it not been for the quick response of the traffic policemen, it could have been much worse. The attack, ironically, brought greater Jewish-Arab/Muslim unity and the congregation continues to employ Arab workers.

CHAPTER 7

Music/Culture

The American Civil War produced songs that are still sung today, as did World War Two. They have become part of American culture and history. In that respect, Israel is no different. For much of its history, the Israeli army has had bands and military musicians whose compulsory service was spent performing songs for soldiers.

Musicians also serve in the reserves and do their service by traveling around the country performing at military bases. The nation's top performers consider it a badge of honor to perform for free wherever soldiers are serving, no matter how few. Sometimes it is only a singer accompanied by a guitar, standing on top of a tank in the middle of the desert, performing for hundreds of battle weary soldiers. One group recalled arriving at a bunker where only five soldiers were stationed. Not only did the show go on, but they let the audience choose the numbers to be performed.

It is said that when the cannons are roaring, the songs stop. In Israel, it is just the opposite. Each war has given birth to songs that have become anthems, songs that are sung at times of national celebration or mourning. The songs have become part of the national culture, almost like religious prayers. The songs reflect the spirit of the nation; the hope for a better, more peaceful time, "All this will come to pass today, and if not today then tomorrow, and if not tomorrow, then the day after tomorrow" ("*Machar*" – "Tomorrow").[81] Songs echo the biblical hope that warriors will return to be farmers, that the land shall witness war no more, and that the young people will grow to be old.

There are songs that reflect the sacrifice of the military medic, as in "*Baladah Lachovesh*" ("Ballad for the Medic")[82] where a medic hears the cry of a wounded soldier and runs into enemy fire to save him. As he drags him to safety, he keeps reassuring the wounded soldier, "You are going to make it." By the end of the song, the soldier is thanking the medic, but the medic is not answering—he has been shot dead, one man giving his life for another, sacrifice without limits.

Another song that stands out is "*Al Shlosha Pishei Damesek*" ("*Three Crimes of Damascus*") dedicated to the soldiers of the *Golani* infantry unit. "You shall not pass; you shall **not** pass because here *Golani* is fighting."[83]

These military songs have become part of the fabric of the culture of this nation and are known by all. The bravery of the soldiers inspires the songwriters and the songs inspire the soldiers. During one of the wars, a top commander called a friend of his, a well-known songwriter, and said, "Do your share, get out your guitar and write us a song, the boys at the front need you."

When the soldiers go out to war, they are accompanied by the songs and prayers of the nation. The songs continue even after the last bullet of the battle has been fired. Israeli air force navigator, Ron Arad, has been MIA since 1986 when he was taken captive after his plane went down in enemy territory. Singer/songwriter, Boaz Sharabi, wrote a song for him, *"K'shetavo"* ("When You Will Come").[84] "When you come home we will present you with flowers, when you come home, home from the cold, home into the light, we will sing for you with joy. For freedom you were born." Ron Arad is still in captivity, but he is not forgotten here in Israel. A missing soldier is a missing family member. We all pray for his safe return.

Israel is a nation that has experienced much war, but yearns for peace. Military songs are about heroism and hope, not about glorifying combat. Side by side with "war songs" are songs hoping for peace. Songs like *"Shir LaShalom"* ("Song of Peace")[85] and *"Noladeti laShalom"* ("I Was Born for Peace")[86] are among the most popular in Israel. *"HaMilchama Ha'Achrona"* ("The Last War")[87] is a prayer that this war will be the last war. The song was written for the 1973 Yom Kippur War, which, clearly, was not the last.

Poet/Warriors

So many of those killed are young idealist men, just finding their way in life. In many cases, after their untimely deaths, songs and poems are found among their personal possessions. Israel started a project to bring these poems by deceased soldiers to life. The songs are matched up with composers and the words are set to music.

This has led to a new tradition. Each year on Memorial Day for Fallen Soldiers, the national radio station sponsors a program called *"Od Me'at Nahafokh le-Shir"* ("Soon We Will Become a Song"). The program features songs written by fallen soldiers and turned into music by Israeli artists. Hearing these songs sung brings part of the personality of the fallen warriors back to life. They may be gone, but their song remains. The parents of the soldiers meet with the composers and the musicians in what is always a very moving encounter.

Yaakov Paz, killed in 1978 while attempting to stop a deadly terrorist attack, left this powerful song, "*Shir Shel Rega Echad*" ("Song of One Moment").[88] "I wrote you a letter, in which I said don't wait for me, because you will be alone. You can wait for me, but then you will be alone."

"Parallel lines go together; they think they will arrive together, to the end, but suddenly, a second before the end, one of them ends. The others continue, and they look for their parallel, and they think they will arrive together, to the end." ("*Kavim Makbilim Meitim*" – "Dead Parallel Lines").[89] These words were written by Shimon Ben Dror, who was killed on the first day of combat during the 1973 Yom Kippur War. He was twenty years old. His family did not know he was killed until after the war was over. His body was never found. Apparently, his tank was hit by a Sager rocket; neither his body nor the tank was ever recovered.

Legendary Israeli composer, Danny Robas, who also lost a brother, loved the text and decided to put it to music. No one had known that Shimon was a writer. When he died, his girlfriend shared his writings with the family. Now he lives through his song.

Slogans and Bumper Stickers

Learning a foreign language is one thing; Understanding the slang is quite another. A great deal can be learned about a society by reading their advertisements and bumper stickers. A New Year's greeting card from my local garage mechanic read, "May this be a year where the only tank you have to deal with is your gas tank, where a 'Top Gun' refers to your ace mechanic and not the point man on your squad, where 'automatic' refers to your gears and not enemy fire, where 'belt' refers to your seat belt and not your bullet belt, where 'campaign' and 'struggle' refer to our efforts to provide you with the best possible service and not to military campaigns. May it be a year of peace and quiet."

This is a New Year's greeting to a clientele where nearly everyone is a warrior, where indeed words like *tank* and *automatic* bring to mind the tank you drove recently in Lebanon and the automatic fire your unit drew from Hizbullah terrorists. Military lingo is everywhere and if you are a non-combatant you will probably understand it anyway, since it is part of the culture, part of the language.

In the United States you might see bumper stickers that read "Born to Shop" or "Shop Till You Drop" or "Hit me, I need the money." This is a reflection of the culture and people understand the references. This is true in Israel as well. You will see bumper stickers proudly displayed: "Once a paratrooper always a paratrooper," "*Duchifat*; the fighting family," "Combat unit is the best, my brother," "Proud Reservist," "*Golani*, brothers forever," and "Follow me, to the paratroopers."

Unit rivalries and loyalties continue long after compulsory service is over. Old soldiers never get discharged—in their minds they are members of their units forever. Often you will see men in their fifties show up at ceremonies to meet the current soldiers in their units. They view them as relatives and tell them stories about how *Golani* stormed the Syrian troops in '67 or '73. The old paratroopers will recount the stories of liberating Jerusalem back in the Six Day War of 1967 and tell the new, young recruits that they must carry on the proud legacy of the unit.

Sadly, not only the heroic memories remain, but trauma as well. A quiet, but significant, segment of the population still wakes up in the middle of the night trying to rescue a friend caught in enemy fire or pull a buddy from a burning tank. Marriages fall apart and families are destroyed. This too is part of the legacy of a nation at war for survival.

CHAPTER 8

Age of Trauma

During a time of war, every unexpected phone call makes you jump; it could be "that" phone call—telling you to come to the hospital to see your loved one, or worse. When you pick up the phone and hear the calming voice of your son or nephew, you can breathe easy; for a moment, you know they are alive and well.

My nephew, Arie, called his parents with a special request; to drive several hours and attend the funeral of his commanding officer, just killed in combat. I spoke to Ari and asked him, "How are you coping with death all around you?"

"There is no time to think about that now, no time to dwell on it, I guess I will deal with it later," he answered. A warrior buries his dead and carries on. In battle, there is no time to mourn. Just as the nation of Israel was born in a struggle four thousand years ago, so was the modern State of Israel born in blood and fire. As soon as it was declared, it was attacked.

While the nation danced in the streets, "The Old Man" was pensive. The first Israeli Prime Minister, David

Ben-Gurion, knew that the dancing would be followed by killing; surely the surrounding Arab nations would not take this sitting down; it was just a matter of time until the fighting began.

In the war that followed, fully one percent of the population of Israel died in battle. Many of those who would be burying friends and relatives had already lost most of their loved ones in the recent European Holocaust. But mourning was a luxury the nation could not afford, and the unwritten and unspoken motto became "No time to mourn, we have a state to build, bury your dead and carry on." Only in recent years would the nation realize that this trauma must be dealt with. Now, the army has begun to provide professional help for traumatized victims who cannot escape their pasts.

There are countless warriors who still cannot be sure if they will sleep through the night. Often, they will wake up believing their injured comrades are calling them from a still-burning tank, begging to be rescued. Thirty years may have passed, but the tank is still burning like the eternal light in the Temple of old. The voices do not die down; the anguish and the pain continue. The outstretched hand and crying voice are still there. The dreaming soldier reaches out to save his friend, only to wake up in a pool of his own sweat.

A war hero in my town was finally able to contact family members of a fallen comrade who died next to him in combat back in 1973. For over forty years, he simply was not able to cope with what had happened when his group of six soldiers in the Sinai Peninsula was attacked by an Egyptian unit.

Sometimes news and videos of new wars or terrorist attacks will trigger a bad memory. Amnon fought as a regular soldier in the Yom Kippur War and belonged to a unit that crossed the Suez Canal. He was exposed to constant attacks by Egyptian warplanes and shelling, he saw many

IDF casualties. In 2004, he was watching the news and saw reports about the terrorist bombing of a hotel in Taba, in the Sinai desert. He suddenly suffered difficulties breathing, saw flashbacks of his war experiences, and burst out crying.

Thirty years after the Yom Kippur War of 1973, the nation finally began to deal with the shell shock of countless soldiers who served in one of the greatest tank battles in history. There are many who cannot get through a day without medication, many who can only hold down the most menial of jobs because since the war they cannot really function. For many, the war never ended. These emotional handicaps are part of everyday life in Israel; the guy who pushed ahead of you in line at the bank may be suffering from nervousness and anxiety that began when his armored personnel carrier was hit by an antitank missile. Israelis can be a bit gruff; we need to understand where they are coming from. Do not yell at them, just offer a smile, they have been through enough already. The trauma is part of everyday living. It is part of society and part of the culture.

Leader in Rehabilitation

I remember our friendly school bus driver from my childhood years. He had a special van designed to accommodate his lack of ability to use his legs. He was paralyzed during the Six Day War of 1967 and was wheelchair-bound. Yet, he was cheerful and always kind to us kids. He seemed to enjoy having us with him for the ride. Sometimes he would show us war trophies; a captured Jordanian flag, or a medal of honor.

One day—a day I will never forget, this kind man had a special treat for us boys—he brought us to his club. It was a beautiful sports facility; with basketball courts, swimming pool, weight room, and balls of all types. It had special bikes, ping-pong tables, ropes and ladders for climbing; a dream place. At first I did not notice what was different, special, about this place, but soon I noticed. There were all sorts of contraptions for handicapped people, such as a way for wheelchair-bound people to get into the pool. There were devices to help the guys use the weights and ropes.

I looked all around and I saw them: men without legs, some missing arms or a hand, some blind, young men in wheelchairs or on crutches, some burned or disfigured, all laughing, having fun. I watched our driver play a very competitive, but friendly, game of basketball. All the men were in wheelchairs, they were passing, shooting, scoring, even smashing into each other. They were having fun and feeling normal.

This was their "home," *Bet HaLochem* (Home of the Warrior). All these men were warriors, combat soldiers who gave a leg or an arm for the safety of this nation. Many had artificial limbs. Here they were comfortable; they did not feel like freaks, missing a limb or an eye was normal. They did not need to cover their scars or hide their fake limbs under long sleeves or long pants; here it was OK, here they were like everybody else.

These men are still warriors; they wear their injuries with pride and they still identify with their units. "On a recent morning the soldiers were easy to spot: young men in T-shirts with military logos, propelling themselves in wheelchairs or striding purposefully on prosthetic legs."[90]

In the 2008 Paralympics, Israel sent many athletes, former soldiers, to participate in the games in Beijing. One of those athletes was a former combat soldier named Shai Haim. He was injured in September 2002 while searching for terrorists. He was shot in the back by a sniper and became paralyzed for life. His best friend, Ari Weiss, my cousin, ran over to help. Weiss was shot through the lungs and died later from his wounds. Shai could not attend Ari's funeral as he was undergoing surgery at the time—he lost one kidney and his spleen. Later on Shai would marry, father a child and compete in the Paralympics.

Israelis love to follow the Olympics on TV. However, truth be told, we rarely come home with many medals. This is not surprising considering the size of our population and the fact that we cannot afford to "sponsor" full-time athletes. There is one exception, the Special Olympics (the Olympics for handicapped/other-abled individuals). In this category, Israel excels. The reason is simple; Israel's team includes many combat soldiers injured in battle. Despite their permanent injuries, their spirit is strong and they are successful in international competitions.

Our war veterans are honored and fully accepted in our society. In another country, when seeing a handicapped person, you might think "car accident." In Israel, you think "war hero." As you see him struggling up the stairs using a cane, you imagine to yourself that at one point this was a young combat commander leading his troops up the Golan Heights against the Syrians. Most likely, an enemy bullet caused the life of challenge he now leads.

Wheelchair ramps and handicap parking are common. People scarred by war, emotionally or physically, are understood and accepted. Israel, as a nation of wounded warriors, is a leader in the manufacture and design of artificial limbs, and a leader in the campaign for handicap rights.

Special Exports

Israel's extensive experience with terrorism and war makes this small nation an international leader in several unique fields.

Trauma Treatment
Israel probably has more victims of terror per capita than any nation on the planet; as such Israel has great

experience and expertise in dealing with traumatized victims. Today, trauma centers all over the world, including the United States, use the Israeli model for treating victims of terror.

Search and Rescue

Israeli search and rescue teams are on the plane within minutes of earthquakes or terrorist explosions anywhere from Turkey to China. Israel's expertise in search and rescue has helped save lives of many—regardless of nationality or faith.

Artificial Limbs

With so many people injured by terrorism and war, Israel has become an international leader in the manufacture of artificial limbs.

Security

Israeli security professionals are in demand all over the world—from kindergarten patrols to hi-tech companies, and as advisers to police units and SWAT teams.

Emergency Response to Attacks

Israel has accumulated a great deal of experience dealing with bombings, shootings, and a wide range of attacks in public areas. Nations from around the world make requests of Israel to come and teach them the Israeli methods. On April 16, 2013, Boston was attacked. Three people were killed and many injured, but it could have been worse. "About two years ago in actual fact we asked the Israelis to come across and they helped us set up our disaster team so that we could respond in this kind of manner," said Alasdair Conn, Chief of Emergency Services at Massachusetts General Hospital, responding to a question about the preparedness of his staff to handle trauma on this scale."[91]

Israel Military Industries (IMI)

From the earliest days of our struggle we have had to be innovators, inventors, and improvisers. Just as the combat fighting systems must constantly evolve, so too must the combat weapons evolve. Today Israel Military Industries is a world-class defense company providing cutting edge products for land, air, and naval forces around the world. Israeli military products are sought after as among the most advanced in the world.

One Bereaved Family

When tragedy strikes, it is said the family of the fallen soldier has now joined the "bereaved family," the family that includes the brothers and sisters, parents and children of all those killed defending this land. The bereaved family is never forgotten. On Memorial Day, my nephew's unit divides up and visits the families of its two commanders who fell in the Second Lebanon War. Even years later, old soldiers still make a point to call and visit the families of their comrades in arms, their buddies whom they trained with and fought with. The bereaved family still feels like part of the unit—they know they are not forgotten. These bonds between soldiers and their fallen friends' families are like an extended family. A warrior does not forget his fellow soldier.

Helping Victims of Terror

Whenever a terrorist succeeds, there are not only the obvious victims, those who die and make the news, there are those who are injured, and those left behind to grieve forever. These people go on suffering for years to come. The injured might no longer be able to work, might have years of hospital visits, surgery, or physical therapy. None of this makes the news, but the suffering continues on a daily basis. A family's income might be severely compromised, emotional issues and flashbacks may plague the family for years.

These people are not forgotten in Israel. The government helps them as do many volunteer organizations. Standard practice is that the government wipes out the family's mortgage. Tutoring is offered for the children. Big Brother programs help children cope with the trauma.

An organization called the One Family Fund is devoted to a single purpose, "rebuilding shattered lives." They provide emotional, legal, and financial assistance to the families of victims. Before the holidays, they will provide extra money so families can observe and celebrate the holidays properly, they will assist with the expenses of a *bar mitzvah* celebration, and they will provide friendship and counseling. One of their programs is "Twinning" where Israeli victims of terrorism are "twinned" with American kids—they will write, share experiences, and meet. The victim is helped by his American twin while the American twin gains a valuable perspective on life.

Free legal assistance allows the families to access whatever insurance benefits they are entitled to, as well as handle debt negotiations. More than anything, the help tells the victims, "You are not alone, you are not forgotten; we are all one family."

Memorial Day

At 8:00 pm, on the eve of Memorial Day, a siren sounds across the nation, marking the beginning of Remembrance Day for the Fallen Soldiers and Victims of Terrorism. At 11 am the next day, a two-minute siren will be heard throughout the country. Everyone will stop and stand at attention. Cars will pull over and drivers will step out and stand by the side of the road. The siren will be heard on all TV and radio stations. The entire country will come to a standstill, united in remembering its fallen.

Dalia Itzik, acting president of Israel in 2006, said, "Tonight Israel weeps. We have no words of comfort, but we embrace you, the families, with endless love. Those who fell defending Israel would want us to be united."

The IDF Chief of General Staff added, "The IDF is a moral army; we are a strong and moral society. The last year (2006) has been difficult for us all. Names were added to those that we have lost; two hundred thirty-three families have joined the list of those who mourn."

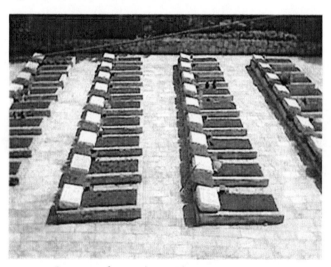

Graves of warriors, Six Day War 1967

Throughout the day, *all* the programming on TV, radio, and at school will be devoted to the memory of the fallen, to those who fell so we can be free. We all know someone who went to battle and did not return; we all know someone who went to work or school and fell victim to terrorism; we share the pain.

Not Forgotten

For many, Memorial Day lasts all year long. Many bereaved parents visit the graves of their loved ones on a regular basis, some even daily. The father of Yiftah Shrier, of blessed memory, my nephew's commander, visits his son's grave every day. These families, however, are not alone, and they are not forgotten.

My brother, Ethan, called Mr. Shrier and said, "My nephew, Arie Katz, served under your son. I heard that your son was a wonderful commander."

"Oh, Arie Katz, yes, he is my son!" said Mr. Shrier.

"Hmm, actually he is the son of my brother and sister-in-law," said my brother, a little confused.

"Since my son's death, his soldiers have become my sons. They call me every Friday afternoon to wish me a good Sabbath; they invite me to their weddings and to all their family celebrations; a birth, an engagement. We have become one family," Mr. Shrier explained. Arie visits the Shrier family on Memorial Day and on the day Yiftah was killed.

During this conversation, Mr. Shrier shared another unusual story. The family of one of the soldiers under his son's command told Mr. Shrier, "Yiftah came to visit me in my home. He asked me many questions about my son. He asked about his childhood, his interests, and his hobbies. Next, he asked to see my son's room. He leafed through his holy books and looked around the room. Next, he wanted to see my son's clothing; what did he wear when he was not in uniform? Finally I said, 'OK, enough is enough, what is going on here?' Yiftah answered, 'If I am going to command your son and lead him into battle, if I am going to inspire and motivate him; then I must understand him, I must understand how he thinks. To be a commander I must be an educator.'"

This is the deep caring an Israeli commander feels for those whose lives have been placed in his charge. When the moment of truth came, Yiftah said to his men, "We are about to enter Lebanon, to fight for the safety of the people of Israel. We do not know who will return and who will not. It is my great honor to lead you into battle, and if it is our fate to die, then it will be my honor to lay beside you."

When I hear his words, I think of the great Shimon Bar Kochba, the last commander of Judea in the year 135 CE. I hear his words echo throughout the generations. The spirit of freedom and the struggle against tyranny has not been lost; it has been passed on across time. Tragically, just like Shimon Bar Kochba, this wonderful young man became yet another sacrifice in our struggle for survival and freedom.

Sharing the Pride and the Pain

In 2007, I stood on a hill at the graves of fallen soldiers. Some have lain there silently for many years; others arrived more recently. They were surrounded by living soldiers, friends who fought with them side by side, and others who never knew them, but came to pay their respects. Their last moments of life were filled with fire and thunder; they died violent deaths. Now they lay peacefully, surrounded by the trees of Jerusalem and a gentle breeze.

The occasion marked a year since the combat medic, Philip Moscow, fell in the Second Lebanon War. Near his grave were the graves of Noam Meyerson, born in the United States, and Yinon, whose mother worked in our local supermarket. They fell in the hell known as Lebanon, defending our people from terrorists who did not value human life.

Friends and strangers surrounded the graves. A unit of new recruits was sent by the military. They were there to pay respect to those who served before them and to hear their stories of bravery. These were not ordinary soldiers; they did not enlist to get a scholarship or pursue a career;

they chose high-risk combat units because they chose to give, to contribute.

High-ranking officers spoke. A police chief spoke of Philip, who volunteered with the local police units as well as with the first aid group. Some of these battle hardened men were so choked with emotion they simply could not speak. The bravery and self-sacrifice of the young is humbling to us all.

As I stood with my brother, we looked at an "empty" plot of land covered with grass. It was pleasant to think that this area was left open so visitors could sit around, but we knew the truth. It was reserved for another generation of fighters, another group of young men and women, who want to live, but know they must serve their people. The reality is that everyone must serve, and space is left...space we hope and pray will forever remain covered with grass.

Philip's father, Ze'ev, rose to speak and thanked us all for coming. He said, "We thank you all for sharing our pain and for sharing our pride." Sharing our pride—they came from Russia to Israel so they could live as free Jews, they made the ultimate sacrifice, their only son, and they are proud. They are warriors; they have no complaints, only pride. Their only daughter followed Philip's example and served in the paratroopers. She stood by his grave in her uniform, a silent testimony to a fallen hero; a family of warriors.

Getting to Know the Fallen Soldiers

A unique aspect of Israeli society is the attempt to get to know as many of the fallen as possible, to learn about them, to meet them through their life stories. Each year on Memorial Day, Israel's two television stations run non-stop video stories about the fallen. Each video report takes you through the life of the soldier, from his childhood to his hobbies, his life outside the army, and the last day of his short life. We meet his family, his parents, his brothers and sisters, wife or girlfriend. We meet his friends and his fellow soldiers who served with him. By the end of the video he is no longer a nameless statistic; he is a friend we have come to know—and we now miss. The entire nation mourns together.

Humans are not the only ones mourned on this day. This past year, one episode was devoted to an Israeli dog killed in combat. Israel's *Oketz* Canine Unit does very important work in searching for bombs and terrorists, as well as search and rescue operations. A unique bond is formed between the soldier and his dog. Dogs work at checkpoints and participate in combat operations. Sometimes they too become casualties of war.

CHAPTER 9

From Pain to Productivity, From Darkness to Light

Our rabbis say the darkest part of night is just before dawn. In our society, out of the darkest tragedies springs new hope, new acts of kindness and generosity. There are some who cannot overcome their personal pain and their lives become tragic struggles to return to normalcy. Many others, however, take that pain and channel it into something useful to society—as part of the national therapy. They take their grief and produce something meaningful out of it; some means of compensating for what they lost by creating something good.

The Leg

A certain combat soldier had his leg blown off in the 1973 Yom Kippur War. He became the "Six Million Dollar Man" as countless medical operations rebuilt the shattered soldier. Clearly he would never be able to fight again. Or could he?

He became a fighter of a different sort—the greatest fundraiser in the country. He travels the world, raising money to build the State of Israel and its academic institutions. He is a well-known figure at Israel's Ben Gurion International Airport due to his constant travel.

Once, on a visit abroad, he was told about a very wealthy Jew, but was warned that the man never contributed anything; it was a waste of time to even try. The soldier-turned-fundraiser is not the quitting type. He never backed away from a challenge in combat and he would not give up now. He called the man and asked to see him; he promised he would never ask the man for a dime. He kept his word. After recounting his experiences in the 1973 war, the fundraiser pulled up his pants and started unscrewing something. Soon, he placed his artificial leg and knee on the table and said, "This is what I have given to my nation, what are you going to give?" The wealthy man quickly took out his checkbook.

The Brothers

Ehud and Nimrod were as close as could be. Nimrod was killed by Hizbullah terrorists in the Second Lebanon War; he was a reservist, twenty-eight years old. "There are really no words to describe how I felt when I heard the news," said Ehud. "I was completely devastated, broken, crushed. He was my only brother, my closest friend, my second half; my everything." From his deep and incredible pain, Ehud came up with an idea to help others and help himself. "I took all the pain that welled up inside of me and I told myself that I had to use this pain to do something to make the world a better place. My brother's death was a message to me."

Ehud decided to devote himself to the cause of world freedom and tolerance, a big task for one person. Still, he felt, when individuals begin to act, change can come. His love for his brother is the fuel that keeps him going; he feels he must do something to make this world a better place for all people. In losing his only brother he has taken on the entire world as brothers. "Starting this project has given me so much more power to deal with the pain of Nimrod's loss. The only thing that keeps me going is the belief in a better future. But the torch I carry is a heavy one and I need as much help as I can get to carry it. We are all of us brothers."

Charities

Many charities and self-help organizations were established as a direct result of warriors being killed. Organizations bearing the names of loved ones were established to provide food for the needy, medical supplies, ambulances, assisted living for injured soldiers, and every possible cause under the sun.

Organizations with names like The Kindness of Meir give help to the needy and perpetuate the name of Rabbi Meir Kahane, killed by an Arab terrorist in New York City while addressing a crowd at a hotel. The kindness done in the name of a deceased is a way of taking that pain and using it to make the world a better place. Parks with names like The Garden of Joshua have been built for children to keep alive the name of a son named Joshua, killed in the line of duty. The sign will say, "In memory of Joshua who died so that young children can be free." When kids play in *his* park it is as if Joshua is alive and taking care of the children.

Dr. Shmuel Gillis was a senior hematologist at the Hadassah University Medical Center; he was also the father of five children. One day while driving home from work, Arab terrorists shot him dead. A few days later Tzachi Sasson, an electrical engineer and father of two was also shot to death by Arab terrorists, driving home on the same road. The two bereaved wives took action. They set up a station where soldiers can come for a hot cup of coffee and a piece of cake. Today, the place is manned by fourteen volunteers and is open from 7 am to 9 pm serving hot drinks, soup, and snacks to weary soldiers. Local residents donate all the food. More than a dozen residents of this area have been killed in recent years.

Ari Weiss, of Blessed Memory

Ari Weiss was my second cousin. My late grandfather, Rabbi Isaac Klein, helped get Ari's grandfather out of Europe. One day while Ari was serving in a combat unit, he was speaking with his mother on the phone. He told her that he and his unit were starving. His mother asked, "How many are you?"

"Thirty-five," he said.

She hung up the phone and went to the main street of her town. She came across a fast food place her son loved. "I went to the manager of the store and said, 'My son is in Shechem, he's stuck in some hellhole with no fridge and he's hungry.'"

He interrupted my sentence and asked the same question, "How many are there?"

"I told him thirty-five." He arranged the package.

Susie Weiss did the same thing with the grocery store, getting free drinks for all thirty-five soldiers. Next, she went to the bakery, same story. Then she went to the frozen meat store. Within half an hour she had the most amazing care package for the thirty-five hungry soldiers. As the story spread, more and more food came in, every bit of it donated. The story made the newspapers. There was even a photograph.

Tragically, just two weeks later, Ari Weiss died a hero's death. He was shot by an Arab sniper while searching for suicide bombers and terrorists' enclaves. His mother continues to organize food shipments to "her boys" serving our country, in memory of her son, Ari, of blessed memory.

Her acts of kindness give her the strength to keep going. Rather than reacting with violence, she responds by bringing more goodness into the world, more kindness, and more light.

Today, there is a synagogue and Torah learning center in Ra'anana, named in his memory, *Ohel Ari* (the Tent of Ari). I was there to celebrate the *brith mila*, the ritual circumcision of another cousin's eight-day-old child. New life of one cousin was being celebrated in the synagogue dedicated to the sacrifice and life of another cousin.

The Boy from Philadelphia

Michael Levin was a typical American Jewish kid. Two of his grandparents were Holocaust survivors. He was named for his grandfather, a survivor of the Auschwitz death camp of the Nazis. "Their stories," said his mother, "motivated him to leave his family and friends behind in the United States, immigrate to Israel, and enlist in the elite paratroopers brigade."[92]

When the war in Lebanon began, his friends were relieved to know he was back in the United States visiting his family. However, as soon as the war began, he cut his vacation short, returned to Israel, and rejoined his unit. It was something he felt he "had to do." During the war, Michael, twenty-two, was shot and killed by a Hizbullah sniper in the southern Lebanese village of *Ayta al Shaab*. Michael Levin died a hero's death. His unit, Battalion 101, had been clearing a building in *Ayta al Shaab* when Hizbullah scored a direct hit with an antitank missile. The human toll was horrific—eleven wounded and three killed.

Michael's comrade, Shanir Turjeman, reported what happened, "I heard on the two-way radio that Michael was wounded, and I remembered the night before, when we'd been talking about girlfriends, family, and life," Turjeman said. "I'd lost eye contact with him during the heavy sniper fire and the antitank attack, and then during the evacuation I spotted him lying there, badly injured."

Another comrade, Shlomi Singer, also an Anglo immigrant, risked his own life and carried his dying friend most of the way back into Israel before they were found and picked up by rescue vehicles, but it was too late. "It was very difficult," Singer said. "We were under heavy fire, and all around us our friends were wounded."

On *Tisha B'Av*, the day we mourn the destruction of the Holy Temple in Jerusalem, Levin was laid to rest in Mount Herzl Cemetery. His family—mother, father, sister Alisa and his twin sister Dara—flew in from Pennsylvania. They were joined by a large crowd of people from all over Israel who came to pay tribute to the young hero.

His mother said she was overwhelmed by the "bear hug" she received from the Israeli people. When they came to Israel for the funeral they did not expect even ten people. More than two thousand mourners came to say goodbye to the soldier. Part of the "bear hug" she referred to comes from other mothers of soldiers who were killed in action. Israel as a warrior nation familiar with death takes care of its bereaved. Other mothers call her on a weekly basis, such as the mother of the soldier buried right next to him. She lights a candle for her own son and for Michael, every week.

To memorialize their son, the Levin family started a fund to help lone soldiers, such as Michael. They sponsored a two-day getaway at a Tel Aviv hotel for lone soldiers. His family is keeping his memory alive by continuing to help others. To commemorate the one-year anniversary of Levin's death, his family hosted a one-day convention to raise awareness of the difficult situation of lone soldiers in the IDF. At the Dan Panorama Hotel in Tel Aviv, three hundred twenty-five lone soldiers gathered to meet each other and to learn about their rights and opportunities upon finishing their service.

Rather than resorting to revenge, suicide bombings, or blowing up buildings, families turn their pain into kindness. That kindness becomes the legacy of the deceased warrior, for after all, a true warrior fights for peace.

Noam Meyerson

Noam and his family immigrated to Israel from the United States. His father works with my brother in the hi-tech industry. Noam completed his obligatory service, and, as is required of all Israelis, became part of the reserves. During the Second Lebanon War, Noam, twenty-three, was called up for reserve duty. He joined a tank squadron unit that merged with a paratroopers force near the village of Bint Jbeil. An antitank missile hit the main tank leading the force, instantly killing Noam and squadron commander, Yotam Lotan, a reservist from a *kibbutz.*

To help cope with their tragic loss, Noam's family decided to honor his memory by establishing a living memorial that would reflect his personality. "Noam loved nature. That's why we chose to build a center for Jewish and environmental studies in the Mitzpe Ramon Educational Center. The new center was named *Darchei Noam* (from a biblical verse meaning the ways of Noam, or the ways of pleasantness, Noam is Hebrew for pleasant) and aims to teach Judaism through observing nature," said Noam's mother, Gila.

Noam's immediate family members were not the only ones to take the tragedy of his death and channel it into positive deeds. Noam was close friends with his cousin Katie, thirteen, of New York. Her mother, Sandy, is the sister of Noam's father, Haim. "Katie used to visit Israel once a year and Noam would take her on trips and spend time with her," a family member said. "They had a very close relationship despite the age difference." The news of Noam's death broke Katie's heart. In her sadness and pain, Katie decided to honor her cousin and the special bond they shared.

"At first, I built a website in his memory," Katie said. "After that, I decided to build a playground in his name and to locate it in one of the country's northern cities that had been hurt by Hizbullah's missiles. I chose Kiryat Shmona for this." Katie began raising funds for the project. She sold teddy bears and T-shirts on the Internet, bearing the slogan "Make Games Not War." She also sent emails to her friends, asking them to donate money in Noam's memory. "He would have been happy," she said. Even Katie's *bat mitzvah* was dedicated to her new initiative, and she asked her relatives for money instead of gifts. The response was rewarding, and soon Katie had raised ten thousand dollars. She also approached the Jewish Agency, which joined in the project and contacted the Kiryat Shmona Municipality, which in turn agreed to build the playground in their town.

Katie and her mother flew to Israel to participate in the playground's cornerstone ceremony. "Noam was only twenty-three when a Hizbullah missile took away his smile. Had he been alive today, he would have been happy to see us building a playground in a city that has suffered from missile attacks," Katie said.

Philip Moscow, Two Years Later

Philip was killed in Lebanon, August 2006. I visited the family during the traditional week of mourning, the week of *shiva*. They could not be comforted. I saw a broken family. I did not know how they would recover.

Philip had taken his maternal late grandfather's last name, Moscow, as he was the last surviving male member of the family after the destruction of the Holocaust. He wanted to honor his grandfather and keep the family name alive.

Two years after his tragic death, his family and friends came together in a united effort to honor his memory and keep it alive. Despite the huge financial undertaking, this humble family decided to dedicate a *sefer Torah*, a Torah scroll, to be donated to the synagogue in which Philip prayed. A Torah scroll takes a master scribe about a year to write. It is a huge expense.

For two years the family raised the necessary funds. Finally, on the second anniversary of his death, the Torah scroll was completed in the presence of friends, family, the mayor, and chief rabbi of my town. The dedication of a Torah scroll is a major celebration for a Jewish community. It is similar to a community wedding. The residents of the town dance with the new Torah scroll from the location where the writing is completed, down the streets of the town, to the synagogue that will house the scroll. There rabbis and community leaders will speak and a festive meal will be served. And such it was for Philip.

Friends and family gathered at the modest home of Philip's family. His sister was given a leave of absence from the army to attend this event. At 6 pm, we gathered for prayer. Then the scribe completed the writing of the scroll. Community members donated money for the honor of writing the final letters, under the watchful eye of the scribe. I had the honor of writing one letter as well.

Some very special guests showed up. Not only the chief rabbi and the mayor were present, but also members of Philip's unit, the 101 Paratroopers. The commander knew Philip; the others did not as they were too young. This is the tradition in Israel; whenever a memorial service of any kind is held in memory of a soldier, members of that unit are sent to honor their fallen comrade. Even years after a soldier fell in combat, current members of his unit will come and honor him. Sometimes these are soldiers who were not even born when this soldier served. This is the loyalty of the unit. They will always honor one of their own.

Moshe writing a letter in the Torah scroll

The chief rabbi spoke, the mayor spoke. And then, when the scroll was complete, we took it out to the streets. Hundreds of well-wishers danced with the Torah scroll in the streets. Periodically, we would stop and the leader would ask the soldiers to touch the holy scroll and pray for safety and well-being. I looked at those young soldiers and I prayed for them as well. Here they seemed so safe and happy, but if trouble broke out, they would be the ones to face it head on; they would be called back to Lebanon or Gaza.

The soldiers danced with the Torah scroll and they reaffirmed their faith. For at least an hour, we accompanied Philip's scroll to its new home, all the while singing and dancing and being joyous. I thought, "What a remarkable people! Their son was killed only two short years ago, but they are not bitter toward the government, they are not becoming suicide bombers and killing Arabs, they are not wallowing in their pain. Instead, they pulled themselves together, worked night and day to raise money, and now are dancing as they dedicate the new Torah scroll. It is pain and joy mingled together. Tomorrow is the official memorial service, but today they dance."

We arrived at the synagogue. Food was served, wine was drunk, and rabbis delivered messages of faith and hope. The Chief Rabbi of the army came to participate in this important event; he drove in all the way from another event in the north of Israel in order to be here. He said, "Our ancient rabbis teach us that only men of faith go to war, the weak of heart stay home in order not to harm the war effort. Only moral men go to war for the Jewish people. We don't send mercenaries, we only send the best, the most spiritual, this is who we are; we are a nation of moral fighters. Philip was a moral fighter. He could have avoided military service, he was issued an exemption, but he volunteered, he chose to serve."

The next morning was the memorial service held at the military cemetery in Jerusalem. Psalms were recited, military commanders spoke. One fellow, a friend of the family, spoke of his experiences fighting in the War of Independence back in 1948. Most of his friends are here, he said, buried in the military cemetery, and it is because of them that we are a free people in our own land.

From Rockets to Roses

Perhaps nothing symbolizes the concept of "from pain to productivity" better than the Rockets to Roses project. Ironically, I learned of this during a visit to the Netherlands. My friends were wearing unique jewelry. I asked where they got the beautiful necklaces with a picture of a rose. They said the necklaces were from Israel. They were made from pieces of metal that came from rockets fired upon Israel.

Israelis took the rockets fired upon them by terrorists and used this material to make beautiful, happy, jewelry—taking rockets and turning them into roses.

The Beat Does Not Stop

Elad Kornfein speaks lovingly of his brothers, Eran and Oded. Eran was killed in an accident and Oded died in combat. "We were five siblings, now we are three." Both Oded and Eran were musicians. Oded played the drums and was already well-known even though he was quite young. He was killed during his years of mandatory service, aged twenty. He was already accompanying famous singers for live performances. Elad will never forget that last time they met, the day before Oded was killed. "The moment that I met him is with me every day when I go to sleep and wake up—that meeting was our goodbye. When I hugged him for the last time, I burst out into tears." The next day the family was notified of Oded's death; he died in an exchange of fire with terrorists in Jenin.

A year after Oded's death, the family arranged an evening in his memory. It was an event to promote and encourage musical talent in their region. Ideas began to develop and eventually they founded the Idan Center to encourage young musical talent in the Jordan Valley region. Years later, it is an established annual event, around the date of Oded's birthday. Scholarships are awarded to young musicians. Oded's music continues; from pain to productivity. How wonderful are your people Israel that this is how you deal with pain.

Death, Pain, and Suffering—Up Close and Personal

I know over thirty people killed in terrorist acts, including a Texas-born cousin who was killed by an Arab sniper. I know many people who were injured; a fifteen-year-old girl who was near a bus blown up by a suicide bomber, she has had many operations and skin grafts and still must avoid direct sunlight. I know a Krav Maga instructor who works in the security field. A bullet went through his cheek, ripping out one eye and leaving him handicapped for life. I know a local man who was stabbed thirteen times all over his body and managed to drag himself to safety. All of these people will bear their scars for life. Many will require multiple operations and emotional support for years to come.

Many young people have paid more visits to cemeteries than they should at this stage of life. Too many people in their late teens and early twenties have already been at most of the military cemeteries in Israel.

Soldiers at memorial service

My nephew, Arie, was born in Los Angeles. Had he remained in sunny Southern California, he would have been in college and his biggest concern might have been final exams or term papers. Instead, he was in Lebanon, defending our democracy and freedom. At the tender young age of twenty, he had already lost one of his youth group leaders, murdered by terrorists while studying in a rabbinical seminary, and two of his commanding officers.

Too many Israelis know a kid who was out having pizza when he was blown to bits by a suicide bomber, or a father and daughter having dinner the night before her wedding when a suicide bomber blew up the restaurant, killing them along with many others, or a nineteen-year-old boy, just out of high school, killed on the front lines, dashing his hopes and dreams. This is a nation that has seen and felt death up close, and if Israeli self-defense is brutal and "in your face" it is because this nation is fed up with terrorists. We need not apologize to anyone. Our cause is just.

CHAPTER 10

Business Mentality

Israelis as Innovators

Few people know that many of the modern technological devices they use every day, and take for granted, were developed here in Israel. The cell phone, instant messaging, voice mail technology, the first DNA computers, drip system irrigation; these and many more modern inventions were first developed in Israel. When anti-Israel elements speak of boycotting Israeli products, they do not realize the toll it would take in their daily lives. They would no longer be able to conduct business or enjoy the lives to which they have become accustomed.

Israel also has one of the highest percentages of hi-tech startup companies in the world—basically, Israelis are great innovators. How did they come to be this way? Part of the answer is their military training.

An Australian newspaper article, in bemoaning the difficult employment issues in their country, wrote the following startling words, "Lessons can be learnt here from, of all places, the Israeli army. In their book, *Start-Up Nation*, Dan Senor and Saul Singer set out to explain how a tiny country perpetually at war and with no natural resources has become a world powerhouse of technology. Israel has more technology companies listed on the Nasdaq than any other country other than the United States. According to the book, between the years 1980 and 2000 Egyptians registered 77 patents in the US, Saudis registered 171 and Israelis 7,652. The answer, they explain, is found in *chutzpah*, the Yiddish word that has become part of our vernacular. We give it to mean gall, guts, audacity, even insolence, but it is impossible to accurately translate with one word."[93]

This attitude, called *chutzpah*, is part of the military training and part of our Krav Maga training. General Ariel Sharon was the epitome of *chutzpah*, and later, during his political career, he became known as "the bulldozer." Full of confidence, Sharon broke rules, did not follow instructions, was unconventional, and upset many people. His superiors wanted him removed from command. While others urged defense against the massive Egyptian onslaught, Sharon was ready to attack and cross the Suez Canal. In the end, his daring actions were decisive in what was probably the greatest Israeli victory in modern times.

In the IDF, creative thinking is encouraged. Israelis from a young age learn to challenge authority. When I teach Americans, I often hear the response "Yes, sir!" to my suggestions. Israeli students challenge me, "Convince me that this works."

"Israelis are taught and encouraged to debate. Young Israeli employees are constantly asking their superiors: 'Why are you my manager; why am I not your manager?'"[94]

No is Not an Answer

Israelis have learned, through hard and bitter experience, that giving up is not an option. Long ago an Israeli professor explained this point to me. "You must understand how to work with Israelis, understand their way of thinking. In America the word 'no' is the end of a conversation, it is the end of negotiations, in Israel it is only the beginning."

In 1948 Israel faced "unbeatable" odds. The American president warned the Israeli leader that there was no way to win; it simply could not be done. Israel declared statehood and, against all odds, won. An Israeli battle position might be down to just a few men, the enemy might possess overwhelming force, yet time after time the Israeli unit would hold out, defying the odds. Simply put, Israeli soldiers learn not to accept defeat, to laugh in the face of the impossible, to reason "I will figure a way out of this."

Sometimes this attitude, when transferred to civilian life, can have a downside. Israelis are notorious for tough negotiations with hotels abroad, always looking for a better deal, always thinking; this is only a starting point in the negotiations, I can hold out for a better deal. It is often difficult to change one's way of approaching matters.

In business, however, this approach has a positive side. Israelis have become among the most innovative people on the planet, accepting challenges, defying the odds, and coming up with innovative solutions.

Teamwork

Another virtue picked up during years of military conditioning is "team play." In American movies, we see the Rambo type—the lone guy who goes in and "cleans up the mess" all by himself. Israelis know this is not reality. No matter what you may think of yourself, you learn quickly that teamwork is the way to survive and succeed in real life combat. It is not your muscles that will save the day; it is clever teamwork.

The total necessity of teamwork becomes truly evident during combat. The one for all and all for one attitude proves itself as a matter of life and death. Your survival depends upon teamwork, trust, coordination, and the understanding that each individual can only achieve so much on this own. As the old Hebrew saying dictates, "The two are better than the one." This reality of teamwork becomes part of the Israeli work ethic. Our ego has to give way to the reality that we need to work with others. When it comes to hi-tech problem solving it is often a fresh pair of eyes and a fresh perspective that leads to the breakthrough. We work together and succeed.

Risk Taking

In the military, Israelis learn that when you are a smaller force you often must take risks. This military reality goes back to biblical warfare where a smaller force will take a daring risk to surprise the enemy and achieve results. "So Gid'on, and the hundred men that were with him, came to the edge of the (enemy) camp...and they blew with their rams horns and broke the jars that were in their hands. Then the three companies blew on the rams horns and broke the jars and held the torches in their left hands and the horns in the right hands to blow on them, and they cried 'The sword of God and of Gid'on'...and all the (enemy) camp ran, and cried, and fled."[95] Without some daring and risk-taking you remain stuck in the same old rut. You must take a risk to move ahead. Again, this risk-taking translates into civilian life.

"Israeli-style innovation probably has less to do with the kind of smarts you pick up at school and university. A lot of the achievement is based on Israeli's oversized appetite for risk-taking as well as our culture of problem-solving and team play. Those values are learned in the street and to a very large extent in the army."[96]

CHAPTER 11

A Family Affair

Compulsory military service creates a unique bond between generations. Whereas a father and son or grandson might not have any common hobbies or share the same taste in music, they share a military history. When the son or daughter enlists, the father or mother will say, "Yes, I remember my first day—the food was so lousy I did not think I could eat it, and then I got latrine duty."

And then, the much anticipated day arrives. With fear, pride, and joy mingled together, the Israeli family drives their eighteen-year-old son or daughter to the enlistment station. They will take the morning off from the work; the boss will understand. He, too, takes the day off when it is his son or daughter's turn to be enlisted. Even Prime Minister Bibi Netanyahu and his wife took the morning off to accompany their son to the enlistment station. They are no different from other parents.

Memories of the parents' own first day in the IDF will flood their consciousness as they offer stories and advice to ease the mind of the soon to be new recruit; what to say, what not to say, where to go. It is a rite of passage.

Then comes the dreaded moment; the painful goodbye. Wiping the tears from their eyes, the parents reassure themselves that everything will be OK, that the new soldier will be back home soon, safe and sound. "When is your first weekend off? How soon will we see you again?"

Somehow, we the parents, uncles, family, feel that "our" soldier is special. He or she will never be added to "that list," our soldier will be protected, but from that moment onward our lives change. We live with fear, for the angel of death knows no favorites, and our fear only dies when we do.

A unique aspect of Israeli society is that nearly all Knesset (Parliament) members have children and grandchildren who served in the army. They know that the decisions they make as politicians will affect them directly as they are sending their own children to the front lines. "In anything you do as a politician, you ask yourself if you are bringing in your own personal bias, your personal feelings," said former Knesset Member, Esterina Tartman, "but especially when it comes to a son in a war; it is not possible to ignore your feelings.... As an MK (Member of Knesset), I have to go home at peace with my decision. I feel a heavy burden on my shoulders for all the parents of Israel."

Golda Meir, former Prime Minister of Israel, was viewed as the classic Jewish mother and grandmother. She often conducted important meetings in her kitchen. Her headquarters were referred to as "Golda's kitchen." When she spoke, you knew her concern and love for "her boys" was that of a Jewish mother and grandmother and not simply a politician uttering rhetoric or thinking about the next election.

In all countries, politicians must think of the boys going off to war and risking their lives, but in most countries very few of the political elite have direct family ties to the military. In Israel, when it comes to military service there is no elite, there are only elite combat units. Everyone is required to serve; no one is above serving. You cannot buy your way out of military service.

Yitzi

October 23, 2012 was a special day for our family. My nephew Yitzi, Yitzchak, Isaac, received his red paratroopers' beret at Ammunition Hill in Jerusalem. He was following a tradition. Not so long ago, we attended the same ceremony for his older brother, Arie. But there is more to it than that—he is named for my grandfather, Rabbi Isaac Klein, of blessed memory; born in Hungary, moved to the United States, where he volunteered for the US Army, and landed in France on D-day, June 1944.

Yitzi is a soft-spoken, quiet boy; I did not imagine he would be joining the paratroopers. I recall when he proudly, yet nervously, told me about his training. He was nervous, not sure what would be. He, and all of us, were so proud when he made the unit; one of the elite combat units of the IDF. With pride and carefully concealed fear, we celebrated with him and his unit.

I saw his shy, smiling face and I, of course, know we can never express our fears—always just below the surface. But with all that, the joy, the fear, there is something so deep, something that I always feel, something that I cannot repeat often enough; when I saw him with his gun, in an Israeli uniform, smiling broadly, I saw many others as well. I saw his forefathers, just a couple of generations ago, in Auschwitz. I saw generations of Jews who could not fight back, who could only, in their greatest fantasies, dream of such a moment. I saw the defenders at Masada shouting at the Romans, "You have not seen the last of us!" I saw Bar Kochba and his men, piously observing Jewish ritual while preparing for guerrilla attacks against the greatest army of that time. I saw all of them reaching into the future, with hands outstretched, saying, "Remember us. Fight for us." Yitzi, Arie, and all the others are the fulfillment of this promise; they are the fulfillment of this dream. They must train for war so that this land and this people shall live in peace and fear none.

A People United

During World War Two, the United States was united in a war against an evil empire. Every American home who had a son, father, husband, daughter, wife, or mother at war had a special star on display. The star announced to one and all, "We are proud to be Americans, we are proud to be serving our country—we stand as one with our troops." Sadly, if a family member fell in combat or was missing in action, another type of star was on display, saying, "We have paid a heavy price for freedom."

During the Vietnam era, the Gulf War, and the wars in Somalia, Afghanistan and Iraq, this feeling has been sadly lacking among some elements of the American population. In Israel, this feeling of unity is one of the cornerstones of our strength.

With nearly every citizen serving in the military, you might think there is nothing special about it anymore, but there is. When you put on that uniform you are putting on a badge of honor, you are making a pledge to protect your people; you are carrying the torch that has been passed down to you. When you stand at the Western Wall, the last remaining structure of the Holy Temple in Jerusalem, you understand that you are a son to a fighting nation, you are a link in a chain that stretches back to King David who resided here, to Samson who fought the Philistines, and to Abraham, the first Hebrew, who came here, to this area with his son Isaac.

The Bible you receive contains your personal history; odds are some form of your name will appear in the Book. You are holding an M-16 rifle; your ancestors stood right here with the latest sword and shield. Their spirit hovers over you as their blood flows in your veins.

If your name is Ari or Aryeh, it means "lion" and you know you must be fierce as a lion in fighting for your people. If your name is Ethan, you know it means "strength" and you must be strong for your people. If your name is Moshe, you know you must be a leader like Moses. If your name is Joshua, you know you must lead the people in war as did the biblical Joshua. If your name is Michal, you know that the biblical Michal was the wife of King David.

You must be willing to stand ahead of the others and lead through raging waters and arid deserts. If your name is Peretz, it means "breaking through" and you know you must break through the enemy's defenses at all costs and stop their aggression. If your name is Noah, it means "calmness" and you must strive to bring calmness to this troubled land. If your name is Meir, it means "one who brings light" and you must bring light to this nation and to the world.

It is as if you can hear God call out to you by name and you respond in the ancient Hebrew, "*Hineni*, here I am, ready to serve." The Hebrew prophet, Isaiah, used that phrase, "*Hineni*" over twenty-eight hundred years ago. God called out to him. "And I heard the voice of God, saying, 'Who shall I send and who will go for us'"[97] and Isaiah responded "*Hinen, shlacheni*" here I am, send me on your mission and I shall serve God and country. The words of Isaiah are still on our lips.

You feel all this when you put on your uniform, but you feel more as well. My nephew, Arie, wrote, "In Israel, just walking in the street with a uniform is something special. You get special treatment. After the war it was insane, people were offering us free meals, rides, patting us on the back... that's something I am going to miss."

You are fighting to protect your people and you know that they are right there with you, in action and in spirit. You know that your actions have a direct impact on those back home. The Arab you are searching might be a suicide bomber on his way to Tel Aviv. Soldiers have expressed that they felt sad having to trouble the Arabs and search them so thoroughly, but they realized it was an *absolute necessity*. These Israeli soldiers are not fighting for some abstract political goal conjured up by politicians; they are fighting for the lives of their people back home, wanting to feel safe going about their daily business. This gives them strength.

Arie Katz, IDF, 2006

Faith and Prayer

There is another source of strength—faith and prayer, as Arie Katz writes, "In Lebanon, in the moments of truth, I'd have to say that religion, faith and friendship are what got me through. That's all you've got, and that's what it comes down to. Suddenly, even those who don't pray regularly are praying. Of course the usual natural drive had to come from Zionist feelings, and the will to serve your country as did generations before us."

You are a link in the chain, the protector of the future, the guardian of the present. You are united; you are one, with the past, the present, and the future. There is strength in unity.

Motivation at Record Highs

After a demoralizing war, in what seems like an endless stream of wars for survival, and the Second Lebanon War in which exactly the same ground had to be conquered, one might think you would witness a lack of enthusiasm. In fact, the opposite is true: Moshe, a paratrooper from a unit that served in the war, says that when his unit was called up to fight terrorists, the turnout was "one hundred percent as usual."[98]

The army reports that motivation is at an all-time high. Seventy-one percent of those who were fit to serve volunteered for top combat units. The *Golani* infantry unit had two applicants for every position, as did similar combat units. For many, it is religious values that sparked the interest. Many rabbis call upon their students to enlist in combat units. Teachers serve as personal examples, as nearly all teachers are combat veterans.

Zohar, the principal of a religious high school, was in a tank unit during the 1973 Yom Kippur War. He was injured in the battle over the Hermon Mountain. He said, "Our teachers emphasize military values. We emphasize meaningful military service. We have an entire program to prepare students for the military. Our alumni who served in elite combat units are invited back to lecture to our current students. They set an example. All our field trips cover grounds where battles took place. We teach combat heritage."

In another school a student said, "The principal's son is in a combat unit. He came and spoke to us. All my friends want to join elite units. The school atmosphere is one of 'combat readiness' we are all excited about serving."

These kids know what they are getting into. They all grew up in a "combat atmosphere." They watched their fathers and uncles, older brothers and cousins go off to war. Those who came back told them stories of heroism and self-sacrifice. They know what they are fighting for, they know the true face of the enemy, and they know there is no other way. The most powerful weapon, the greatest weapon in our arsenal, as US President Ronald Reagan said, is the human ingredient—the courage and morals of a free people, a people willing to fight for truth and freedom.

Soldiers at a memorial service for a fallen comrade, honoring those who paid the highest price.

Although every position in the army is of importance, there is special prestige reserved for the combat units. One can sense this pride when seeing stickers such as, "Combat is the best, my brother" (in Hebrew this rhymes).

Thus, it was with great pride that my local newspaper announced that one of our high schools in Maaleh Adumim, *Dekel Vilnai*, came in thirty-seventh place in the country in terms of percentage of students enlisting in combat units. Seventy-eight percent of the students have enlisted in combat units for the upcoming draft. The mayor was very proud and came out with a statement saying that this amazing result is a testimony to the values and education we provide in this town. He added that from a young age we teach the value of volunteerism, making a contribution to society, Zionism, and Judaism.

The principal of the school, Harel Horowitz said, "We shall continue to educate according to the vision of excellence and contribution to the Israeli society. We are proud of all of our graduates who are taking meaningful positions in the IDF, and we wish them to return home safely and peacefully."[99]

The Bus Station

I was at the Central Bus Station in Jerusalem. The place was swarming with kids and young soldiers in uniform, carrying their full backpacks and their assault rifles. Some were on their way home to a well-deserved break; others were on their way back to their bases. How wonderful it was to see them, to talk to a few of them. These kids are defending our country, defending our freedom. Each of them, in their own way, is carrying the burden. They are our golden youth. I felt like shaking each one's hand and thanking them personally for their sacrifice, for their dedication and devotion to all of us, for each one of us needs each of one of them.

I saw the camaraderie between them. For those who were going home for a break, the farewell was always accompanied with a warm embrace. This silent hug spoke volumes, without a word it said so much. These were combat troops; border police, *Golani*, paratroopers, they have been to hell and back, they have seen death and faced the moment of truth. That silent hug says, "Be strong brother, I will always be there for you, we will always watch each other's back." Life for them is such that you never know who will be tomorrow's hero or who you will accompany on their last journey. Life can be short and uncertain. You look at their faces and you memorize the smiles, you want to hold them forever.

I look into their eyes and I see people living the moment, living for today, for you don't know what tomorrow will bring. They are here today; tomorrow they may be facing terrorists hellbent on death and destruction. Today they are smiling; tomorrow they may find themselves under a hail of bullets. They hug each other, silently praying, "May God watch over you and bring you back safe, my brother." I look at their smiling faces, so youthful, but yet having seen and felt so much pain, and I pray with them, "May God watch over you and bring you all home safely."

Without saying a word...so much is spoken; the pain, the uncertainty of life, the power of life itself and the hope for tomorrow.

Without saying a word...

"Soon he will be going back to the war, without saying a word. She can't believe he is leaving. She will stand there silently; he wipes the tear off her cheek. She can't believe he is leaving. Another moment and the door will close; he thinks he heard her screaming. And he is going, without saying a word" (*"Bli Lomar Milah"* – "Without Saying a Word").[100] This is our youth and this is how they have to live. So much is placed on their young shoulders. I look at them and I ask God to watch over them, please.

Motivated Girls

The intense motivation to serve is not limited to guys; teenage girls are also highly motivated. It is not a matter of feminism or "proving what girls can do"; it is a matter of feeling that you are contributing something to your people, that you are shouldering part of the burden. It is a desire to give, not to receive. Speaking to young female soldiers you will hear the same themes again and again; "I was looking to fulfill myself and find a way to contribute to my country. I chose this unit because it is challenging and I feel that here I can really make a difference. I know this job involves danger, but my parents support me in my decision and encourage me."

Michal

I took Michal out for the traditional pre-army dinner. Together with her mother, we talked about the army and what lay ahead in the days, weeks, and two years to come. "Do you have everything you need? Any last minute shopping? Warm socks, underwear?" Yes, she has everything. Her older sister, an officer in the IDF, made sure she had everything she needed. She is all set.

Michal took a little extra time before enlisting. She spent a year in a pre-military academy; she spent some time growing up. Now she knows what she wants. Like her mother, she will be a fitness instructor. But unlike her mother who grew up in England, she will be a *combat* fitness instructor. She has been preparing for this for a long time. Her years of karate and Krav Maga with me, and her training with her mother have given her a solid background, but still she says, "I heard the course is hell."

Her first stop will be Ammunition Hill in Jerusalem. This pickup point was not randomly chosen. In 1967, the famed Jordanian Legion held this post. The post consisted of tens of bunkers and a trench system surrounding the hill, with fortified gun emplacements covering each trench. The Israeli forces suffered serious casualties in this battle. The battle and the falling of one of the commanders was described in *"Givat HaTachmoshet"* ("Ammunition Hill"), a song by Yoram Taharlev, which became one the most famous songs in Israel. "The sun had not yet risen, half the unit already lay in blood, but we were already there, on Ammunition Hill....Whoever went first fell, one needed a great deal of luck, on Ammunition Hill."[101]

IDF soldier

The Battle of Ammunition Hill was one of the turning points in the war and the liberating of Jerusalem. When Michal is dropped off there, her first step in becoming a soldier, she will become part of this tradition. Today, it is a peaceful place, but we must remember that this is only due to those who gave everything for the people of Israel. "I sent Eitan, Eitan did not hesitate for a moment, he went up and started using his machine gun...Eitan would cover and we would clear out the bunkers from inside, until he took a bullet to the head and fell inside. Perhaps we were lions, but whoever wanted to live should not have been on Ammunition Hill."[102]

Kayla

From the time Kayla was a little girl, she knew she was going to be a soldier in the IDF; there was never any doubt in her mind. "I remember seeing soldiers in uniform, looking at them and thinking to myself, 'I want to be like them. I want to serve my country.' From that point on it never entered my mind that I would not be a soldier." When she reached military age, she enlisted with the hope of making a major contribution. At first she wanted to be a combat soldier, or in a combat support role, but her talents led her elsewhere. She was earmarked for intelligence work. Her outstanding high school grades caught the attention of the military and she was assigned to an exclusive intelligence unit involving translating Arabic information.

"I was very, very motivated, I was willing to spend three years in some godforsaken place in some combat position." Kayla accepted that she would have to serve in another capacity, one equally important. "It made me very proud to be a soldier. It gave me an overwhelming sense of joy and pride."

Her basic training lasted two weeks. It was a coed program and was "hard times, but I loved it!" Her job in intelligence was no less demanding; stuck in the same room with the same people day after day; sometimes she had to work for twenty-four hours straight. She was on call night and day. She describes the feeling as being "very fulfilling." Recently, Kayla was discharged and now she is training to be a Krav Maga instructor.

Ilana

Ilana wanted to be accepted as a combat fitness instructor. Every day I would see her outside in her running gear with her timer and heart rate monitor. She would run up and down the hills, and then do other exercises. Eventually she made it. She is currently an officer in the IDF.

Dvora

Dvora was offered a job that involved greeting foreign dignitaries, wearing nice clothing and high heels. The job would lead to contacts that could help her career after her military service. She rejected this offer and kept pursuing her dream of serving with a combat unit. Eventually, after several attempts, she was accepted as a combat instructor; working long hours, sleeping very little, and often living in combat conditions. She is now an officer and a combat instructor.

Danielle

Danielle is a vivacious, attractive, fun-loving, typical Israeli high school senior. Her parents immigrated to Israel from the United States. Her maternal grandmother survived the European Holocaust. She participated in the March of the Living, a program whereby high school students visit the concentration camps in Europe and learn about the mass killings committed by the Nazis and their allies during World War Two. When she came home, she decided she would be joining the Israeli army. She simply felt that she had to be part of the promise made to the victims; never again would we be helpless, everyone must contribute to our national defense. Her great-grandparents were killed in such camps, their exact fate was never known, nor did they ever receive a proper burial. Our history teaches us that we must all take responsibility, each and every one of us.

The Question of Women and Combat

Since the middle of the War of Independence, women no longer serve as active combat soldiers, meaning that they are not sent into a war zone to attack the enemy. "Women had been fighters in the *Palmach* until the Arabs conquered Kibbutz Gezer in June (1948). But in that battle, the Arabs raped the girls. So the *Palmach* decided not to put women on the front lines anymore."[103] However, women are still sometimes attached to combat units. Of the one hundred-nineteen soldiers killed during the Second Lebanon War, one was female. When you visit Mount Herzl Military Cemetery, you will notice several female names, all around the age of nineteen or twenty at the time of their deaths.

These days, there have been attempts to reintroduce women into combat type roles, although they do not participate in actual combat. The *Nachshol* unit deals with field intelligence; they are an infantry unit where the women must attain "level three rifle" proficiency (a rather high level). There is observation and gathering of intelligence in the field. The *Shavit* unit is a "combat unit with search and rescue training, integrating boys and girls, and is operational in Judea and Samaria and provides search and rescue services in Israel and around the world."[104]

In 2015, the IDF opened a third mixed-gender combat battalion. The total number of female conscripts volunteering for combat service jumped one hundred twenty-three percent from 2012 to 2014. The IDF hopes to see seven percent of female soldiers serving in combat positions.[105]

Many women also serve in the *Oketz* Canine unit, a very important unit actively involved in locating explosives and preventing bombings.

Karakal is a mixed male/female unit with a ratio of two-thirds women and one-third men. The main task of this unit is to patrol the Egyptian border and block the infiltration of terrorists as well as to prevent smuggling of weapons, drugs, and other illegal items. In September 2012, the *Karakal* unit had to deal with a terrorist cell that infiltrated into Israel. In open combat, they killed all three terrorists. One of the soldiers who killed a terrorist was killed during the exchange of fire. A female soldier stormed the enemy position, shooting and killing another of the armed terrorists.

For women who join combat units, there are pluses and minuses. They serve longer than other women; they must sign on for two years and eight months—eight months longer than other women. They must agree to serve in the reserves until age forty-five and, of course, there are greater risks. On the plus side, they receive higher pay and upon release they receive an increased "release package" (more money). They also receive greater aid in purchasing top quality training sneakers. So why would anyone want to volunteer for such service? As it says on the sticker they proudly display, "Because combat is the best, my sister."

CHAPTER 12

Warriors Make the Nation

Israel, as a nation of immigrants from so many countries, has a great deal of cultural diversity. People arriving from the former USSR, United States, Ethiopia, Yemen, Morocco, France, India, Britain, Germany, Poland, Australia, and, of course, native Israelis, would be hard pressed to get along at a party, let alone as a unit that must go into combat together and count on each other to protect their lives. The army, however, serves as a unifying force, a force that forges these diverse elements into one unified nation. "The army is the threshold people need to cross to join Israeli society," said Brig. General Avigdor Kahalani.

Former Immigration Minister, Ya'acov Edri, said, "Army service is the rite of passage into Israeli society."[106]

New immigrants speak of their desire to enlist, not only for pure patriotism, but also for cultural reasons. The army is a leveling ground; it creates a culture common to all Israelis, it is the fastest way to integrate into Israeli society. You may come from Spain or Ethiopia, the United States or

Russia, but after serving in the IDF, you have become an Israeli. You have picked up military slang, you understand our difficult security situation, you have tasted military food and cleaned the latrines; most likely you have lost a few friends in combat. You have become part of the Israeli family. The military creates more than a common bond; in many ways it creates Israeli society. Warriors not only make the army, they forge a nation.

The Restaurant as a Battlefield

Conventional wars are fought on battlefields. The participants are trained soldiers. Unconventional wars are fought everywhere, and everyone is a participant.

When my brother, Ethan, a combat veteran, visited Jordan, he surveyed the land as a combat spy would observe the layout of the land. He looked for weak points where an enemy could attack, points where a solid defense could be mounted. He was doing this because by then, after years in the military, it had become second nature to him; it had become part of his way of thinking. In Israel, a wise person treats every place as a potential combat zone because our enemies treat every place as a potential point of attack, and every Israeli as a potential victim.

When choosing a restaurant, the first thing one should take into account is the element of time; what times are the threats greater, what times of day are terrorists most likely to attack, and which days of the week are likely to be chosen. Saturday night, for example, is most likely to be chosen as an opportune time to attack.

In choosing a restaurant, one should think of the clientele; is this clientele a likely first choice for a target? Location should be taken into account; is it on a quiet side street or in a large commercial area? The size of the location is also a factor; every establishment has a security guard, but how much can he do? In most cases when the guard spots a suicide bomber—the bomber will quickly detonate the bomb, killing himself, the guard, and everyone around him. In a large restaurant or a mall, you can be seated far enough away from the door to avoid the effects of the bomb and the shrapnel, but in a small, street-side café you have no chance, you are too close to the scene of the explosion to avoid harm.

Just as a soldier would not walk carefree into a battle zone, no civilian should walk carefree into a restaurant, he should remember that he is a warrior and everywhere can be a battle zone. A warrior never leaves himself unprotected or exposed.

The "Neighborhood Watch"

Most communities in Israel have round-the-clock security. It is the citizen's responsibility to protect his own community. As such, each male citizen is assigned to second or third shift; from 9 pm to 12 am, from 12 to 3 or from 3 to 6 am. He will be joined by several other men and will be driven around in a jeep. From time to time, he will get out and patrol by foot. When I explained this to a friend visiting from the United States, he commented, "Oh like a neighborhood watch. We have that too!"

I said, "Not exactly, here volunteers will be handed an M-16 rifle and will be expected to be familiar with how to fire it and how to use it as a blunt weapon. Here, citizens are assumed to have completed at least basic military training in the IDF. Many have served in the Russian or other armies as well; most have combat experience. No, this is not your ordinary 'neighborhood watch.'"

In a nation of warriors, every citizen is ready and able to join an armed patrol; he is capable of handling an assault rifle, apprehending a suspect, and working as a team with other citizen/soldiers. Most importantly he has the attitude; the fearless aggressiveness to pursue the enemy, sticking to the goal, and functioning well under stress.

Rabbis and Guns

Most rabbis have served in the military. Many trained in a five-year *hesder* program that combines advanced religious studies with military combat training. One of the unique aspects of this program is that they study war from a religious/ethical perspective. The students grapple with moral and spiritual issues that a soldier may face. This has a doubly profound effect; it affects the behavior of the soldiers during combat and, later, it affects the perspective of the rabbis who have become community leaders. A man who has stared death in the eyes has a heightened spiritual perspective.

The religious warrior is a unique phenomenon. The IDF has a chief military rabbi, but there are also many rabbis on the front lines. During the Gaza war against Hamas, rabbis were on the front lines in full military gear side by side with the combat troops. The rabbis strengthened the spirit of the fighting men and encouraged them with biblical stories that matched their current situation. Many centuries earlier, King David fought the Philistines here, now his descendants were fighting the current enemy in the same area. Faith and a deepened sense of history helped the soldiers during this difficult time.

The rabbis give out copies of the *Prayer Before Battle*. The soldiers, both religious and secular accept and recite the words, "Be with the soldiers of Israel, emissaries of Your people, who are going to war today with their enemies. Strengthen us and embolden us, fight our battles, hold the shield and rise up to help us."

Girls and Guns

A group of visiting Americans came to watch a military demonstration. Five female soldiers appeared; all beautifully groomed. The crowd commented on their attractiveness. All were carrying guns and proceeded with a demonstration of their martial skills. Next came a team of search and rescue soldiers. They proceeded to drill through thick metal and cement, knock down walls, climb over hurdles and crawl through tiny spaces. When they emerged, they took off their protective helmets and it was those same beautiful young women, IDF soldiers. One of the visitors in the audience commented to his friend, "I have a daughter that age—all she does is hang out at the mall!"

The message is that in Israel the typical eighteen-year-old girl might be firing a rifle, running an obstacle course, training a unit of new recruits, or teaching martial arts to soldiers. She will still be putting on make-up and thinking of what to do with her hair, but she will also be actively contributing to making her country a safer and better place to live.

Israeli women have long played a part in our national struggle. They were members of all the pre-state underground militias; *Nili, Irgun, Lehi,* and *Haganah.* They did not shy away from any role; gun smuggling, intelligence, smuggling in illegal Jewish immigrants past British blockades, combat medics, bomb making, and active combat.

Sara Aharonson joined the *Nili* organization in 1916. The purpose of this organization was to gather military intelligence for the British against the Turks. (At the time, the Jews of Israel sided with the British against the Ottoman Turks as the British had promised the Jews a homeland; a promise left unfulfilled.) She was captured by the Turks in 1917, and after severe torture shot herself to avoid giving away any information.

Ella Izbuzki was born in Poland and came to Israel as a child. She joined the *Irgun* in 1945 and participated in gun smuggling and bombing of bridges and trains that served the enemy. When the actual combat began, she served as a combat medic and was shot in the stomach. She told the other medics to treat the fighters first. As a result, she died from her wounds on the battlefield.

Rachel Zeltzer was born in Romania. When the Germans conquered her town she was transferred to the ghetto. Her mother managed to get her smuggled out of the ghetto in 1941 and from there she joined the "illegal immigration to Israel" (as it was illegal for Jews to flee to the one place where they could truly be safe). In 1948, with the outbreak of the War of Independence, Rachel joined the fighting forces, serving first in Jerusalem. She served as a sharpshooter in the Old City of Jerusalem, where she was shot and killed.

The *Haganah* was one of the three pre-state militias; the *Palmach* was its elite commando unit. Women fought in this unit and thirty-three were killed in combat. Today, the mixed male/female unit, *Karakal,* is officially known as Unit Thirty-Three; in honor of the thirty-three women of the *Palmach* who fell in combat.

During the 1948 War of Independence, the women fought side by side with the men. In biblical times, Debra the Prophetess inspired and conducted the war against the Philistines, guiding the people of Israel in battle.

Tradition

In the classic film, *Fiddler on the Roof,* Tevya the milkman is asked many questions. "Why do we Jews do this? Why do we Jews do that? Why do we wear certain garments? Why do we observe certain practices?"

How does Tevya answer? "Tradition! Tradition!"[107]

Indeed, our tradition is very important and teaches us many vital lessons about who we are and how to survive. Every year during the holiday of Passover, Jews gather round the table and recite the story of the exodus from Egypt and the lessons learned. Some of the lessons are written in code.

There is a passage about five rabbis who were up all night telling the story of the Exodus when suddenly a student runs in and says "Rabbis! It is time to recite the morning prayers." On the surface, the point of this story is the importance of recounting the story of the Exodus, but there is a hidden meaning. My father, of blessed memory, while leading the Passover *seder*, would say that the rabbis were, in fact, planning the revolt against the Romans who had conquered and occupied the Land of Israel. Religious and political freedoms were intertwined, and the leaders of the revolts against foreign occupiers were always religious leaders.

The rabbis used the holiday as a pretext for this dangerous gathering to plan the revolt against the foreign occupiers. Otherwise, the gathering of such prominent religious leaders would have aroused suspicion. The student who came running in to tell the rabbis to pray raises a question. Did not the rabbis know when to recite the morning prayers? Do rabbis need to be reminded to pray? The student was the "look-out guy," and his warning was a code that the Roman guards were approaching and the rabbis had better stop their secret session.

There is more to this story. Old rebellions inspire new ones. That rebellion against the Romans took place nearly two thousand years ago. That was the last time in two thousand years that the Jewish people had an army of their own in an independent Land of Israel. But as we are commanded to read the story of Passover, the wise amongst us understand the message—freedom is never free, you have to fight for it.

The rabbis instruct us, "Every man should see himself as if he personally came out of Egypt." That means that over these thousands of years, when one reads the Passover story of liberation he must visualize *himself* becoming free. Each reader of the story is, in fact, *visualizing* becoming free, mentally *training* himself to be the leader of freedom fighters, a movement of liberation.

The Jew may have been a poor oppressed minority, without land or army to protect him, but in his soul he was commanded to be free. The rabbis instructed him to read the Passover story each year, on the anniversary of our exodus from Egypt and to remember that feeling of becoming free, to feel that freedom in his own soul.

This book, this evening once a year, kept the dream of freedom alive in one's heart; it prevented one from falling into a slave mentality. It guarded one from despair. As long as one can visualize freedom, hope still remains. Reciting these stories kept the spark of freedom alive, even when the physical reality was harsh. Natan Sharansky, one of our greatest "Refusniks," spent many years in a Soviet prison and yet he always remained a free man.

Old rebellions inspire new ones. My father, of blessed memory, made a point of reminding us that the famed Warsaw Ghetto Revolt also began on this night; the night of Passover, the night of liberation from Egyptian bondage. For over three weeks, the starved Jews of the Warsaw ghetto in Poland fought back the Nazi war machine, just as the starved Jews fought off the Romans in Jerusalem in the year 70 CE. Using homemade weapons and an assortment of weapons purchased from other resistance movements, the outnumbered and outgunned Jews defeated the powerful enemy day after day. They sent the Nazis out, retreating from the ragtag army of the Jews. The Jews held out for longer than the entire Polish army!

At the time of the revolt, most of the Jews of the ghetto had already been sent to their deaths in concentration camps. The number of Jewish fighters was actually very small. Once again, as in ancient times, it was the few against the many, the pure against the impure, the David against the Goliath. The ancient tradition inspired a modern rebellion; the biblical Hebrew warrior arose once again to grab his sword and face his enemy.

On the night of Passover, we read how "In every generation they rise against us to annihilate us." Some people may not understand the purpose of our enemies; they might say we can reason with them, make concessions, give them "land for peace," or other such nonsense. The *Haggadah*, the Passover liturgy, reminds us of the enemy's purpose: to annihilate us. The Passover ritual reminds us that there is no logic or reason, but simply that "in each generation someone will rise up against us."

My dear father reminded us that on this night not only did our forefathers leave Egyptian bondage and slavery and march to Israel, but on this night, just a few short years ago, a starved and oppressed people, abandoned by the entire world, cornered into a ghetto, and deprived of all human dignity, rose up to say, "You may herd us into trains like cattle, you may starve us and murder us, but never, never can you take away our human dignity. You may take our body, but you can never crush our soul."

Year after year the *Haggadah* is recited. Year after year the stories are told. In Poland, in Siberia, in Auschwitz, the story is recited. Under harsh Muslim rule in Iraq, Syria, Egypt and Yemen, the story is recited. The spark, the spirit, was kept alive, passed on from generation to generation until finally the moment came when the spark became a flame and the flame became a fire. In blood and fire Zion fell and in blood and fire Zion arose once again.

That is why we must read it every year, lest we forget. That is why Israeli military commanders want their soldiers to read it; to remind them what kind of enemy they are fighting against, to remind them what kind of nation we must be. These soldiers may soon find themselves at war and they must know the purpose of the enemy, and the spiritual strength of our people.

The Warrior and the Bible

In some cultures, there had always been a warrior class and a scholarly class. From their youth boys were divided and raised accordingly. The two groups seemingly had nothing in common; one was raised to be a soldier, the other a scholar. Soldiers did not rise up the ranks to become generals; the general came from the scholarly class.

Among the people of Israel this has never been the case. From the days of the Bible, we have always had the warrior/scholar. Even the rugged warrior was bound by the laws and morals of the Torah, even the scholar had to be trained for war. The Bible enumerates very specific, and rare, cases where a man could be temporarily exempted from military service.

Our ancient prophets were warriors and scholars. King David was the epitome of the warrior/scholar. The judges of Israel; Samson, Ehud Ben Gerah, Deborah, were all warriors. This tradition continues today. In the religious academies of Israel, this tradition is part and parcel of daily life. The study of Torah and preparation for military service go hand in hand. It is well known that religious soldiers have been in the forefront of the most dangerous battles and have risen to the highest ranks.

The State of Israel and the IDF recognize that religious training should be provided for all, even the self-proclaimed secularists who do not follow a traditional Jewish lifestyle. The army provides training in basic Jewish concepts and values; they understand that, in Israel, this is an essential part of being a complete soldier. We are a people's army and this people must know what they are fighting for.

Perhaps the most moving moment in a soldier's career is the moment he or she is sworn in as a soldier of Israel. Standing at the Western Wall of the destroyed Holy Temple or at the ruins of Masada where brave warriors held out, the young recruit receives his/her basic survival tools—the M-16 rifle and the Hebrew Bible. These two tools will be with them throughout their service. Both are an essential part of who we are as a people.

In this Bible, this Torah, they will read about their ancestors who fought on the same land, for the same causes, the same values, and the same principles as they are fighting for today. The soldiers must understand that the Torah, the Hebrew Bible, is their history, their guidebook, and their inspiration. Here they will learn how their ancient forefathers stood up for justice and fought tyranny and oppression. Here they will learn about the scholar/warrior who carries the holy book with him into battle. The heroic tales of old will inspire and guide them.

CHAPTER 13

Warfare in Biblical Times

In July 2006, two Israeli soldiers were taken captive by Arab terrorists operating out of Lebanon. Obtaining the return of prisoners, alive or dead, has always been a primary Jewish value. It is part of our respect for life, for the human being "created in the image of God." The Israeli forces responded with overwhelming military firepower, not only in an attempt to get the boys back, but also as a deterrent for the future.

This is not the first incident of this kind. Around four thousand years ago, there was a similar occurrence. "And they took Lot, Abram's brother's son, who dwelt in Sodom... And a refugee came and told Abram the Hebrew."[108] The story of Abraham as a warrior is rarely told. Abraham was but the first of many Hebrew warriors, and it is this tradition that we continue today.

Biblical Warriors

Abraham – the first Hebrew, the first Hebrew warrior, man of God, man of war

The story of Israeli self-defense begins with the very first Hebrew—the patriarch Abraham, born over four thousand years ago. His nephew, Lot, was taken captive by four victorious kings known for their fierceness. They hoped to receive a ransom from the wealthy Abraham. Abraham *would not negotiate*. He knew that negotiating with terrorists and kidnappers is not a good policy. He had to think of the future—to set a precedent. He responded in a different way, "And when Abram heard that his brother had been taken captive (it was his nephew, but he treated him like a brother) he led forth his trained servants...three hundred and eighteen, and pursued them to the extreme north of Cana'an, to the area of Dan."

The Bible uses a somewhat rare term in this verse, "*WaYarek.*" The biblical commentator, Rabbi Abraham Ibn Ezra, notes "that he gave them weapons." Ibn Ezra brings other sources to show variations of this word used in the context of a spear and a sword. Abraham had an army of three hundred-eighteen men, all well-trained in the art of war, "For he had trained them many times in the art of war even if it is not mentioned (in the biblical text)."[109]

Abraham was thus the first Hebrew martial arts instructor. He personally trained all the members of his household in the art of warfare, for he knew that at times it would be necessary to defend his family and his property. He armed them with swords and spears and they pursued the enemy. "and he divided his forces in an attack against them at night, in order to throw them into confusion...and he defeated them and pursued them... he brought back his kinsman, Lot."[110] Clearly, Abraham was well versed in the tactics of war, although he was a spiritual man.

Jacob – our first wrestler

Abraham's son, Isaac, led a peaceful life, as did his grandson, Jacob. However, even a man of peace must sometimes fight. "And Jacob was left alone; and there wrestled a man with him until the break of day. And when the man saw that he did not prevail against Jacob, he touched the hollow of Jacob's thigh and it was put out of joint, as he wrestled with him."[111]

One thousand years ago, the biblical commentator explained, "As it is the way of two opponents who make an effort to knock each other down, that they grab each other with their arms, shake each other, moving their legs about and try to wrestle the other down."[112]

Sounds like our Judo of today. The biblical narrative tells us that Jacob's wrestling opponent was none other than an angel of God. After the match, the angel blesses Jacob and tells him he now will have a new name; *Yisrael* (Israel). The Hebrew word *Yisrael* is composed of two words: *yisra* (to struggle) and *El* (God). "For you have struggled with God and man and have prevailed." Thus, the name Israel was born of this early wrestling match close to four thousand years ago. In a sense, the nation of Israel and the earliest Israeli self-defense were born together. "Israel" was born in a struggle. The struggle with "God and man" has continued to this very day.

Shimon and Levi – the brothers of Dina, masters of the sword

One of the more controversial issues in the book of Bereshith, and one still debated today, is the episode of Shimon and Levi. The sons of Jacob and the brothers of Dina, they "negotiated" for her release (after she was abducted by Shechem and his clan) and ended up wiping out all males of that clan. The verse reads, "And two sons of *Ya'akov* (Jacob), Shimon and Levi, the brothers of Dina, each took his sword and turned on the city with confidence and killed every male."[113] We see from this verse that each one had a sword and was obviously quite adept at its use (as they killed an entire clan, although it is true that the males of the clan were in pain after their circumcisions, as agreed upon with the clan of *Ya'akov*).

Although the sons of *Ya'akov* are described mostly in terms of being shepherds, herdsmen, and farmers, we see here without any doubt, that just like their grandfather, Abraham, they were well-trained in the art of warfare and were expert swordsmen.

Moshe (Moses) – the redeemer of the people

The Hebrews had become slaves to the Egyptians. The Egyptians feared an uprising and decreed harsh measures against them.

Moshe was hidden by his mother to avoid death by the Egyptians who had decreed that all newborn Hebrew babies were to be killed. He was found by pharaoh's daughter who adopted him and raised him in the palace. Our rabbis teach that this was divinely ordained so that he should not grow up as a slave, but as a prince. As the ordained future leader and redeemer of the people of Israel, *Moshe* must think like a prince and not like a slave.

He always knew who he was and did not forget his own people. When he grew to be a man, he went out so see his brethren, slaves to the Egyptians. "And *Moshe* went out to his brothers, and saw how they were suffering under harsh conditions, and he saw an Egyptian taskmaster beating a Hebrew man, one of his brothers."[114]

Moshe viewed the Hebrew slaves as brothers; he felt their pain and he had to act. These were true signs of leadership. Without thinking of his own safety, without worrying that he would be throwing away his status as a prince of Egypt, he acted. "He turned to all sides to see if anyone would come to the aid of the Hebrew, when he saw there was no man, he fought with the Egyptian, slew him, and hid him in the sand."[115]

Moshe displays all the important qualities of leadership. He goes out to the people, he "sees" their suffering, he feels their pain, and he knows he must act. Without fear for his own life or his own political position; he takes decisive action, knowing that after this he must flee Egypt. This is the man God will choose to lead the people out of slavery. This is the man who, until this very day, we call *Moshe Rabeinu, (Moshe* our rabbi).

Pinhas – man of war, man of peace, master of the spear

The Israelites were battling the nation of Moab. Moab had tried every trick in the book to stop the advance of the people of Israel, including the use of magicians and spell casters, but nothing worked. They feared the Israelite foe. They resorted to man's weak point—young women. The daughters of Moab were sent out to distract and weaken the fighters of Israel, and it was proving effective. "And the people began to commit harlotry with the daughters of Moab...and the anger of the Lord was kindled against Israel....And *Moshe* said to the judges of Israel, 'Slay every one his men that have attached themselves to *Baal – pe'or* (the god of Moab).' And, behold, one of the children of Israel came and brought to his brethren a Midianite woman in the sight of *Moshe* (Moses), and in the sight of the congregation of the children of Israel...And when Pinhas, the son of Elazar, the son of Aaron the Cohen (priest), saw it, he rose up from among the congregation, and took a spear in his hand; and he went after the man of Israel into his chamber, and thrust both of them through, the man of Israel and the woman, through the belly."[116]

This act of violence ended the plague and ended the problem. Pinhas was clearly an expert in the use of the spear, as exhibited by his accurate shot, killing both the man and the woman with a single blow. Pinhas is rewarded by God and is given a covenant of peace for ending this immoral episode. Again, we see the fusion of military might, the ability and willingness to act, and spiritual closeness with God.

Ehud Ben Gerah – judge of Israel, master of the short sword

In the book of Judges, God appoints Ehud, son of Gera, to judge the people and return them to the path of God. This spiritual mission does not preclude violence toward the enemy. Ehud personally kills the enemy king with a new kind of weapon; a double-edged sword. "Ehud made him a sword which had two edges, of a cubit length."[117] This sword was a major innovation. All swords had only one sharp side, this was sharp on both sides, an innovation designed to facilitate a quicker and swifter death. Ehud was to meet the King of Moab privately and had to make it quick, before the guards returned.

All swords were long; this sword was designed as a shorter version so he could hide it under his clothing when he went to meet the enemy king. "And he girded it under his clothes on his right thigh."[118] He wore it on his right thigh, as he was left-handed, and had it designed for a quick and easy draw. "He took the sword from his right thigh, and thrust it into his belly."[119] The entire sword became submerged in the large belly of the king. Ehud left it there and made his quick retreat. Had he pulled the sword out, blood would have dripped on his clothing, drawing attention to himself.

When Ehud returned to the Israeli side of the border, he blew the ram's horn, the *shofar*, as a prearranged signal for the people to gather for war. The warriors of Israel came down from the mountains and Ehud led them in victorious battle. "Moab was subdued that day under the hand of Israel and the land rested for eighty years."[120]

Deborah – judge, prophetess, military leader

Thirty-two hundred years ago, there was a Hebrew woman who led her people politically, spiritually, and militarily. "And Deborah, a prophetess, woman of Lapidoth, she judged Israel at that time."[121]

The people of Israel were being subjugated by the Philistines. Although life was tolerable, the proud Hebrew nation could not stand being under the thumb of a foreign ruler. Deborah decided to act. Deborah initiated, organized, and planned the military campaign against the great Canaanite general, Sisra, in order to conquer the valley of Jezre'el. After Israel had been subjugated to the Canaanites for twenty years, Deborah decided to change things.

Deborah had no intention of personally leading the troops in battle, however, after some pressure; she agreed to be present at the military camp of Israel. Deborah plays a major role in the military campaign, deciding the number of warriors needed, planning strategy, defining military parameters and goals. "Go and gather your men to Mount Tavor, and take with you ten thousand men of the children of Naftali and of the children of Zebulon and I will draw out to you to the wadi of Qishon Sisra, the captain of Yavin's army with his chariots and his multitude, and I will deliver him into thy hand."[122] She is, of course, speaking in the name of God when she promises redemption and victory.

The plan is to draw Sisra's army into the open field, the *wadi*, the low-lying valley, and then to attack them there. Barak Ben Avinoam, the Israelite commander, is to come down from Mount Tavor in a surprise attack. "And Deborah said to Barak, 'Up, for this is the day God has given Sisra to your hands...so Barak went down from Mount Tavor and ten thousand men after him."[123] Barak's troops routed the Canaanite army and Sisra fled on foot, looking for a place to hide.

Yael – the final heroine

The final blow was struck by a woman named Yael, as prophesied by Deborah. Yael was not of the people of Israel, but of the Keini tribe. The Keini tribe had been close with the people of Israel since the days of Moshe (Moses). In general, they tried to remain neutral, but in this case sided with Israel. Sisra accepted Yael's hospitality because relations had been good between the Canaanites and the Keini tribe. Yael lured Sisra into her tent, where she first offered him hospitality. "Turn in, Sir, turn in to me, do not fear."[124] Then, when he was resting, she killed him. "Then Yael, Hever's wife, took a tent peg, and took a hammer in her hand, and went softly to him, and drove the tent peg into his temple...so he died."[125] The war ends with complete victory for Israel. "And the land was quiet for forty years."[126]

Yael, the heroine, is still honored today as the name Yael has become one of the most popular names for Jewish girls.

Samson – great warrior and judge, master of guerrilla warfare

Samson was a great warrior, the strongman of the Bible. He served as a judge and spiritual leader for the people of Israel for twenty years. These were hard times; the southern part of Israel was controlled by the Philistines. The people of Israel felt downtrodden and powerless to resist. They were full of desperation and feared the Philistines.

Unlike other leaders, Samson did not lead the people in battle; perhaps they were simply not ready for it. Instead, he fought a one-man battle and engaged in guerrilla warfare against the Philistines. He was careful to make it look like a personal vendetta so the Philistines would not retaliate and use collective punishment against the entire people of Israel.

To learn their ways, he lived among the Philistines, married their women, and played their games. Samson's tactics were unusual and his behavior a bit unorthodox, yet he is viewed as a hero. These were unusual times and unusual methods were necessary to raise the spirits of the people. The rabbis of the Talmud refer to him as "the protector of Israel" and "Samson the Brave." He is said to have been a selfless man who never used his position or his power for personal gain.

Samson was a powerful man who beat the Philistines time and again with various tactics. "And the spirit of the Lord came upon him and he went down to Ashkelon, and slew thirty men of them."[127] After he agreed to be taken away, to avoid Philistine retaliation against the community of Israel, he was tied up and taken captive. The Philistines shouted at him and offended him, "And the spirit of the Lord came mightily upon him, and the cords that were upon his arms became as flax that was burnt with fire, and his bands melted from off his hands, and he found a new jawbone of an ass, and put out his hand, and took it, and slew a thousand men with it."[128] We can just imagine the powerful circular motions he must have used in combating so many men at once.

Samson was a proud man. When he was blinded by the Philistines, after his Philistine wife betrayed him and revealed to her people his source of strength, he was brought as entertainment to the palace. He decided to avenge his dishonor. He called out to God asking to restore his strength for one last heroic blow against the enemy. "O God remember me, and strengthen me, only this one time O God that I may avenge against the Philistines for one of my two eyes."[129] He cried out, "Let my soul perish with the Philistines," as he knocked down the two central pillars of the palace. The palace crumbled and fell upon the three thousand guests, "So the dead whom he slew at his death were more than those whom he slew in his life."[130]

It is said that for twenty years after his death, the fear of Samson was still upon the Philistine people. For twenty years they behaved themselves, fearing another Samson. Although Samson did not bring total freedom to the people of Israel, his actions were the beginning; the first weakening of the Philistine stronghold on Israel. Others would continue the work.

Today the name Samson, *Shimshon* in Hebrew, is associated with strength and bravery. There is a unit in the Israeli army called *Shimshon*, as well as several gyms and boxing clubs with his name, all a tribute to the man who raised the hopes of the people of Israel during those difficult times.

King Saul's first victory – the battle of Michmash, Judea

King Saul put together a professional army of three thousand men, but he was still badly outnumbered and outgunned by the ruling Philistines. The Philistines had "thirty thousand chariots, six thousand cavalry and people as numerous as the sands of the sea."[131]

The Philistines were the dominant power. King Saul planned to rebel. The rebellion began with his son, Jonathan, attacking the Philistine garrison. The Philistines heard of this and planned a counterattack. King Saul blew the *shofar* (ram's horn) and gathered his warriors at the Gilgal. The Philistines encamped at Michmash. The Hebrew soldiers hid "in caves, and in thickets, and in rocks, and in strongholds, and in pits."[132]

The Philistines were better armed, as the Hebrews had nearly no metal weapons. "Now there was no smith found throughout the Land of Israel, for the Philistines said, lest the Hebrew make them swords or spears."[133] The ruling Philistines did not allow any smiths in the Land of Israel, much like the Japanese would ban all swords in Okinawa in the 19th century. This was a common practice to prevent the people from rebelling. Only Saul and his son Jonathan had swords.

Jonathan, who was known as a brave and fearless warrior, and a God-fearing man, took his aide and went over to watch the Philistine camp. "Between the passes, by which Jonathan sought to go over to the garrison of the Philistines, there was a sharp rock on the one side, and a sharp rock on the other side."[134]

After a few divine signs the two men attacked the Philistine camp. They killed about twenty men, but the main effect was to cause tremendous confusion in the Philistine camp. The Philistines did not know where the attack came from or where the Hebrew warriors were. This caused a panic in the camp. "And there was trembling in the camp, in the field, and among all the people."[135] As a result, the confused Philistines attacked each other, thinking they were Hebrews, "And behold, every man's sword was against his fellow, and there was a very great confusion."[136] At this point the regular troops of King Saul descended upon the confused Philistines and achieved a great victory.

Centuries passed, armies came and went, but the land remained as it was. The biblical name of the Hebrew town, Michmas, was preserved by Arabs who invaded and occupied the land; they called it Mahamas—without realizing it, they provided another proof of who the original inhabitants of this town were.

In 1918, toward the end of World War One, General Allenby was with the British troops and was to conquer this village from the Turks. His assistant, Major Vivian Gilbert, was troubled. The name of the village sounded familiar. He opened his Bible, found the name Michmas in the book of Samuel, and began to read. He wondered, "Would those two sharp rocks and the narrow pass still be there?" Indeed they were! It was occupied by only a small group of Turkish soldiers.

He realized that very little had changed over the years, and decided to change his battle plan. Instead of sending a full brigade, he sent only one unit. They ran into only a few Turks and easily overcame them. Then, in the middle of the night, the British troops climbed the mountain, just as Jonathan had done three thousand years earlier. The Turks woke up startled; they thought they had been attacked by the entire British brigade. All were either killed or taken captive; not one escaped.

Samuel – prophet, man of God, master of the long sword

The prophet Samuel was a man of God in the truest sense. God had given King Saul, via the prophet Samuel, very specific instructions as to how to handle the enemy. King Saul, instead, acted on his own judgment. Among other things, he did not kill Agag, the vicious king of Amalek, who had been tormenting the people of Israel. God knew that the evil nation of Amalek had to be destroyed and that their king must be slain in order to avoid future wars. Sometimes violence is needed to secure peace. King Saul did not heed the word of God and thus was destined to lose his kingdom.

Samuel strongly rebuked King Saul, "The Lord has torn the kingdom of Israel from you this day and has given it to a neighbor of yours."[137] Samuel then calls for Agag, king of Amalek, "Then said Samuel, 'bring here to me Agag the king of Amalek.' And Agag came to him in chains. And Agag said, 'Surely the bitterness of death is past.' And Samuel said, 'As thy sword has made women childless, so shall thy mother be childless among women.' And Samuel cut Agag in pieces before the Lord in Gilgal."[138]

Those who have studied the art of the sword know that to be able to cut apart a human being with a sword requires a great deal of skill acquired from years of intense training. The Japanese arts of the sword, *Kendo* and *Iiado*, are lifetime pursuits. Clearly the prophet Samuel, besides being a man of great spirit, was also a skilled swordsman.

David – shepherd, king of Israel

"And David was the son of a certain man of Efrat of Beth-lehem in Yehuda, and the name of this man was Yishai and he had eight sons, and during the days of King Saul the man was quite old, an aged man."[139]

This is the humble beginning, the first mention, of the man who would come to embody the ideal Hebrew/Jew. This is the man who would become king and represent the proper balance between mind and body, philosophy and combat readiness, the world of the spirit and the world of hard core realpolitik and war. It is David who would write the words in the book of Psalms, "Blessed be God my rock who teaches my hands to do battle, my fingers for war."[139] It is David who conquers the city of Jerusalem and makes it the eternal capital of Israel.

David's first test, first fight, is with Goliath the Philistine giant, but before then, as a shepherd, he already showed his courage and prowess. King Saul at first doubts David's ability to take on Goliath, "And Shaul said to David: you cannot go against this Pelishti (Philistine) and fight him for you are but a youth and he is a man of war from his childhood."[141]

David responds, "Your servant (David) has been a shepherd for his father, tending the sheep, and when a lion or a bear would come and take a sheep from the flock, and I would go after it and smote it and saved it from its mouth. And when it arose against me, I caught it by its beard and smote and killed it. Your servant killed both the lion and the bear, and this uncircumcised Pelishti shall be as one of them, seeing as he has mocked the armies of the living God."[142] David then proceeds to take on and defeat the giant.

David shows early on this quality of the warrior/man of God, "And David said to the Pelishti, you come at me with a sword, and with a spear and with a javelin but I come at you in the name of God the head of the army of Israel which you have mocked."[143]

He then adds a great deal of bravado! "This day God will deliver you into my hand and I will smite you and take off your head from you and I will give the carcass of the camp of Pelishtim (Philistines) this day to the birds of the sky and the wild beasts of the earth that all the earth may know that there is a God in Israel."[144] As Goliath approached, David took a stone from his bag and slung it at the Philistine and caused him to fall down. Then David took another stone and killed him. David did not have a sword so he took Goliath's own sword and cut off his head. At this point, the men of Israel and Yehuda charged against the Philistines and achieved a great victory. And when David and the men came back from the battle, they were greeted by the women of all the cities of Israel, with song and with dance. "And the women answered one another as they danced and said Shaul has slain his thousands and David his ten thousands."[145] David's reputation as a great warrior was now fully established.

David would fight many more successful battles against the Philistines, "And there was war again, and David went out, and fought with the Pelishtim, and slew them with a great slaughter, and they fled from him."[146] David ruled as king in Hebron for seven and a half years at which point he conquered Jerusalem from the Yevusi (Jebusites) and became king over all of Israel and Yehuda. "And David took the stronghold of Ziyyon, that is the city of David."[147]

Deterrent

The concept of deterrent was well known to our biblical ancestors. "Now Dinah, the daughter of Leah, whom she had borne to Jacob, went out to see the girls of the country. Shechem, son of Hamor the Hivite, the chieftain of the land, saw her and took her by force; he lay with her and violated her."[148] Dinah's brothers, Shimon and Levi, were outraged. As a small and outnumbered clan they knew they must make a stand, lest this sort of thing happen again. So they plotted.

They agreed to Shechem's peace proposal that the two clans intermarry and share the wealth. The brothers, however, insisted that Shechem and his entire clan become circumcised, as is the Hebrew tradition going back four thousand years. In his desire and passion for Dinah, Shechem agreed and convinced his clansmen to join him. "And every male was circumcised."[149]

Shimon and Levi knew that the third day after surgery was the most painful, and that would give them the greatest advantage. "On the third day, when they were in pain, two sons of Jacob, Shimon and Levi, Dinah's brothers, each took his sword and turned on the city. They were confident, and they killed all the males...and they took Dinah from the house of Shechem and they left."[150] We see from this verse that Dinah was in "the house of Shechem"; she was being held hostage. Our rabbis say that Shimon and Levi are given the honor of being referred to as "Dinah's brothers" because they acted as brothers; they came to her rescue in her hour of need.

Jacob was troubled by this act, not because of the act itself, but by the fact that "I am but few in number, they will gather against me and attack me."[151] The brothers retorted with their own perspective, "Shall we allow our sister to be treated as a harlot."[152] "Let this be a warning to all who want to make harlots of our sisters."[153]

Rabbi E. Perr of Brooklyn offers the following insight, "One act does not make a woman a harlot, so why do the brothers use the term harlot? Because if they would not act now, surely this violation would repeat itself again and again until she in fact would become a harlot. They had to act now to nip it in the bud, to show that the sons of Jacob would not tolerate such behavior." As a small clan they had to make a big stand.

Just a few verses later, we see the practical results of this policy, "And they traveled, and the fear of God was upon the cities around them and they did not chase after the sons of Ya'akov."[154] Shimon and Levi understood the nature of their neighbors and that only a daring act of force would bring them freedom from future attacks. They knew that their bold action would not soon be forgotten.

Biblical Weapons

Throughout the Bible we find many weapons mentioned—the sword, spear, bow and arrow, and various daggers. Other weapons appear occasionally, such as a slingshot and a jawbone. There is mention of body armor, chariots, and cavalry. One unique aspect is the use of horns.

The ancient Israelites, or children of Israel, faced many enemies and all indications are that they were a warlike nation. Kings such as David and Saul regularly led the troops in battle. Even the prophet Samuel was handy with the sword. The Bible teaches that the ideal ruler should combine this necessary war readiness with softness. The ideal leader is a warrior/scholar—a man who combines the virtues of a holy man with the practical requirements of war.

The Stone

There is no doubt that the stone was one of the earliest weapons used, and its use goes back to antiquity. The stone was not only commonly available, but did not involve any work to prepare it as a weapon. Stones were used with slingshots, as in the famous episode with David and Goliath. The biblical text speaks of stones, "shooting stones," that were thrown at the enemy by using a slingshot make of leather or a strong cloth material. The tribe of Benjamin is noted in particular as being adept at the use of this weapon. "Every one of them could sling a stone at a hair and not miss."[155]

Stones at the Masada fortress, remains of the struggle nineteen hundred years ago

A sword required close contact, but the slingshot could be used from a safe distance, however, this required great skill and considerable practice. We read in the book of Kings that the king of Moab rebelled against Israel. The kings of Israel called for a man of God, Elisha the prophet, "and the hand of God came upon him." Elisha gives them instructions on how to fight Moab, which include "And you shall smite every fortified city and every choice city and shall fell every good tree, and stop all wells of water, and mar every good piece of land **with stones**. Every man threw a stone into each fertile field, so that it was covered over; and they stopped up every spring and felled every fruit tree. Only the walls of Hareshet were left, and then the slingers surrounded it and attacked it."[156]

As a matter of general practice, throwing stones from the top of the walls was the first line of defense against an invader or an attacker mounting a siege, (this was still done in the days of the Masada fortress in the battle against the Romans in 73 -74 CE). Therefore, stones were always prepared and at the ready on top of the walls. "And Uzziyyahu prepared for them throughout all the host shields, and spears, and helmets, and coats of mail, and bows, and **stones for slinging**. And in Jerusalem he made engines, invented by skillful men, to be on the towers and upon the bulwarks, to shoot arrows and great stones."[157]

Among the stones that were used for warfare, one can distinguish several different shapes and sizes. For example, when the Bible discusses the law of the murderer[158] several weapons are mentioned including "and if he smite him by hand with a stone." The Hebrew phrase *"even yad"* is not totally clear. This was apparently a stone with some sort of handle, or it is possible that it was a sort of Stone Age type brass knuckle. Or it could simply mean a common stone that was small enough to be held by hand, the type that one can find on the ground.

The Fist

The fist is mentioned, but not as a weapon of war. It is mentioned in the context of two men fighting, quarreling. "And if men strive together, and one hit another with a stone or with an *egrof* (fist)..."[159] The word used in Hebrew is *egrof*. In modern Hebrew, this is the word we use for fist, but when this verse was being interpreted by the rabbis of the 11th and 12th centuries it was not at all clear what this biblical verse meant. Some felt it meant some type of stone. Rabbi Abraham Ibn Ezra felt it meant a sweeping motion "as one who grabs something in his hand and sweeps." Rabbi Moshe son of Nachman[160] writes, "It is the hand where the fingers are gathered together into the palm in order for one to hit with it." He then compares the types of weapons mentioned in this verse, the stone and the fist, and says both require a certain force, unlike a sword. When making a judgment as to the damage the aggressor owes the victim, the presiding judges need to ascertain how much force was used. The stone and fist are similar in that depending on the force used and the part of the body struck, both can or cannot, cause death. Thus, we see that the fist was seen as a potentially deadly weapon, and a skilled practitioner could kill his opponent with a punch.

Noise and Horns

Self-defense expert, Professor Arthur Cohen, often says that loud, sudden noises are one of the things we fear most. It startles us and causes momentary confusion. It is an excellent self-defense tool; easy to use, very effective, and creates a window of opportunity for either escape or attack.

The ancient fighters of Israel were aware of this. They always went into battle with horns. In the famous battle of Jericho, the fighters circled the city seven times, blowing horns. The Bible records that this actually caused the walls of Jericho to come tumbling down. "And it shall come to pass, that when they make a long blast with the ram's horn, when you hear the sound of the horn, all the people shall shout with a great shout; and the wall of the city shall fall down flat."[161]

In the book of Judges, we read that the angel of the Lord came to the town of Ofra and found the young man, Gideon, threshing wheat. "And the angel of the Lord appeared to him, and said to him, 'The Lord is with thee, thou mighty man of valor.'"[162] The angel appoints Gideon to battle the Midianites. Gideon accepts the mission. "So Gideon and his men came to the edge of the camp in the middle of the night...and they blew the ram's horns, and broke the jars that were in their hands. The three companies blew on the horns and smashed the jars and held torches in their left hands…and they shouted 'The sword of the Lord, and of Gideon'…and all the camp (of Midian) ran and fled. And the three hundred blew the horns, and the Lord set every man's sword against his fellow throughout all the camp."[163]

A surprise attack in the dead of night, the use of loud, sudden noise caused by blowing trumpets and smashing jars, charging in with flaming torches and drawn swords—all these added up to victory. The much smaller force of Israel was thus able to defeat and rout the larger force of Midian. The "sword of the Lord and of Gideon" was the battle cry, symbolizing the spiritual and the physical elements.

In Bamidbar (the Book of Numbers) we find a similar approach and the value attached to noisemaking instruments, as it is written, "And Moshe sent them to war, a thousand of every tribe, them and Pinhas the son of Elazar the priest, to the war, with the holy instruments, and the **trumpets** to blow in his hand. And they warred against Midian and they slew all the males. And they slew the kings of Midian."[164]

The Sword

The most often mentioned weapon in the Bible is the sword—it was the standard sidearm. "David said to his men, 'Let each man gird his **sword**.' And they girded on every man his sword; and David also girded on his sword."[165] When building the Temple, the men were concerned about attacks, so they were armed. "For the builders, everyone had his sword girded by his side, and so he built."[166]

Yoav, Son of Tzruya, was commander in chief; "Yoav was girded with his military coat, and upon it was strapped his sword fastened around his waist in its sheath."[167]

Spear, Bow and Arrow, Sword and Shield, Javelin

Both the spear and bow are mentioned frequently throughout the Bible, "And Saul raised the **spear**."[168] "I stationed them according to their families, with their **swords**, their **spears**, and their **bows**."[169] "The **bow** of Jonathan turned not back and the **sword** of Saul returned not empty."[170] "To teach the children of Yehuda the use of the **bow**, behold it is written in the book."[171]

King Saul died at the hands of the feared enemy archers. "The battle went hard against Saul, and the **archers** hit him, and he was greatly in dread of the enemy archers."[172] "The sons of Re'uven, and the Gadi, and half the tribe of Menashe, of men at arms, able to bear **shield** and **sword**, and to draw the **bow**, and skillful in war."[173] "And the Lord said to Joshua, 'Stretch out the **javelin** that is in thy hand toward 'Ay'; for I will give it into thy hand.'"[174]

Sticks and Stones

While it is clear that professional warriors carried swords, the non-warrior was not adept with this weapon. Young David, long before he came to be king, was not yet of military age. He was just a boy when he heard about the giant Goliath mocking the armies of "the living God" and challenging the Israelites to a contest of strength and courage.

"Why should you come out to engage in battle? I am the Pelishti (Philistine) and you are servants to Shaul (Saul), choose a man for yourselves and let him come down to me. If he beats me and kills me, then we will all be your servants, but if I prevail against him and kill him, then you shall be our servants and serve us. And the Pelishti said 'I defy the ranks of Israel this day; give me a man that we may fight together.' When Shaul and all Israel heard these words they were dismayed and filled with terror."[175]

This taunting took place for forty days. Three of David's older brothers were soldiers. His elderly father sent him to inquire about his brothers. "And Yishay said to David his son, 'Take now for your brothers an *efa* of this parched corn, and these ten loaves, and run to the camp to your brothers;

and carry these ten cheeses to the captain...and inquire of your brothers' welfare.'"[176]

David came to the front lines and heard the arrogant challenge of Goliath, mocking the armies of Israel. David said, "Who is this uncircumcised Philistine that he should taunt the armies of the living God."[177] He was furious and decided to accept Goliath's challenge. He went to Saul, the king, who was commanding the troops and said "Let no man's heart fail because of him; your servant shall go and fight this Philistine."[178]

Saul said to young David, "You art not able to go up against this Philistine to fight with him for you art but a youth, and he is a man of war from his youth."[179] David tells Saul that as a shepherd, he had to defend against a lion and a bear and he was not afraid of Goliath, despite his size and reputation.

At first Saul armed David as a warrior, "And Saul armed David with his armor, and he put a helmet of brass upon his head; also he clothed him with a coat of metal. And David girded his sword upon his armor but could not go." David was not familiar with these items and did not feel comfortable fighting this way. He removed the entire outfit and instead, "He took his **wooden staff** in his hand, and chose five smooth **stones** out of the brook, and put them in a shepherd's bag and his **sling** was in his hand, and he drew near the Philistine."[180]

The rest is history. Goliath had used psychological warfare and no one was willing to fight him. The young David was not familiar with fear. Alone in the woods with his flock of sheep he had battled lions and bears, since no one had taught him to fear them. He was not afraid of Goliath; he knew that every man could be beaten. This passage indicates that while a "man of war" could easily handle a sword and a spear, a common shepherd was more adept at the use of the wooden staff and the slingshot.

The stick is also mentioned in the book of Exodus, Shemoth, "And if a man smite his servant or his maid with a **rod**."[181]

Jawbone

Sometimes unconventional, improvised weapons were used, such as the jawbone of a donkey. "Samson found a **jawbone** of a donkey, and took it and slew a thousand men with it."[182]

Armor

From the story of David, we see that the ancient Israelites used armor; from the descriptions of Goliath we learn about the armor of the Philistine warriors. "And there went out Goliath, of Gat, whose height was six cubits and a span. And he had a **helmet of brass** upon his head, and he was armed with a **body armor** of scale; and the weight of the body armor was five thousand shekels of brass. And he had **brass** upon his legs, and a javelin of brass between his shoulders. And the staff of his spear was like a weaver's beam, and his spear's head weighed six hundred shekels of iron."[183]

Man of Valor – Use of Wooden Staff Against a Spear

During the Second Lebanon War, there was a great tank commander called Benaya. The name brings back memories of another Benaya—he too was a warrior, but from many years ago. "Benaya the son of Yehoyada, the son of a valiant man of Qavze'el, who had done many acts; he slew two lionhearted men of Mo'av; and he went down and slew a lion in a pit in a time of snow. And he slew a Mizrian man, a man of great stature, five cubits high; and in the Mizrian's hand was a spear like a weaver's beam: and he went down to him with a **staff**, and plucked the **spear** out of the Mizrian's hand, and slew him with his own spear...and David set him over his guard."[184]

Military Transportation

For the purposes of war, armies used horses and chariots. Many passages mention the chariots and cavalry of Egypt and the Philistines. "And the Philistines gathered themselves to fight with Israel, thirty thousand **chariots** and six thousand horseman."[185] When the children of Israel left Egypt, pharaoh, king of Egypt, came after them. "And he took his **chariot**, and took his people with him and he took six hundred chosen chariots."[186] They later drowned in the sea. "And the waters covered the chariots and the horseman."[187]

I could not find any mention of the Israelite warriors using chariots or cavalry.

Spies and Ambush

We see in the Bible effective use of spies sent to learn "the weaknesses of the enemy." "And Joshua the son of Nun sent out of Shittim two men to **spy** secretly, saying, 'Go view the land, and Jericho.'"[188]

Great value was placed on military strategy, the use of ambush, and siege. However, the ancient Hebrews always left one side of a city open; to allow for escape and a non-violent conclusion, unless there was a specific divine order to the contrary.

This plan was followed exactly and succeeded. A small group of Israelite soldiers attacked the city of Ay and drew out the overconfident forces who decided to chase them and wipe them out once and for all. Joshua himself led this group, just as modern Israeli commanders lead their troops in battle. Joshua and his men acted defeated and scared,

"And Joshua and all Israel made as if they were beaten before them, and fled by the way of the wilderness. And the people that were in Ay were called out to pursue after them, and they pursued after Joshua and were drawn away from the city. And the Lord said to Joshua, 'Stretch out the javelin that is in your hand toward Ay, for I will give it into thy hand.' And Joshua stretched out the javelin that he had in his hand toward the city. And the ambush rose quickly out of their place, and they ran...and they entered the city, and took it and hastily set the city on fire. And the men of Ay looked behind them, they saw, and behold. The smoke of the city ascended up to the sky, and they had no power to flee this way or that way. And the soldiers of Israel that had fled to the wilderness turned back upon the pursuers... and they slew the men of Ay."[190]

CHAPTER 14

Post-Biblical Fighting

The fighting tradition of the people of Israel did not end with the closing of the biblical period. The year was 586 BCE. The capital, Jerusalem, and the Holy Temple, the center of Jewish life, were destroyed. The greater part of ten of the twelve tribes had been exiled and scattered. Of the remaining tribes most had been destroyed by war, famine, enslavement, and disease.

Fugitive Israelites were killed by many enemies or handed over to the conquering Chaldeans (Babylonians). Judea was almost completely depopulated. And yet the people of Israel survived and would fight again, against all odds.

In 539 BCE, Babylon falls to Persia. Cyrus (Koresh) the Great defeats Babylon and allows the Israelites to return to the Land of Israel and rebuild Jerusalem and the Temple. It is significant that Cyrus is referred to as God's Messiah, "God's anointed one."[191] "Thus says God to his anointed, to Koresh." Unlike modern times, the idea of a messiah is simply a redeemer of Israel and not a supernatural creature from heaven or a miracle doer.

The ancient people of Israel were a proud and fierce people, deeply spiritual and deeply committed to freedom and independence. With trust in God, they raised armies and fought those who came to oppress them.

The Maccabees

In the year 168 BCE, the Syrian Greek king, Antiochus Epiphanes, sought to impose a policy of spiritual genocide and assimilation on the people of Israel. He was determined to uproot the ancient religion of the Jews. The Jewish state was attacked; the Holy Temple defiled with idols. Evil decrees backed by the military might of the most powerful army of its day forced Jews to worship heathen idols, eat the flesh of the forbidden swine, and refrain from observing the holy Sabbath day. The Jewish tradition of circumcising all boys was outlawed. "The king issued a decree throughout his kingdom that they should all become one people and abandon their own laws and religion...sacrificing to idols and profaning the Sabbath...they must leave their sons uncircumcised, and defile themselves...whoever would not obey the order of the king was to die."[192]

The Revolt, 167 BCE

The revolt, led by a band of farmers/warriors of deep faith, has almost no parallel in human history. It was a true liberation movement. "In those days Mattathias, son of Yohanan, son of Simeon, a *cohen* (priest) of the family of Yoarib, moved from Jerusalem and settled in Modiin. He had five sons." Mattathias the priest and his sons rose up and led a national liberation movement. They were known as the Hasmoneans or the Maccabees. The elder Mattathias shouted out, "Whoever is for God, come with me! It was then that they were joined by a company of devout followers, strong Israelite loyalists, each one willingly offering himself in the cause of Jewish law."[193]

In an age of mercenaries or men who were raised to be warriors, the army of Mattathias the elder was like no other of its time. The men were neither mercenaries nor professional full-time soldiers; they were simple farmers, gentle scholars, devoted to Jewish law and values, to God. They were citizen/soldiers. These men took up the sword, as had their biblical fathers before them, to fight for freedom. Mattathias began by tearing down pagan altars, and reinforcing Jewish law.

As Mattathias grew old and was ready to die, he called forth his sons and inspired them with the stories of bravery and faith from Abraham to the present. "Was not Abraham faithful in time of trial...Pinhas, our ancestor, for his zeal... consider how throughout every generation, none who trust in Him lack strength." (Pinhas was his ancestor as all *cohanim*, the Cohen family, are related.) Leadership of the revolt was passed to his son, Judah, known as the Maccabee. "Judah Maccabee has been strong and brave from his youth. He shall be your captain and fight the people's war...repay the pagans for what they have done, heed the laws of the Torah. Then Mattathias blessed them and was gathered to his fathers."[194]

Judah, the Hebrew Hammer

It is not known for certain what the word Maccabee means. Nowhere else is it used. It is believed that it means "The Hammer." Judah the Hammer would lead the freedom fighters in battle against the greatest power of the day. Apollonius, leader of Samaria, gathered a large army to fight against Israel. Judah heard of this and marched out to meet him in battle "and he defeated and killed him." Judah took the sword of Apollonius, and fought with it for the rest of his life.[195]

Judah's soldiers were known as faithful men, devoted to Jewish law, brave, and experienced in the art of warfare. They won battle after battle, defeating larger forces. "The fear and dread of Judah and his brothers began to spread among the pagans around them."[196]

King Antiochus Epiphanes was enraged. He gathered the largest army possible, "All the forces of his empire, a very powerful expedition." The forces of Judah the Maccabee were badly outnumbered. He and his men placed their faith in God and prepared for war. Judah spoke to his men, "Prepare yourselves for action and show yourselves to be brave men. Be ready at dawn to fight against the pagans who are gathered together against us, to destroy us and our Holy Place."[197]

The king's troops, led by Gorgias, came to attack the camp of Judah, but they had left. At daybreak, Judah and his troops came to attack another pagan camp. "Judah's men sounded their trumpets and attacked." They routed the pagans and killed about three thousand men. When Gorgias and his troops returned to camp and found the victorious army of Judah, they fled.[198]

The king gathered an even larger force, sixty thousand troops. Judah with his ten thousand men defeated them, killing five thousand men. The Greek commander, Lysias, feared the bravery of Judah and his men. "When Lysias saw that his army was routed, and that Judah had grown bold, and was ready either to live or to die nobly, he departed."[199]

In the year 164 BCE, Judah and his brothers took back Jerusalem and rededicated the holy Temple. Judah said to the warriors, "Now that our enemies are crushed, let us go up to Jerusalem to purify the Holy Place."[200] The holiday of *Hanukah* (rededication) commemorating this event, is observed by Jews to this very day.

The enemy continued to send forces. In the year 161 BCE, in a lopsided battle, Judah the Maccabee was killed. The enemy numbered twenty thousand foot soldiers and two thousand cavalry. Judah had barely three thousand men. Judah refused to surrender or retreat, "If my day to die has come, it will be with honor."[201] The men pleaded with Judah to back down and retreat, but Judah would not hear of it. His brothers Yonatan and Shimon took over.

By the year 142 BCE, complete Jewish independence was finally secured under the last of the surviving brothers, Simon, who signed a formal peace treaty with the Greeks. Countless Jews had died martyrs, fighting bravely against the enemy. The Syrian Greeks had finally realized they could not defeat the people of Israel, despite vastly superior forces.

After the Greeks came the Romans. The Romans conquered everything in their path, including the Land of Israel. But the stubborn Jewish warrior nation would not be quiet.

The Great Revolt, 66-73 CE (or 74 CE)

Perhaps no other war shows the spirit of this nation of warriors more than the Great Revolt, for in this case we have a written document of the conditions they faced. This comes in the form of the great speech delivered by Agrippa the Second.

The Jewish people had been provoked by Roman governors who were creating excuses for more massacres. Indeed, the Jewish people had every right to be free and to live by the Torah, but Agrippa knew that the situation was hopeless. His speech was a work of art. Step by step, he outlined the logic of the situation.

> Think of the Athenians...the liberty of Greece...think of the Macedonians. Other nations...bursting with greater determination to assert their liberty, no longer exist. Will you refuse to serve the masters of the whole world?

Where are the men, where are the weapons you count on? Where is the fleet that is to sweep the Roman seas? Where are the funds to pay for your expeditions? Do you think you are going to war with Egyptians and Arabs? Look at the far-flung empire of Rome and contrast your own weakness.

How justly Bithynia, Cappadocia, Pamphylia, Lycia, and Cilicia might demand liberty! Yet without armed pressure they pay their dues.

Then there are the Thracians, spread over a country five days' march in width and seven in length, more rugged and much more defensible than yours, a country whose icy blasts are enough to halt an invader. Yet two thousand Roman guards suffice to maintain order.

Which of you has not heard of the Germans, with their inexhaustible manpower? You have, I am sure, seen their magnificent physique on many occasions, for on every side Roman masters have German slaves; yet this people occupies an immense area, their physique is surpassed by their pride, from the bottom of their hearts they despise death, and when enraged they are more dangerous than the fiercest of wild beasts. Yet the Rhine is the limit of their aggression and the Romans with eight legions have tamed them, enslaving the prisoners and driving the entire nation to seek refuge in flight.

Consider the defenses of the Britons, you who feel so sure of the defenses of Jerusalem. They are surrounded by the ocean and inhabit an island as big as the land which we inhabit, yet the Romans crossed the sea and enslaved them...

Almost every nation under the sun bows down before the might of Rome; and will you alone go to war, not even considering the fate of the Carthaginians, who boasted of great Hannibal and their glorious Phoenician ancestors, but fell beneath Scipio's hand?[202]

And yet, that is exactly what they did; against all odds, the people of Israel rose up and fought the Romans in a war that lasted four years. It took the Romans another three years to fully suppress the rebellion. The great Roman army was beaten back again and again until they sent for the finest Roman general, Vespasian, together with his son, Titus.

The outnumbered and out-armed Jews knew they had no chance in the open battlefield. They barricaded themselves in their towns. The Romans laid siege to town after town. Some towns fought heroically to the last man, other towns surrendered in order to save their lives. Those who escaped fled to Jerusalem, where they believed the redemption would begin.

In the spring of the year 70 CE, the Romans laid siege to Jerusalem. Titus led four top Roman legions. "The Romans, from the moment of their arrival, had the painful experience of the daring spirit of their opponents (the Jews). While the tenth legion, which had advanced from Jericho to Jerusalem, was still occupied with the strengthening of its camp on the Mount of Olives, it was attacked with such violence that it had well-nigh suffered an utter defeat."[203]

The Romans battered the walls of the Holy Temple with their battering rams. "Jews took torches and threw themselves into the Romans' machines. They went forward as if to greet a lover. No one exceeded this bravery. They jumped into the enemy's machines and set them on fire, all the while arrows and stones were being shot at them. They did not attempt to leave the place of danger until the machines were set on fire. The bravery of the Jews set the Romans back."[204]

The Romans built new batteries, the hunger within Jerusalem increased. Many Jews went up to the Holy Temple to wait for redemption; there they found their death. Titus could not break the walls of the Temple, so he ordered to burn the gates and break in from there. It took five months of siege for Titus to take the city of Jerusalem. Finally, the starved and exhausted defenders were taken. The city was burned and the population mostly slaughtered.

"Together they brought down the walls of Jerusalem and burned the Holy Temple, losing tens of thousands of legionnaires in the process. A million Jews fell in their struggle for Zion, but not in cattle cars or led to gas chambers. Rather in proud battle and, at the end, with the dignity and honor of Masada as the Jews—seeing that the final moment had come and having taken so many lives of the enemy—took their own, rather than be humiliated."[205] The revolt ended in the year 73 CE (or 74, there is uncertainty on this point) with the fall of the last Jewish stronghold, Masada.

The fortress Masada, located on an isolated mountaintop deep in the Judean desert, was built by Herod the Great years earlier. In the year 66 CE, the Jewish commander, Menachem, conquered the position from the Romans. His nephew, Elazar Ben Yair, together with a group numbering nine hundred sixty-six Jewish men, women, and children found refuge there.

Masada was surrounded by a huge Roman force, estimated at between eight up to fifteen thousand troops including the famous Roman Tenth Legion. The situation for the Jewish defenders looked bleak, but they used every means at their disposal to fight back. They had large stones to roll down on the Romans and they manufactured arrows at Masada itself.

Moshe looking upon Masada, the last stand of the Jews against the Romans in the year 73 or 74

Although the Holy Temple in Jerusalem had already been destroyed and most of the country lay in ruin, a small number of Jews continued to fight back. As Americans would say nineteen hundred years later, it was a matter of "live free or die." Under the command of Elazar, employing guerrilla warfare, the Jewish freedom fighters attacked the Roman garrisons whenever possible and then retreated to the safety of Masada.

In the year 73 or 74 CE, the Roman general, Flavius Silva, laid siege to Masada. After several months of siege with no results, he built a ramp to reach the top of the mountain and brought up a battering ram. When all hope was lost, the Jewish defenders took their own lives, denying the Romans their great victory.

Archaeological finds indicate that, without a doubt, these last defenders lived a life in strict accordance with

Jewish law. Even as they were surrounded, night and day, by overwhelming forces intent on their destruction they continued to observe the minutest details of Jewish law and custom. Like their ancestors before them, they were "men of God and men of war."

The physical evidence found by archaeologists teaches us that the biblical laws of tithes were strictly observed. A potsherd was found with the Hebrew words, "*ma'aser cohen*" meaning the tithe for the *cohen*, the priest. This is living evidence that biblical laws of tithes were observed on Masada. Numerous ritual baths were found, indicating that biblical laws of family purity were maintained. Parts of biblical scrolls were found and many other religious artifacts. In the shadow of death, these Jews sanctified life.

The Second Jewish – Roman War

In the year 114 CE, the Romans conquered many areas with large Jewish populations. Some estimate as many as one million Jews lived in these areas. In the years 115-117, the Jews of Libya (Cyrenaica), Cyprus, Egypt, and other areas would rise up against their Roman oppressors in another bloody revolt. This war began in the Diaspora and was mainly fought by the Jews outside of Israel, but it soon spread to Israel as well. In Jerusalem, the Jews were provoked by the Roman procurator, Lucius Quietus, who set an idol up on the Temple Mount, where the Holy Temple belonged.

Known as "The Rebellion of the Diaspora" or "The War of Kitos," this too would be brutally put down, but not before the Jews caused untold damage to the Romans. "When their resentment finally broke out with ferocious violence in different parts of the eastern Mediterranean, the uprising caught the Romans by surprise."[206]

"The Jews in the region of Cyrene had put a certain Andreas at their head, and were destroying both the Romans and the Greeks."[207]

By all accounts, this was considered extremely violent even compared with the other revolts. The Jews were angry and attacked, causing great damage. The revolt was described as "unprecedented not just in its savagery but in its geographic spread."[208] The Jews, perhaps as revenge, destroyed or damaged many pagan temples; of Apollo, Zeus, Demeter, Artemis, and Isis. The Roman general, Lucius Quietus, eventually crushed the rebellion. It was his name, Quietus, misspelled Kitos, which gave the war/revolt one of its names.

Hadrian was appointed Roman emperor and needed to put an end to this chaos and bring some calm. He had Quietus put to death in 118 CE on charges of conspiracy, and made promises to the Jews that he would allow them to rebuild the Temple, *Beth HaMikdash*.

Despite the vast destruction and massive loss of life, the Jews of Israel would rise again and stage one last brilliant revolt.

The Bar Kochba Revolt, 132-135 CE

The end of Jewish Independence until the rebirth of the State of Israel.

The Jewish tradition of fierce independence and a warrior nation continued, despite being outnumbered and despite the devastation of the previous revolt/war against Rome. In the year 117, Hadrian was appointed emperor of the Roman Empire, ruling Rome and the conquered lands from 117 to 138. Only one war was fought during his reign and that was the Third Roman-Jewish War in Judea; it consumed all his men and all the might of the Roman Empire.

Hadrian's policies in Judea led directly to the Bar Kochba revolt. Hadrian did not care for the religions in this area. His policies affected both Jews and the early Christians, although most Christians did not join the war effort against Rome.

Hadrian built a large temple to the goddess, Venus, on top of what the early Christians venerated as the tomb of *Yeshu* (Jesus), whom they saw as the Messiah. This was done to suppress Christian worship there; later this site was rebuilt as the Church of the Holy Sepulcher after the Christian Empress Helena ordered the temple of Venus be demolished.

Hadrian, at first, seemed inclined to kindness toward the Jews. Matters changed, and he decided to build a Roman pagan city on the ruins of the city of Jerusalem, (destroyed by the Romans in 70 CE) the holy city of the Jews, and a temple to the pagan god, Jupiter, on the site of the Holy Temple. "The Judea that Hadrian had in mind was not to be Jewish at all: At Jerusalem he founded a city in place of the one which had been razed to the ground, naming it Aelia Capitolina, and on the site of the temple he raised a new temple to Jupiter."[209] These actions were followed by harsh decrees such as a ban against Jews living in Jerusalem, a law against circumcision, and bans on the practice of the Jewish religion and the study of Torah.

Hadrian felt he should leave Jerusalem empty in order to avoid giving the Jews hope and an "invitation" to agitate for their former glory. This time, he would leave no doubt. Hadrian planted a pagan Roman colony on the site where the Jewish Temple once stood, thus making it quite clear that there was no chance of rebuilding the Temple any time soon. He turned the site of Jerusalem into a smaller version of Rome, filled with Roman religious practice and totally inhabited by gentiles. He felt these actions would cause the Jewish agitation to evaporate. He could not have been more wrong!

He did not understand the nature of the Jews and their fierce desire for independence and even more so for religious freedom. The Jews began to prepare for war. They were, at first, pacified by the words of one of the leading rabbis, Rabbi Joshua ben Hananiah, who urged restraint against the powerful enemy and discouraged another revolt, but soon they could take no more.

The commander of this revolt was a man known as Shimon Bar Kochba. His original name was Shimon Ben (or *bar*, son of) Kosba (pronounced Kosiba). Rabbi Akiva believed that Shimon was the Messiah, the anointed one, and called him Bar Kochba, Son of Star, as in the biblical verse "There shall come a star (*kochab*) out of Ya'akov (Jacob) and shall arise a tribe from Israel who shall smite the corners of Moav and destroy all the children of Sheth."[210] Bar Kochba was a descendant of King David. According to Jewish tradition, all kings must be from the line of King David. Years later, some would refer to him as Bar Kosiva; *kosiva* means false, or one who falsely led the people to a doomed war.

The war would last three and a half years. He was determined not to repeat the mistakes of the previous Great Revolt. Unity among the Jewish fighters was a must, and was achieved. Organization and efficiency were impressive. Having the backing of the leading rabbis was essential, and this too was achieved. It is believed that none other than Rabbi Akiva was the spiritual force behind the revolt. Direct, conventional combat with the Romans was to be avoided.

General Shimon Bar Kochba was regarded as a brilliant tactician, a powerful man, a strict disciplinarian, and a messianic religious leader. Letters reveal that he was a devoutly religious man who went to great lengths to take care of the religious needs of his soldiers. In all the letters found, Bar Kochba is referred to as Shimon Ben Kosiba, president of Israel. In these letters, he deals with every aspect of the war and any disputes between people; issues of property, cattle, food, and how to deal with those who did not cooperate with the war effort. These discovered correspondences, found near the Dead Sea, also reveal that he personally adhered strictly to the laws of the Torah. It is truly amazing that actual letters written by Bar Kochba were found—signed by him! The climate in the Dead Sea area is uniquely dry and perfect for preserving such material. They were found by Bedouin nomads in caves deep in the Judean desert.

Along with letters, the researchers later found, deep in the mountains, piles of bones and skulls; the remains of some of Bar Kochba's fighters who died of starvation while hiding in the mountains. In one cave, seventeen skeletons were found; men, women, and children. So we now know that entire families, not only fighters, hid out in these caves. They had all starved to death.

Carpets and clothing were also found among the remains. This gave us insight into the clothing of the time. It was found that the biblical laws of *sha'atnez* were strictly adhered to. *Sha'atnez* refers to "mingled garment" or a garment made of wool and linen. "Neither shall a garment mingled of linen and wool come upon thee."[211] It was also found that the clothing had a particular type of stripes, amazingly similar to the stripes still found in the *tallith*, (prayer shawl) worn by Jewish men to this very day! Prayer shawls were also found, but they lacked the ritual fringes. "Speak to the children of Israel and tell them to make fringes in the corners of their garments."[212] This can be explained by the fact that fringes must be removed when one is near the dead. Even today, when in a cemetery, a Jew is required to tuck in his ritual fringes.

Researchers found partially completed fringes, indicating that the inhabitants followed the biblical laws of ritual fringes, even in their most difficult circumstances. There was also a distinct difference found between men's garments and those worn by women, again a biblical law. Arrowheads were found in the caves, as well as coins minted during the Bar Kochba revolt; on one side engraved with "Shimon" and the other side "for the freedom of Jerusalem."

The cooking utensils found in the cave were another indication of the religious piety of Bar Kochba's followers. In one tied bag, nineteen different cooking utensils (pots and pans) were found. What surprised the archaeologists was that they had pagan images on them—clearly prohibited by Jewish law! "Thou shalt not make for thyself any carved idol or any likeness of anything that is in heaven above, or that is in the earth beneath."[213] Upon closer examination, it was determined that all the images had been scratched, or partially rubbed out. In some cases, the rubbing out was very clear, in other cases only the nose of the creature was wiped out. All this fits in perfectly with the laws written in the Talmud, that one may use a utensil belonging to any idol worshiper as long as it is deformed. "How does one erase it? Break the edge of the ear, the head of the nose, the head of a finger, even if not complete—it is 'canceled.'"[214]

These utensils had been Roman and were probably taken by Bar Kochba's men during one of their victories. Some of the utensils were used by the Romans as part of their idol worship ceremonies. Many Jewish laws, some on the books until today, date back to those days and are designed to keep Jews away from idol worship, so prevalent at the time. For example, Jews are prohibited from drinking wines of Gentiles out of suspicion that perhaps these wines were used for the wine libation in idol worship ceremonies. The caves also contained fragments of written texts. The first found, by a young man named Shlomo, was a fragment that read, "Who shall abide in thy tent. Who shall...uprightly and acts justly...not slander" It was just a fragment, but it was certainly Psalms, chapter 15. The warriors of General Bar Kochba had been reading the Psalms of the Bible. Sadly, the young man, Shlomo, would also die in combat, like his heroes in the Bar Kochba war. He was killed in action during the Six Day War of 1967, he fought with great bravery and self-sacrifice, much like those he so admired.

Perhaps the most amazing discovery were the packages of letters dictated by Bar Kochba himself. Written in Aramaic and Hebrew, they give orders about supplies and policy. Some of the letters pertain to religious obligations such as providing the four species for *Sukkoth*, (the Feast of Tabernacles). In one letter, he orders a certain man sent to him, but emphasizes that he is to arrive before the Sabbath begins.

General Bar Kochba and his men prepared well for this rebellion. They decided not to use the failed tactic of the "Great Rebellion" of holding out in fortified cities. Instead, they would fight in the open field, but in an unconventional way. Bar Kochba and his fighters developed a new form of warfare—guerrilla warfare. The Jews knew they were terribly outnumbered and could not fight the Romans in the open field.

The fighters converted the caves in the mountains into hiding places and fortifications which they connected by subterranean passages. Every effort was made for a sustained and successful war. They spent years digging underground caves. These caves served both the soldiers and the general population. They were hidden and not visible on the outside. These caves contained many rooms and passageways, air ventilation, living quarters, vast supplies; weapons, food, and water.

They would ambush and surprise small groups of Roman troops and return to their underground dwellings. When the Roman forces approached, the Jewish forces disappeared into the hidden underground caves. The Romans lost tremendous numbers of their finest troops until they learned how to conduct anti-guerrilla warfare. They eventually discovered the hidden caves and set fires in them. Archaeologists found caves with dozens of bodies in them; all burned to death.

The rebellion succeeded at first; the Jews reestablished their independence and minted new coins of freedom. The new state was named Israel; a name the Romans refused to use when they referred to the Jews. In this war, the Jewish forces did not wait in the cities, they took the initiative and attacked the Roman forces everywhere. Tinius Rufus and his men had to flee to Caesarea. The Roman twenty-second legion was beaten so badly, it was never mentioned again in the Roman chronicles.

The Romans sent in more legions and better generals. Hadrian took personal command, thus drawing in the greatest military minds of his age. They learned the tactics of the Jews and slowly beat them back. The Jews had to flee to fortified cities. Sieges were laid and destruction followed. "The (Roman) victory was won indeed at a very heavy cost. So great were the losses that Hadrian in his letter to the Senate omitted the usual introductory formula, that 'he and the army were well.'"[215]

Five hundred eighty thousand Jews died in the war—martyrs in a struggle for independence. The destruction of the Jewish community was so great that no further rebellions were attempted. Only small pockets of Jewish independence continued to exist. Areas formerly inhabited by a Jewish majority would now become Christian areas, as the Christians had not joined in the struggle and had rejected Rabbi Akiva's idea that Bar Kochba might be the Messiah.

The rebellion was crushed and all hope was lost, but the Jewish bravery would not be forgotten. "In the face of an almost total peace, quiet, and tranquility inspired by the universal awe and fear of the mighty legions of Caesar, the Jews, the Zionists—living in Zion, their home—rose up against Roman oppression of body and soul and revolted. Under the sainted and martyred Rabbi Akiva and the legendary general Shimon Bar Kochba, they drove the Roman armies from Jerusalem, from Judea, sending the

Roman governor Tinius Rufus along with the governor of Syria, Publius Marcellius, and the legions rushed from Egypt, scattering in flight. It was only a desperate call to the greatest of the generals of Rome, Julius Severus, arriving from far off Britain with legions from the Danubian lands that forced the Jews back step by step, with ferocious struggle and heavy losses to the stupefied Romans. Bitterly these Jewish warriors fought and bitterly they died. Stubbornly they struck at the invader of their land—the aggressors and imperialists of imperial Rome, and blood washed the paths and streets of the mountain-city of Bethar where the beleaguered Jews of freedom, retreated for the final battle—to die or to conquer the land, their land, Zion."[216]

The Jew and his land; bound by Divine promise, blood, sweat, toil, and tears. The memory of these struggles would never die, they would be passed on from generation to generation, from soul to soul wherever the Jew wandered, wherever he found his temporary home...until someday another Jewish soldier would return, to this very same land and continue this very same struggle for freedom and independence.

Not much is recorded from this time. We know that Bar Kochba died during the rebellion The oral history was that a certain Cuthean brought his head to Hadrian, the Roman ruler. Hadrian was a great admirer of the Jewish general. He asked the man, "Who killed him?"

The man said, "I killed him."

Hadrian said, "Let me see his body." Upon examining the body, Hadrian saw that Bar Kochba had a snake wrapped around him and had actually died from a snake bite. Hadrian said, "Had it not been that God killed him, who could have ever killed him?"

The sources from this period are weak and meager and it is often difficult to separate fact from legend. Perhaps it was the hundreds of years of exile, oppression, and yearning that would turn Bar Kochba into a legend of Jewish bravery, a national hero. Stories were told of his incredible strength, pulling trees out with their roots while riding on a horse, bouncing the heavy stones fired by the Romans off his knees back at the enemy.

The legend of Bar Kochba would inspire Jewish children during the long, dark years of the exile. On a certain holiday, *Lag Ba Omer*, the children would play with bows and arrows, reenacting the Jewish revolt, dreaming of returning to their homeland. For a moment they were warriors again, back in their homeland, soldiers of the great Bar Kochba, president of Israel, *Nasi Yisrael*, hiding out in the Judean Desert, striking fear in the Roman legions. They would dream of return, even though it was far off.

And return they would, after a long, dark night of unspeakable horrors, they would return home. The Jew would return to *his* land; he would pick up the sword of Bar Kochba again and reclaim what was his. The Romans would be relegated to the dustbin of history, empires would rise and fall, but the Jew would never forget his homeland, he would return...but first, he would wander the earth for close to two thousand years, an "exiled man" with no home to call his own. He would become the "wandering Jew," a pariah among nations, hated by all, moving from one country to another, wherever he could find some temporary peace; some rest from persecution. Sometimes he would be a welcome guest, sometimes a tolerated taxpaying foreigner, and sometimes a hated enemy. He would be hated for being "different." He would be despised for trying to fit in. But he would never forget his roots, he would never forget who he is, he would never forget his true name or his home.

The Roman, Hadrian, tried to erase the memory of the Jew from "The Land." He would rename Jerusalem, Aelia Capitlina, he would rename Judea "Philistia" (Palestine, and thus years later giving the name to the false nation of

"Palestinians"), and he would forbid the Jews, on pain of death, to enter Jerusalem. But the Jew would never forget, the Jew would *never* forget. "If I forget thee O Jerusalem let my right hand forget its skill. If I do not remember thee, let my tongue cleave to the roof of my mouth; if I do not set Jerusalem above my highest joy."[217]

Jerusalem, the word would be uttered every day in prayer, the word would be uttered whenever a Jew said the blessing after a meal, it would be remembered under the wedding canopy as a glass was smashed to remember the destruction of Jerusalem. Jerusalem, Jerusalem...if I forget thee...

The Bones

Bethar was the last stronghold of the Jews. The bones found in the caves were followers of Bar Kochba, probably some of those who escaped from Bethar when all hope was lost. They had hoped for help, for reinforcements, but none could come. They starved to death in these caves and their bones lay there. Empires rose and fell and others rose in their place and these bones lay untouched, their souls still hovering where they once fought so bravely; the remnants of the freedom army of Israel.

Hadrian was wrong, the Jews did not disappear, and Bar Kochba was not forgotten. Eighteen hundred and twenty-six years would pass, and their spiritual descendants did come to get them. Yigael Yadin, the archaeologist, (and former chief of staff of the IDF) and a team of students and soldiers found the remains of these brave warriors. The remains were finally removed from the caves and buried according to Jewish custom and ritual. These warriors were given an official state funeral with full military honors, eighteen hundred and twenty-six years after they died. The burial was witnessed by members of the new army of Israel, the new army of liberation. One generation of warriors was honoring another. The great warriors of Bar Kochba's army were finally laid to rest, by soldiers of the free and independent State of Israel; our hope is not lost.

Bar Kochba had fought for an idea and an ideal and these survived. The final victory was his. He believed in something greater than himself and this idea survived his physical demise. In the end, the Romans could not crush the spirit of the Judeans. In the end, they could not sever the ties between the people of Israel and the Land of Israel. The stories of Bar Kochba would be passed down from generation to generation and the spark remained alive. Today, Bethar is a thriving city in the modern State of Israel, and the new army of Israel, and the people of Israel lives.

Some of Bar Kochba's men would find refuge in the lands of Arabia.

Jewish Revolts in the Middle East

The flame of revolt was never extinguished. At every opportunity, whenever the circumstances permitted, the Jews formed alliances and attacked their oppressors. The goal was always the same—religious and political freedom, and to return to Jerusalem.

Jewish Revolt Against Gallus in the Land of Israel – 351 CE

The Jews of Israel never accepted their status as a conquered people. In the year 351, the Roman emperor, Constantius Gallus II, showed a strong preference for the Christian religion. This was expressed in many ways such as allowing Christians to persecute the pagans and the Jews. Christian clergy practiced intolerance toward non-Christians, attacked pagan temples and Jewish synagogues, and actively sought to convert Jews to Christianity.

The Jews, under Yitzhak of Sippori, (Sippori was a town in the Galilee) attacked the Roman garrison. The revolt spread to other cities. Gallus sent in his men and the uprising was violently suppressed; entire towns were destroyed.

Jewish Self-Defense and Independence in Babylon (Iraq) – 513 CE

"The new exilarch, Mar Zutra II, did not obtain the right to autonomous self-defense from King Kovad (r488-531 CE). He raised an army including an elite group of four hundred soldiers for the defense of the Jewish community. Being denied autonomy, he declared independence. He succeeded in maintaining an independent state for seven years (513-520 CE), collecting revenue even from the non-Jewish population of Iraq. Active measures by King Kovad put an end, at length, to the exilarch's state: Mar Zutra, only twenty-two years of age, and Mar Hanina were crucified (520) on the bridge of Machoza, his capital; and his infant son, Mar Zutra III, was carried to Israel, where he founded a new line of *Nasiim*, Patriarchs."[218]

Jews in the Persian Army, and the Victory Over the Byzantines in Jerusalem – 608 CE

In 602, the Roman army revolted and marched on the capital, with Phocas Augustus at its head. Soon after, Phocas was acclaimed as emperor. In 608, General Heraclius, in Africa, rebelled against Phocas. Civil war broke out in the Byzantine Empire. The Persian king, Khosrau, saw this is a great opportunity to attack the Byzantine Roman Empire. The Land of Israel, called Syria-Palestine at that time, was in between Persia and Egypt. He needed allies and troops. The Jews, always eager to fight for their homeland and return to Israel, could be natural allies.

"Khosrau developed a plan: he could gain Egypt, settle his domestic problems, and gain a powerful ally behind the lines of Roman troops if he declared the Jews be entitled to all their hereditary rights; more than this they could reclaim their ancestral homeland."[219] He placed a Jew, Nehemiah ben Hushiel, as symbolic leader of the Persian troops. It is said Nehemiah raised an army of twenty thousand Jews to fight alongside the Persians and liberate the Land of Israel. When the armies reached Israel, they were joined by local Jews. Benjamin of Tiberius was a key figure; a wealthy man who recruited and armed Jewish soldiers. Together, the Judeo-Persian army liberated Jerusalem in the year 614.

Nehemiah was appointed ruler of Jerusalem. Preparations began for the rebuilding of the Holy Temple. Genealogies were studied and sorted out in order to establish a new high priesthood. But this was not to be as Christians attacked Jerusalem, killed Nehemiah and his council, and the remaining Jews escaped to Caesarea.

The Jews and Persians returned and again attacked the Christians of Jerusalem. The Judeo-Persian forces took Jerusalem and killed the Christians and their monks. The land was free from the Christian yoke and it appeared that Israel would be independent again. This was to last only fourteen years.

The Roman response was swift. To counter the Jewish insolence, there was the largest ever meeting of Merovingian Bishops, the Fifth Council of Paris in Gaul (France). They decided that all Jews holding military or civil positions must accept baptism, together with their families. Massive Jewish persecutions began to occur throughout the Roman Empire.

Khosrau panicked and betrayed the Jews. The Persians withdrew their support and allowed the Romans to attack the Jews, killing an estimated twenty thousand Jews in Jerusalem in the year 619. The Roman general, Heraclius, then proceeded to rampage throughout Israel, killing every Jew in sight. Heraclius turned the site of the Temple into public latrines and a garbage dump. Muslims would no longer pray in this direction, but the Jews kept the faith, and continued to pray in the direction of Jerusalem, to this very day. Jerusalem, even in its shame, remained holy to the Jews.

The Years of Exile, False Messiahs

During the years ahead, in nearly every land, from time to time a new false leader would arise—promising redemption. In 1160, it was David Alroy or Al-Rai, who was born in Kurdistan and declared himself a messiah. He asserted that he had been sent by God to free the Jews from the Muslim yoke and to lead them back to Jerusalem. In more recent times, there was the false messiah, Shabbatai Svi.

Some would claim prophecy, some would believe they were the Messiah, and some would claim descent from a king or past leader. Jews would become excited, sell their homes, and sometimes raise armies, and the results were disastrous.

"These movements did not arise at times of acute distress or trouble; they seem to have come at times of change, times of rising expectations. In fact, going against the conventional wisdom which associates messianic figures with times of deprivation, it can be argued on the basis of much evidence from Jewish history that messianic movements do not arise at times of great distress, but at times when hope is rising."[220]

Wisely, the rabbis began to discourage messianism. They knew the time was not yet right or ripe for redemption. They censored history and destroyed records of Jewish rebellions and wars. Emphasis was shifted to prayer. The Jew was encouraged to turn his eyes to heaven, and...wait.

The Expulsion from Spain

After the massacres of 1366 and 1391 and the Inquisitions that began in 1492, the Jews of the Iberian Peninsula were forced from the lands where they had lived for over thirteen hundred years. Some of the surviving Jews decided to fight back and punish the evil Spanish empire. Jews became pirates and sought to destroy Spain by destroying its fleet. Jewish pirates operating with other enemies of Spain in fact "brought the Spanish Empire to its knees" in the late 1660s.[221]

During the centuries following the expulsion of the Jews from the Spanish empire, the Jews actively fought back and helped found colonies in the New World. Jews participated in an unsuccessful Dutch attack on Brazil on May 8, 1624. The hope was always the same; to find a place where a Jew could live openly as a Jew without fear from the Christian Church.

Ukraine

Although history tends to paint a picture of Jews as helpless victims, this is not true. Even during massacres, Jews often fought back. In 1768, in Uman, Ukraine, the Haidamak army attacked Jews and Poles with the intention of destroying them all. The Jews actively fought back and put up a courageous defense. As the situation became worse, the last Jews gathered in the synagogue. The defense efforts were led by Leib Shargorodski and Moshe Menaker. Tragically, they were destroyed by cannon fire and slaughtered.

Jews of Arabia

Dhu-Nuwas, a cousin of Mar Zutra, became ruler of the area in Saudi Arabia now known as Medina, between the years 517-525. After many stunning victories, he was eventually defeated by the combined armies of Ethiopia and Rome.

Many Jewish tribes had been living in the Hijaz, western Arabia, for centuries. Thus, Jews predated Muslims in the birthplace of Islam. No one seems to know for sure how they came to live there; possibly they were sent by Joshua to fight the Amalek, or perhaps they escaped Roman persecution in the Land of Israel.

Two of the tribes were *cohanim*, descended from the priests of the tribe of Levi, those who served in the Holy Temple of Jerusalem. The rise of Islam led to attacks on these tribes and their loss of independence, but many did fight back. It is said that when the Muslims attacked the Jews of Khaybar they fought back with fierce opposition. In particular, the Jewish archers of Khaybar were known as the best in Arabia. They held back the larger Muslim forces for five days. It was only the capture of a Jewish spy and his revealing vital information that led to the Jewish defeat.

Habbani Jews of Southern Yemen

"The Jews in these parts are held in high esteem by everyone in Yemen and Aden. They are said to be courageous, always with their weapons and wild long hair, and the names of their towns are mentioned by the Jews of Yemen with great admiration—Shmuel Yavnieli, 1912."[222]

There are a number of legends about the origins of the Jews of Habban. The most prominent is that they descend from Judean soldiers who were stationed in southern Arabia by King Herod of Jerusalem during the Second Temple Period. Herod dispatched a unit of Jews in the region to assist the Romans with fighting wars in the area. Unlike the Jews of northern Yemen, the Habbani Jews wore *jambiyya* (curved knife), *matznaph* (turban), and *avne't* (sash).

Mountain Jews

There were isolated communities of Jews throughout the Caucus Mountains and through Central Asia into Tibet, with small independent Jewish mountain kingdoms. They often lived in impenetrable strongholds to prevent enemies from invading their lands.

The American Revolution

America became that "great experiment in self-government." America was certainly not without its anti-Semites and racists, but whenever Jews were permitted, they participated fully in all aspects of early American life, including in the fighting. October 25, 1765, at the state house in Philadelphia a group of merchants gathered to sign the non-importation agreement to fight against the hated Stamp Tax of the British government. The first man to step forward to sign his name, Mathias Bush, was the president of Mikve Israel Congregation, Philadelphia's only synagogue. Aaron Solomon fought in the front ranks of the Battle of Bunker Hill on June 17, 1776. Francis Salvador, a Jewish soldier in the South, was killed by Indians on July 1, 1776, thus becoming the first Jew to die for America. Jewish merchants turned their ships into war vessels for the war effort. They ravaged the British at sea.

"Men such as Aaron Lopez were bankrupted supporting the Revolution when their ships were lost to the British. In the area of finance, the young American government might have foundered too, except for the financial genius and personal financial risk and support taken on by Hayim Solomon. Solomon was to die bankrupted by his total support of the American cause. Though small in number the Jews chose to cast their fate with America."[223]

Some feel that the actions of a small group of Jews were instrumental in the great American victory against General Cornwallis. There was a free island, the Island of Dutch St. Eustatius. Jewish merchants and arms traders were a major presence on the island. From this island, Jewish merchants shipped supplies for the American war effort. The

British decided it was paramount to destroy this community. They attacked the Jews, burning every house, including the synagogue. While this was going on, the French, (allied with the Americans), under Admiral DeGrasse, attacked the now weakened British fleet. As a result, Cornwallis never received his badly needed supplies. General George Washington, seeing his opportunity, trapped and besieged Cornwallis. In short course Cornwallis surrendered. The war was over. Jews have fought side by side with their fellow Americans in every war America was involved in, including, tragically, both sides of the Civil War.

The Exile and the Transformation

From Peddlers and Scholars to the World's Best Warriors

During our long exile, many Jews lost the tradition of the warrior nation. The proud nation of Israel found itself exiled, homeless, stateless, and powerless. The rabbis tried to discourage any feelings of warrior-ship, as this could only lead to tragedy and false hope under their current unfortunate circumstances. Perhaps it was also fear of the host nations, both Christian and Muslim, which taught the people to keep a low profile and downplay the historical militarism of the Jewish people. Truly what purpose would it serve to celebrate the military aspects of the Jewish tradition? Surely the best policy would be to come across as a pious, book-centered people, not a people with a propensity for war and revolution.

So the Jew accepted his new role and did what needed to be done to survive. The Jew became an expert at survival and maintaining his unique faith. More than that would have been nearly impossible. So the Jew became the "fiddler on the roof," trying "to eke out a miserable tune without falling off the roof," that is to say, trying to maintain his body and soul, his faith and religion without being physically destroyed.

Who has not seen "Fiddler on the Roof," the classic screen adaptation of Sholom Aleichem's Yiddish stories? Tevya is a classic Jew; praying, reading the holy books, trying to make a living, and trying to survive the unpredictable outbursts of the local anti-Semites. He does not fight back; he prays to God and keeps a low profile as he waits for the Messiah. "For though he may tarry, I believe he will come." The Jew longed for the Messiah, the redeemer—even if he should tarry, the Jew would wait.

The joke is told: a Jew comes to the rabbi; he needs a job. The rabbi says, "I have a job for you. Go on the roof of the synagogue, look to the east, look to the west, to the north and to the south. When you see the Messiah coming, let me know."

"Very good," says the man, "I can do that. How much does this job pay?"

"Two kopecks a day," says the rabbi.

"Only two kopecks! That's not very much," says the disappointed man.

"Yes," says the rabbi, "but it is steady work."

In biblical days, we had plenty of warrior heroes. During the years of exile and persecution there were certainly instances of Jewish self-defense, but on the whole, the Jews were defenseless. They were a scattered people, living by the grace of some local lord or king—just trying to survive, make a living, and maintain their traditional way of life. They could not fight the local armies. The Jew used his wits and intelligence to survive; forming an army was not an option.

During much of this time, Jews were not allowed to become citizens and were not permitted to serve in the military. When the opportunity did arrive, they served with gusto. Many Jews in Germany, for instance, received the highest awards for bravery while serving in combat units during World War One. We know this because when the Nazis came to round them up for execution during the years of the Holocaust, these Jewish/German war heroes pulled out their medals of honor to prove their service to the fatherland. Of course, this did not prevent or even delay their murder. One such Jew was Otto Frank, the father of Anne Frank, whose diary told the story of a Jewish girl in hiding during the Holocaust. Otto was an officer in World War One and earned the Iron Cross fighting for Germany, the "fatherland." Otto was eventually sent to Auschwitz.

Jews in other lands also enthusiastically joined the military as they were eager to prove that they were worthy citizens. Jews fought for many countries and on many fronts. The tragic result of this was that on some occasions Jewish soldiers ended up killing "enemy" soldiers who were also Jewish. They knew the victim was Jewish when they heard him recite the martyr's final words in Hebrew as he died; *Shma Yisrael* (Hear oh Israel!).

It is not commonly known that Jews not only participated in every war, fighting for their host country alongside their "countrymen" but they also participated in wars of national liberation. "A unit known as the Beardlings, composed of staunchly religious Jews, distinguished itself in the revolt of 1830-1831. Jews participated in the Polish Rising of 1860-1863 and a Jewish legion led by Berek Joselowicz fought for Poland against the Czar with 'exceptional valor, against overwhelming odds.'"[224]

Although no in-depth studies seem to exist of Jewish self-defense during these years, we do know from oral stories that Jews did, at times, stand up to their tormentors. My late grandfather, Rabbi Isaac Klein, was born and spent his youth in Hungary. He related the following story, "There was a gang of Cossacks that went from town to town attacking Jews. Word reached us that they would soon be arriving, via train, to our village. Men who had served with the

Hungarian army in World War One arranged a group to 'greet' these Cossacks at the railroad station. Armed with sticks with nails in them, knives, and other makeshift weapons, the Jews waited. When the Cossacks arrived and saw the 'welcoming committee' they got right back on the train." My grandfather loved telling this story.

With the birth of political Zionism in the 19th century, the Jewish attitude toward their homes in the exile began to change. Some Jews came to the conclusion that living in Europe, or under any foreign power, would never work. Various plans were devised for the development of an independent state for the Jewish people in the Land of Israel, our ancestral homeland.

Among the paths advocated was that of Ze'ev (Vladimir) Jabotinsky who felt Jews must become a nation that can fight for its own survival and protection. In the 1920s and 1930s, he began urging Jews to arm themselves and train in the use of firearms. He penned a famous and controversial essay, "Jewish youth, learn to shoot!" or in Yiddish, "*Yiddin, learn tzoo shissin!*" "Of all the necessities of national rebirth, shooting is the most important....We are forced to learn to shoot and it is futile to argue against the compulsion of an historical reality."

World War One – Jewish Units

Jabotinsky also believed that until a Jewish state was reestablished, Jews should form their own units and fight alongside the allies in World War One. "The Jewish nation's place is therefore on all the fronts where countries fight for those very foundations of society whose Magna Carta is our Bible."[225]

In December 1914, Ze'ev Jabotinsky and Joseph Trumpeldor, a legendary Jewish veteran of the Russian army, raised the idea of forming a Jewish unit to fight as part of the British forces. They wanted to help conquer the Land of Israel, then controlled by the Ottoman Empire. Trumpeldor, the one-armed hero of the Japanese-Russian War, had been awarded the St. George Order, the highest Russian military award for bravery, four times. He was also the first Jew to become an officer in the Tsarist Army.

From around the world, the two men raised a force of over six hundred Jewish soldiers, which became known as the Zion Mule Corps. Both Jabotinsky and Trumpeldor actually served in this unit, leading by example. Trumpeldor, known by all as a fearless warrior, was injured during one of the battles. One of the men to volunteer was Private David Ben-Gurion, later to become Israel's first prime minister. This was the first Jewish fighting force, with a Jewish flag and emblem, to participate in a war since the days of General Bar Kochba, eighteen hundred and six years earlier.

The Zion Mule Corps saw action on the Gallipoli front. Of the valiant Jewish contingent, six were killed and fifty-five were injured in combat. Three were awarded military honors. When this unit was disbanded, its soldiers formed the nucleus of what would become the Jewish Legion.

In 1917, the formation of the Jewish regiment was formally announced. Again, Jabotinsky personally served with the troops. "The only conditional demand was that Jews should be allowed to fight as Jews; that it should be recorded in the annals of this war that the Jews were one of the peoples fighting for the common good cause."[226] Jabotinsky's idea was that at the end of the war, the Jewish nation would be rewarded for its efforts with an independent state, not as a gift, but as part of the victor's share.

A change was taking place. Jews realized that prayer alone was not enough; they must fight for their freedom. Young Jews in Europe began preparing for life in Israel by learning skills Jews had forsaken for a long time—farming, agriculture, and military training.

World War Two

Sadly, they did not have to wait for their arrival in Israel to use these skills. The rise of Germany and the plan to exterminate the Jewish nation awakened the greatest heroism and bravery among the Jewish people.

The notion that the Jewish people went quietly to their graves is an incorrect simplification of a very complex and multifaceted issue. In fact, even during the dark years of World War Two, the spirit of resistance was everywhere—despite the hopelessness of the situation. In the Warsaw ghetto, the Jewish resistance fought off the Nazi war machine for over three weeks. A few hundred poorly armed, starved Jews managed to humiliate the mighty German industrial war machine. Echoes were heard from nearly two thousand years earlier when the starved defenders of the Holy Temple in Jerusalem held back the mighty Roman army. Echoes were heard from the defenders of Masada. The same warrior heart was still beating; the same warrior spirit was still fighting.

Armed with a few guns purchased at a heavy price from smugglers, merchants, and gentile partisans, and with home-made Molotov cocktails and other homemade weapons, the Jews beat back the Nazis day after day. They were only defeated when the Nazis leveled the ghetto, destroying building after building. The ghetto went up in flames, just as the Temple had two millennia earlier.

Two months later, Jewish snipers were still firing at Germans from sewers and hiding places. Those Jews who managed to escape the ghetto joined the partisans and continued to fight the Nazis. Countless chapters of heroism were recorded during those times. "Far from going to their slaughter like sheep, the Jews resisted in Warsaw, Vilna, Bialystok, and others, and in concentration camps such as Treblinka, Sobibor, and the rest, and in the forests."[227]

What makes the Jewish resistance even more remarkable during these difficult times is that it had been so long since Jews had fought. Nearly two thousand years of exile had taken their toll. They were simply not prepared. And yet, in a short amount of time they made the transition. "The Jews in dispersion did not have warlike traditions. They had not been brought up in the spirit of war and bearing weapons. They had not been taught to value weapons and to use them. They had received an education emphasizing love for peace. Jewish youth were not imbued with the military spirit; e.g., using weapons in defense of Jewish national pride and taking merciless revenge against an enemy. Jewish youth were not taught the (biblical) command 'If someone comes to kill you, get up and kill him.' In short, young Jews were not reared in a Spartan, militaristic tradition."[228]

In addition, the young Jews faced serious dilemmas; should they leave elderly family members behind and join the fighting partisans? Should an able-bodied man leave his wife and children and go fight? Should the most able and fit abandon a community? And yet, "In spite of these dilemmas there emerged a Jewish partisan movement of tens of thousands of fighters, with the common purpose of preserving the honor of Israel. Jewish partisans were daring men, imbued from childhood with love of Torah, Israel and the dignity of man.... In eastern Europe, in Russia, in the western Ukraine there was hardly a single town without some underground nucleus from which sprang a Jewish partisan group."[229]

The Bielski Brothers

One of the exceptional partisan groups was known as Bielski Partisans. Under the command of Tuvia Bielski, who had served in the Polish army from 1927 to 1929, and led by the four Bielski brothers, this group fought back against the Nazis and their allies.

Following the Germans' Operation Barbarossa invasion of the Soviet Union that began on June 22, 1941, the Nazis began murdering the Jews who now fell under their control. The Bielski brothers had witnessed their parents and three other siblings being taken away by the Nazis. They were killed in the ghetto in December 1941. The four remaining brothers fled to the nearby Zabielovo and Perelaz forests and began their struggle for revenge and survival. Most of their group were women, children, and elderly. Only about one hundred fifty members engaged in armed operations.

In 1943, with the increased danger of being discovered by German patrols, the Bielskis took their entire group deeper into the most inaccessible regions of the forest. In the Bielski camp, everyone worked—some built huts, others fixed clothing, guns, and tools. There were shoemakers, metal workers, nurses—everyone did what they could. They set up a school, metalworking shop, synagogue, kitchen, mill, bakery, bathhouse, and a medical clinic. The group became a real community.

"At the same time that it saved lives and protected the noncombatants in the camp, the Bielski group carried out several operational missions. It attacked the Belorussian auxiliary police officials, as well as local farmers suspected of killing Jews. The group disabled German trains, blew up railbeds, destroyed bridges, and facilitated escapes from Jewish ghettos. The Bielski fighters often joined with Soviet partisans in operations against German guards and facilities, killing many Germans and Belorussian collaborators."[230]

On June 22, 1944, Soviet troops initiated a massive offensive in Eastern Belorussia. Within six weeks, the Bielski group was free. During this period, they saved twelve hundred thirty-six Jewish men, women, and children from certain death. None of the Bielskis ever sought any recognition for their actions. In 1948, Tuvia and Zus Bielski would fight again, this time it would be in Israel—against the Arabs.

The Warsaw Ghetto Revolt

The most famous instance of Jewish resistance was in the Warsaw Ghetto in Poland. On April 19, 1943, the Warsaw ghetto uprising began after German troops and police entered the ghetto to deport its surviving inhabitants. For a long time, many of the Jews held on to the belief that some of them would survive; that the Nazis did not plan to kill them all. Surely, they said, the Nazis would not kill so many valuable factory workers, these workers were vital to the Nazi war effort, it simply made no sense! The Jew held on to his sense of logic and could not fathom the Nazi plan of genocide. The signs were there. In retrospect, they were very clear, but the idea was so unthinkable to normal civilized people that most Jews were simply unable to draw the correct conclusion. Others realized that logic was dead, and soon so would be the Jew. Now there was no longer any doubt. Now they knew that the trains that arrived daily were not taking them for "resettlement." The destination of the deportations was now known to the Jews—it was the Treblinka Death Camp.

Survivor, "witness," Marek Edelman, describes some daily events in the ghetto.

> Three children sit, one behind the other, in front of the hospital. A gendarme, passing by, shoots all three with a single round.

> A pregnant woman trips and falls while crossing the street. A German, present during the accident, does not allow her to rise and shoots her right there and then.

> Dozens of those smuggling across the ghetto wall are killed by a new German technique: Germans clad in

civilian clothes, with Jewish arm-bands and weapons hidden in burlap bags, wait for the instant when the smugglers scale the wall. At that very moment machine-guns appear from the bags and the fate of the group is settled.

Every morning a small Opel stops at Orla Street. Every morning a shackled man is thrown out of the car and shot in the first house entrance. It is a Jew who had been caught on the "Aryan side" without identification papers.[231]

The Jewish revolt was led by two twenty-three-year-old men, Pavel Frankel and Mordecai Anielewicz. Seven hundred fifty fighters fought the heavily armed and well-trained Germans. The Nazi combat troops entered the ghetto expecting an easy job. The well-trained troops, however, suffered heavy losses as they were repeatedly ambushed by Jewish fighters who fired at them with an odd assortment of rifles, machine guns, and pistols; and launched Molotov cocktails and hand grenades from alleyways, sewers, and windows.

Marek Edelman describes the opening of the uprising.

At 4 am the Germans in groups of threes, fours, or fives, so as not to arouse the ZOB's (Jewish fighting group) or the population's suspicion began penetrating into the "inter-ghetto" areas. Here they formed into platoons and companies. At 7 o'clock motorized detachments, including a number of tanks and armored vehicles, entered the ghetto. Artillery pieces were placed outside the walls. Now the SS-men were ready to attack. In closed formations stepping haughtily and loudly, they marched into the seemingly dead streets of the central ghetto.

Their triumph appeared to be complete. It looked as if this superbly equipped modern army had scared off the handful of bravado-drunk men, as if those few immature boys had at last realized that there was no point in attempting the unfeasible, that they understood that the Germans had more rifles than there were rounds for all their pistols.

But no, they did not scare us and we were not taken by surprise. We were only awaiting an opportune moment. Such a moment presently arrived. The Germans chose the intersection at Mila and Zamenhofa Streets for their bivouac area, and battle groups barricaded at the four corners of the street opened concentric fire on them. Strange projectiles began exploding everywhere (the hand grenades of our own make), the lone machine-gun sent shots through the air now and then (ammunition had to be conserved carefully), rifles started firing a bit farther away. Such was the beginning.

The Germans attempted a retreat, but their path was cut. German dead soon littered the street. The remainder tried to find cover in the neighboring stores and house entrances, but this shelter proved insufficient. The "glorious" SS, therefore, called tanks into action under the cover of which the remaining men of two companies were to commence a "victorious" retreat. But even the tanks seemed to be affected by the Germans' bad luck. The first was burned out by one of our incendiary bottles; the rest did not approach our positions. The fate of the Germans caught in the Mita Street-Zamenhofa Street trap was settled. Not a single German left this area alive.[232]

The Nazi commander, General Stroop, was to lose his post over this defeat. The job of liquidating the ghetto was supposed to take three days. With the initial repulsion of the German troops the freedom fighters put up two flags, one for Poland and one, blue and white, for the Jews. These flags were well-seen from the Warsaw streets and remained atop the house for four entire days, despite German attempts to remove them. This greatly angered the Germans.

The matter of the flags was of great political and moral importance. It reminded hundreds of thousands of the cause of freedom; it excited them and unified the population; both Jews and Poles. Flags and national colors are a means of combat exactly like a rapid-fire weapon. Heinrich Himmler bellowed into the phone: "Stroop, you must at all costs bring down those two flags."[233]

Another German armored vehicle was destroyed in an insurgent counterattack after Stroop's ultimatum to surrender was rejected by the defenders. The Nazis resorted to systematically burning houses block by block with flamethrowers and by blowing up basements and sewers. "We were beaten by the flames, not the Germans. The sea of flames flooded houses and courtyards....There was no air, only black, choking smoke and heavy burning heat radiating from the red-hot walls, from the glowing stone stairs," recalled Marek Edelman in 2003.

The ZZW lost all its leaders, and on April 29, 1943, the remaining fighters escaped the ghetto through the Muranowski tunnel and relocated to the Michalin forest. This event marked the end of the organized resistance, and of significant fighting.

The remaining Jews, civilians, and surviving fighters, took cover in the "bunker" dugouts which were carefully hidden among the largely burned-out ruins of the ghetto. The German troops employed dogs to discover the hideouts, using smoke grenades and tear gas to force Jews out. In many instances, the Jews came out of their hiding places firing at the Germans, while a number of female fighters lobbed hidden grenades or fired concealed handguns after they had surrendered. It is important to note that Jewish women fought bravely side by side with the men. Small groups of Jewish insurgents engaged German patrols in nighttime skirmishes. However, German losses were minimal following the first ten days of the uprising.

Grave of the fighters of the Warsaw Ghetto uprising

On May 8, 1943, the Germans discovered the main command post of the Jewish fighters, located at Mila 18 Street. Most of its leadership and dozens of remaining fighters were killed, while others committed mass suicide by ingesting cyanide. The ghetto fighters were able to hold out for nearly a month, but on May 16, 1943, the revolt ended. Pockets of resistance remained until August of that year. The Jewish fighters of the ghetto held out longer than anyone could have expected.

The Bialystok Ghetto Revolt

The Jews of the Bialystok Ghetto, as well, organized a resistance movement, although by this time the Nazis were better prepared. Nonetheless, the starved and poorly armed Jews put up a courageous fight. The day chosen for resistance was the day the Germans were to come in for the final liquidation of the ghetto. The Jews' only hope was to die bravely and inflict damage upon the enemy. At this time, the entire Jewish arsenal consisted of twenty-five German rifles, roughly one hundred rifles and pistols, a few Tommy guns, some hand grenades, and one heavy machine gun. There were also a few sticks of dynamite, bottles filled with vitriol (Molotov cocktails) and an unspecified number of axes, knives, and bayonets. With these weapons and a great deal of courage, the Jews would take on the Nazi army.

When the Nazis entered the ghetto, SS officers were in an armored car escorted by three light tanks; a young Jewish girl named Dora ran up and shot an SS officer dead. She was then shot and killed, along with others, in a burst of machine gun fire. At every turn, the advancing Nazi columns were attacked by Jewish fighters hiding in buildings. The Germans withdrew and sent in the air force.

Bravery was everywhere. In one instance, a group of elderly Jews armed with nothing but stones and a few Molotov cocktails tried to storm a tank. They were cut down before they could get close enough to throw their homemade weapons. In the end, the ghetto was bombed and destroyed. Some of the surviving fighters managed to escape to the forests and join the partisans. The rest were rounded up and taken to death camps.

The Partisans

The partisans were irregular troops fighting the Nazi occupiers of their countries. There were Soviets and Yugoslavs, Albanians and Poles, Ukrainians and French, and there were Jews. The Jewish partisans were unique in two ways; one, they really had no country to fight for, and two; they often faced anti-Semitism from the other partisans.

The Jewish fighters often joined the partisans after the ghetto uprisings. When there was no hope in the ghetto, they left for the forests. Some joined "mixed" partisan groups consisting of Soviets or Slavs, while others formed independent Jewish partisan groups. Some groups consisted only of fighters while others had non-combatants as well—women, children, and the elderly. Many women participated as brave and valiant fighters, often many died in combat.

The partisan groups engaged in guerrilla warfare and sabotage, rarely facing the enemy head on. They blew up German convoys, derailed trains, damaged railroads and bridges, sabotaged communication lines, and attacked small groups. They even managed to free some Jews from the ghettos and concentration camps.

They fought the Nazi occupation any way they could. In some cases, they helped organize uprisings in ghettos. An estimated twenty thousand to thirty thousand Jewish partisans fought the Nazis, killing an estimated three thousand German soldiers in Lithuania alone, and causing great damage.

Life for the partisans was difficult, harsh. Food was hard to come by, shelter was no more than a hole in the ground, and there was the constant fear of being discovered by a Nazi patrol. Their clothing was inadequate and they had to deal with the severe cold. It was difficult for the Jews to join the partisans; first they had to escape, constantly fearing detection by local residents. They had to move in small groups. Then they had to find the partisans in the forests. Once they arrived and were accepted they were eager to fight back. Life was always perilous and usually short. One never knew who to trust, or what the next day would bring. "Never say that this is the end of the road," wrote Hirsch Glick, the young Jewish poet who authored the song that would become known as "The Partisans' Anthem," but for many Jews—it was.[234] And yet the Jewish people marched on.

Slave Laborers

One of the lesser known aspects of Jewish resistance is the story of forced Jewish laborers who served with the Hungarian army. Many of these men were former soldiers, many had no military background. From the spring of 1942, they were forced to work as slave laborers for the Hungarian army. Eighty percent died as a result of the harsh conditions, starvation, and outright murder.

On rare occasions, the Jewish laborers were given weapons to fight the Soviet enemy and the partisans. The Jewish laborers fought valiantly, although this was against their own cause. Some still felt pride in being Hungarian nationalists, despite being stripped of citizenship and deprived of all rights, and some felt that by proving their loyalty they would secure better living conditions and have a higher chance of survival.

Mor Heller, a Jewish survivor, tells us, "As forced laborers we were also given weapons by the Germans. Once, we sensed movement in the bushes and shot...and they (the partisans) returned fire. We lost twenty men in the ensuing combat...the Germans arrived and praised us for daring to fight the partisans."[235]

On other occasions, they fought without permission. A Hungarian officer who kept a diary wrote, "Our men were routed and ran away, leaving behind the wounded and the dead; the unarmed Jews (the forced laborers), under heavy enemy fire, went back to the battlefield and fetched the wounded and dead soldiers back, and of the Jews in the company, about fifty were killed and twice as many wounded."

Another diarist wrote, "When close combat was fought at the bridge-head, the very 'core,' they did not care about having a yellow armband, but seized Russian machine-guns, and with these...they fought the battle to the end, without permission. A number of them fell."[236]

Another chapter of Jewish bravery came when many of the Jewish forced laborers were taken captive by the Soviet forces. While most ended up being treated as enemy soldiers, not different from Germans or Hungarians, some were privileged to serve as a fighting unit within the Red Army.

Former labor service men born in prewar Czechoslovakia were allowed, after a thorough interview, to join a special Czechoslovak unit under the Soviets. The Czechoslovak Brigade, under the command of Ludvik Svoboda, later president of Czechoslovakia, went into action in May 1943. Jews held many of the key positions in this unit. They fought many important battles where Jews distinguished themselves for bravery. The result was a very high casualty rate. In 1944, the corps crossed into Slovakia and liberated Prague in May 1945.[237]

Jewish Soldiers in World War Two

During World War Two, while the Nazis and their allies were murdering six million Jews, there were other Jews, in free lands, who joined the armed forces in droves. It is estimated that almost one million five hundred thousand Jews fought in the allied armies. Some three hundred thousand Jewish soldiers, sailors, airmen, and marines died serving in the allied armies in World War Two; among them eleven thousand American Jewish soldiers.

Many Jewish scientists played decisive roles in developing the atom bomb; saving millions of Americans and allies from dying in a potential invasion of Japan. Twenty-nine hundred and fifty-six British Jewish servicemen and women were killed fighting in World War Two. More than seven hundred Jews from the Land of Israel died serving in the British Commonwealth Forces; there was a five thousand strong Jewish infantry brigade in the British army that fought in Italy in 1945. At least thirty-five Israeli generals served in this unit.

Jews from the Land of Israel also served in a special British commando unit in North Africa; called SIG, "Special Interrogation Unit" but also known as "The Lions of Judah." The year was 1941 and the British were in a desperate situation. They were facing Erwin Rommel, the genius general of Germany, who had already conquered most of North Africa and was ready to invade Egypt.

Captain Herbert Buck, a British commander who was fluent in German, was put in charge of creating a special unit that could go behind enemy lines and wreak havoc on the Germans. He recruited German Jews who were fluent in German. Some were "Palestinian Jews" who had escaped Nazi Germany, gone to Israel, and gained military experience by serving with Jewish militias—the *Haganah, Irgun,* and *Palmach.* Others had been with the French Foreign Legion. Many had lost their families to the Nazi genocide. All wanted revenge. Captain Buck explained to them that the operation would be extremely difficult and if they were caught and their true identity was found out, there would be no hope for them. They succeed in destroying a Nazi airfield and causing great damage, but part of the unit was betrayed by a German POW and they died heroically in battle.

Between two hundred thousand and two hundred fifty thousand Soviet Jewish servicemen were killed in the war (five hundred thousand served in all).

Thirty thousand Polish Jews were killed in action in the 1939 campaign to defend Poland during the German invasion that started World War Two; with many more killed serving in the Free Polish Forces in Italy, North Africa, and other fronts. "More than one hundred thousand Jews were members of the Polish army in the campaign of September 1939; about thirty thousand fell in the fighting and sixty thousand were captured by the Germans. Despite this, and with no connection to the Jews' warm welcome of the Soviet forces, their Polish comrades-in-arms turned their backs on them the moment they were taken captive and harassed and humiliated them in front of their German captors."[238]

In Czechoslovakia, Jews fought in every possible way, despite anti-Semitism on every level. "Some sixteen hundred Jews had participated in the Slovak uprising and had fought as partisans and soldiers against the Nazis and their accomplices, and hundreds of Slovak Jews had seen action on the western and eastern fronts while serving in the Czechoslovak army."[239]

The Jews of Germany, despite their hopeless situation, also managed to participate in the fighting and contribute to the allied war effort. No one was waiting for the world to "come and save them." The Jews did everything they could. More than twenty thousand German Jews and over fifteen thousand Austrian Jews found ways into regular armies to fight the Nazis. Many of them joined the British forces, some even managed to join the US forces. Other armies that they joined included the Red Army, the Free French, the Eighth Australian Division, and the home guard in New Zealand.

"It is important to note that these German Jews took upon themselves a much greater risk than other soldiers. While every soldier faced the risk of death in battle or the risk of being taken prisoner, Jewish soldiers knew that if they fell into German hands, they would receive 'special treatment' and not be treated as regular POWs. In particular, a special fate would await Jews who were once German citizens and now were fighting against the fatherland. Indeed, this took great courage."[240]

Thousands of Jewish soldiers died in the French army in 1940, as well as in the Free Greek, Czech, Free French, Belgian, Commonwealth (i.e., Canada, New Zealand, etc.) armies that fought on many fronts. There were even Jewish soldiers in the British Indian army who fought in Italy, Burma, and other countries. Jews fought back wherever they could.

My grandfather, Rabbi Isaac Klein, served as a chaplain in the US army, my uncle M. Bernard Resnikoff served, and we lost a cousin, Irwin Wilburt (Willie) Newman, in the Battle of the Bulge. Five days after the Japanese attack on Pearl Harbor, my grandfather, a congregational rabbi in Massachusetts, stunned his congregation with the message that "Jews should join the war." A woman in the congregation said, "Easy for you to say, Rabbi, you're too old to be drafted." He then informed her that he had already volunteered. He would eventually land with the US forces on D-Day at Utah Beach, Normandy, France. Another Jewish soldier recalled "waking up on the beach at Normandy and seeing a man draped in *tallith* and *teffilin* and a prayer book in his hands."

Cousin Willie served with the 315th regiment, 79th Infantry Division. He died on January 17th, 1945, in one of the toughest battles of the war. His final resting place is in the American military cemetery in St. Avold, France. Jews served with valor on all fronts.

Some say the Jews waited for the "world to rescue them." They did not. The Jewish people did all they could, as part of the conquered lands such as Poland and France, as part of the Soviet army, and as part of the Allied Forces. Sadly, this was not enough—two-thirds of the Jews of Europe were murdered; one of every three Jews on the planet was gone.

Back Home

Those who survived long enough to make it to the promised Land of Israel found that the Middle East was not very hospitable to Jews either. Survivors of the ghettos and the partisans now had to fight the Arabs and the British. The road to freedom was a long and bloody one. The fight was far from over.

To borrow a Christian phrase, this was a "baptism of fire." Many men and women had fought the Nazis in the ghettos and in the forests. They came to Israel and joined one of the pre-state underground forces. Then, in 1947-1948, they fought the Arabs again in the War of Independence. Some would fight again in the war of 1956. By the Six Day War of 1967 and the Yom Kippur War of 1973, it would be their sons who would carry on the fighting. Their grandsons would fight in the Lebanon Wars and in Gaza.

From the peddlers of Eastern Europe to the battle-fields of Israel a transformation took place. The Jew returned to his biblical roots and reclaimed his role as a warrior. A true warrior believes in a cause and is willing to sacrifice everything for it. "Who is the fighter who believes in what he fights for? Surely it is the man who is always prepared to begin anew in order to implement his beliefs. This preparedness is imprinted in the history and traditions of the most militant among nations—the Jewish people."[241]

The Jews of Israel would fight war after war over the next sixty-seven years. Officially, there have been seven wars, but in between wars we have the constant war on terrorism and "campaigns" against terrorists in Gaza and Lebanon. And still, our enemies have not come to terms with our existence. Sadly, this land has not known peace. Today, the Israelis are known for being among the fiercest and most innovative warriors. We have no choice.

The Battle for Independence

The story is told that future Israeli prime minister, David Ben-Gurion, met with United States president Harry Truman. BG, as he was known, wanted to declare an independent state to be called the State of Israel—Truman objected. He said Israel did not have the manpower or weapons to defend against and defeat the vast Arab armies, and the United States would not send American boys to die for Israel. "Pressures were exerted on the Jewish representatives in Washington and elsewhere to postpone what might precipitate action and thus avoid forcing the Arab armies to go to war. But David Ben-Gurion, head of what was known then as the "People's Directorate," decided that the historic opportunity that had been created must be seized, and his view prevailed."[242]

Our rabbis say there are those who earn their place in the world to come in one instant. This was Ben-Gurion's moment—he declared the State of Israel. He said in Israel we do not pray for miracles—we *count* on them (even though he was not a religious man).

The Jewish community numbered only six hundred thousand individuals—men, women, and children. The total force that could be mobilized was about forty-five thousand individuals. Of these, Chaim Herzog says about thirty thousand had functions limited to local defense. Thus, there were only about fifteen thousand active combat soldiers. Ammunition was so low that only two of every three soldiers could be armed. The air force consisted of eleven single engine, light aircraft and the Navy consisted of a few motorboats. This force, with its limited combat experience, was all that there was to fend off the regular armies of five Arab nations plus the local Arab gangs and militias. The Arab armies facing Israel were: the Transjordan Arab Legion, the Arab Liberation Army, the Mufti's Army of

Salvation, and the regular armies of Lebanon, Syria, Egypt, and Iraq, plus contingents from Saudi Arabia.

Photos from this war show men, women, teenagers, and old people fighting side by side. Defending the cities of Jerusalem and Safed, there are photos of rabbis with long beards, their guns sticking out from the barricades. Truly this war was fought, and won, by a people's army. Anyone who could fight—fought. It was a fight for survival. As the Arab leaders pointed out, it was going to be a fight to the finish and "woe to the vanquished."

The Grand Mufti of Jerusalem, Haj Amin al Husseini, wanted to "Settle the question of Jewish elements in Palestine and other Arab countries in accordance with the national and racial interests of the Arabs and along the lines similar to those used to solve the Jewish question in Germany and Italy."[243]

The Iraqi air force, alone, consisted of one hundred planes. The Egyptian air force had over thirty Spitfires, four Hawker Hurricanes, and twenty C47's modified into crude bombers. The Syrian air force had fifty planes. They had men, tanks, complete armies, but Israel had a true people's army.

The young state in formation fought back. Israel lost a full one percent of its total population. The modern State of Israel was born. In blood and fire Zion fell and in blood and fire Zion arose again. After nearly two thousand years, the Jewish people had a free and independent homeland. Despite all the efforts of emperors, generals, new religions that emerged from Judaism, (Christianity and Islam), and every form of persecution, the passionate ties between the Land of Israel and the Jewish people never weakened. Israel, Zion, Jerusalem, was constantly on their lips and in their hearts. Whenever the opportunity arose to "return home," to a home most had never even seen, the Jew risked everything to return to his homeland.

CHAPTER 15

Principles of Krav Maga/Israeli Self-Defense

Along with the reemergence of the Israeli warrior nation came the Israeli unarmed combat style known as Krav Maga. Today, Krav Maga is taught all over the world. It is perhaps the leading "reality self-defense" in the world today. Martial arts experts, police, military, and special forces from many nations come to Israel to learn this art firsthand from Israelis.

History of Krav Maga

Krav Maga means "combat – contact" or "close quarter combat." Krav Maga has no single "founder" and no official beginning. It is the product of the needs of the times and the efforts of many instructors over the years, each adding and modifying based on his skills and experience.

The roots of modern Krav Maga began with the need for self-defense in the Land of Israel. The Jews living here were regarded as weak and helpless. They were considered fair targets by Bedouin Arabs and other Muslims who did not care for them. The Jews, who had come in peace, were unprepared for these attacks and were seen as a "soft" target by the hardened Arabs. The Arabs did not respect weakness and referred to the Jews as *walid el mita*, "the child of death," someone too weak to deserve life. Jewish blood was considered cheap. The Jews lived in their own quarters, scared and at the mercy of others. Often, they hired Arabs to protect them.

The Jews immigrating to Israel from around the world, coming home to their ancestral homeland, found this situation shocking, intolerable, and unacceptable. These Jews were not the same proud warriors of two thousand years earlier; the years of exile took their toll. They began to "adjust" to the Middle East. In time, the warrior spirit would burst forth again.

In 1903, the Maccabi Union was formed to teach Jews physical fitness and strength. They wanted to end the era of *walid el mita*. They soon began training with sticks (early KAPAP) but the goal was rifles, live weapons. In 1907, a group was formed called *Hashomer Hatzair* (The Guard), with the purpose of defending Jewish settlements. From this point is a constant exploration and evolution of hand-to-hand self-defense techniques and strategies. This process continues to this day. In 1919, Ze'ev Jabotinsky founded the *Haganah* (Defense), for the purpose of defending Jews against the increasing Arab attacks.

Jabotinsky was one of the great Jewish leaders of the 20th century. He foresaw doom for European Jewry and urged them to relocate to the Land of Israel (*aliya*, ascension). He founded the *Betar* youth movement and the *Herut* (freedom) political party. Future prime ministers Menachem Begin and Yitzchak Shamir were among his disciples.

Jabotinsky, or Jabo as he was known by the Jewish masses, was not only a great leader and speaker, he was also a writer and poet. He wrote in many languages; novels, poems, and textbooks on the Hebrew language. His works inspired his generation and those that followed. Jabotinsky formed the Zion Mule Corps as part of the British army in World War One, and he himself enlisted as a private.

While Jabotinsky was the philosophical force behind Jewish military revival, as well as an active participant, others were the hands-on Krav Maga instructors. Various instructors were instrumental in developing what would become known as KAPAP and eventually Krav Maga. In January 1941, a self-defense course took place. The chief instructors were Maishel Horowitz, Menashe Harel, Gershon Kofler, and Yitzhak Shtibel. The course marked a key point in the organized development of Israeli self-defense.

In Czechoslovakia in the 1930s, Imi Lichtenfeld, an expert in boxing and wrestling, together with other Jews, formed a Jewish self-defense group. He was influenced by his father, Shmuel, a detective and defensive tactics instructor with the local police force. Shmuel Lichtenfeld was known as a tough officer with a reputation for arresting the most violent criminals. Young Imi grew up in a tough area and had to deal with Fascist thugs, violent gangs, and anti-Semites. On the street, he learned to distinguish between sporting techniques and real-life self-defense.

When Europe became unbearable for Jews, Imi left. He eventually ended up in the Land of Israel in 1942, then controlled by the British. Israeli self-defense was already well in the process of development. As a member of the *Haganah*, he joined this ongoing process and made significant contributions.

Lichtenfeld's talents were noticed and he was assigned to join the unarmed combat instructors' team. Eventually, he became a KAPAP instructor and was among those who trained the *Palmach* and *Palyam*. He is credited with a shifting of emphasis from use of the stick to the greater incorporation of jujitsu. When Israel became a state in 1948, all the pre-state militias joined together to form the IDF. Imi was recruited into the staff of the IDF physical training school where he was one of eleven KAPAP instructors.

Krav Maga includes techniques from judo, jujitsu, karate, western boxing, and elements of wrestling. With the establishment of the State of Israel, Krav Maga was adopted as the official fighting style of the IDF and the Israel Police Force.

In 1964, Lichtenfeld retired from the IDF and opened a private Krav Maga club. He became the first to offer Krav Maga to civilians, although nearly all Israeli civilians serve in the military and have some Krav Maga training. His fame came from his initiation of the development of civilian Krav Maga. This is a process still going on today.

Krav Maga is free flowing; all styles of punching, kicking, chokes, and take-downs are employed with the aim of neutralizing the enemy in the shortest amount of time possible. Unlike competitive martial arts, where limits are placed on the type of techniques used or the areas targeted, Krav Maga has no limitations. Groin shots, eyes, throat, face, are all fair game. Therefore, Krav Maga does not hold competitions and does not seek to be represented in the Olympics. The danger to the participants would simply be too great.

Krav Maga is designed for self-defense, combat, and worst-case scenarios. A major part of the training involves the ability to handle such stressful situations, both physically and mentally. The style is easy to learn and apply. Krav Maga chooses simple movements that are natural to the body, based on instincts that are already established within us.

A unique aspect of Krav Maga is the emphasis on aggressiveness, sticking to the goal, even when it is hard, even when you feel you have nothing left, and a no compromising attitude toward the enemy. Our goal is to neutralize the enemy; the specific technique does not matter.

Krav Maga knife defense

Krav Maga is taught to all units of the IDF; the amount depends upon the unit. As such, nearly everyone in Israel has some Krav Maga training. Depending on the unit, knife and gun disarms are also taught. All training involves strict discipline, aggressiveness, and a warrior mindset.

Attitude

If there is a quality you sense right away when dealing with Israelis, it is attitude and confidence. They *know* they are the best. You can see it in the way they walk, talk, and interact. In a real fight, attitude makes all the difference.

I was at the *dojo* looking for a training partner and spotted Yossi. I soon discovered he was a member of an elite police unit that had an excellent track record for apprehending dangerous terrorists. I figured he must be some sort of real-life Rambo, a deadly fighting machine. We squared off for a kickboxing match...well, clearly this was not his forte. We moved to freestyle, then wrestling—still no magic fighting powers. Finally, I asked him, "How do you manage to capture so many wanted terrorists? What is your fighting secret?"

He told me, "Our attitude and spirit. We barge into a wanted terrorist's home in the middle of the night—catch him unsuspecting in his pajamas while we are wearing fierce-looking uniforms. We come in kicking and shouting with a feeling of invincibility and they usually give in without a fight." In a word: attitude.

*The "Davidka" – a key weapon in the
defense of Jerusalem, 1948*

In the 1948 War of Independence, Israel did not have many weapons. They bought what they could and improvised the rest. A fellow named David invented a small canon; it became known as the *Davidka* or "Little David." It proved to be a failure, and a success. The weapon had a lot of attitude; it created a large boom and a lot of smoke, but very little gunpowder. It caused no real damage. However, the Arabs feared this weapon, believing it to be a powerful new invention. As such, it helped spread panic among the Arab troops and played a key role in the war. The *Davidka* symbolizes the attitude of the Israeli fighters—small, but gutsy. Today, it is on display in central Jerusalem as a reminder of the bitter battle for freedom. Carved on the stone in the background is the beginning of a biblical verse, "And I shall protect and defend this city."

Intensity – Act Forcefully and Prevail

Elisha is a slightly built teenager serving in an elite commando unit. He completed a basic course in Israeli fighting and feels invincible. Often while walking, he will spot a large, muscular fellow and say, "I can take him, easily." He is not very strong and does not have much martial arts training. So what is his secret? He has been trained to charge in without fear or hesitation and take the bull by the horns. His few basic techniques work well because they are applied without the slightest hint of hesitation. He moves with total confidence. He is relentless in his attack and does not let up until it is over.

Toughness – Body, Mind, and Spirit of a Warrior

I have seen wimpy, skinny teenagers transformed into heroic warriors. A major factor in Israeli combat self-defense is toughness. I was talking to a student of mine, now serving in an elite unit. He said they had already had a few Krav Maga sessions. "What techniques have you learned?" I asked him.

"None. What we do is lots of push-ups, running, pull-ups, more push-ups, no rest." What does this have to do with self-defense, you might ask? This has everything to do with real-life self-defense, because if you are too tired and beaten to execute the technique it is of absolutely no use to you. Israeli self-defense first trains the body, the mind, and the spirit, to be those of a warrior. The actual techniques will come later. It is the person more than the technique that matters.

Time and again, the soldiers stressed to me that self-defense in the IDF focuses on mental and physical toughness rather than individual techniques. They describe their training—doing push-ups on their knuckles and holding the position without moving for a very long time, being attacked by thirty soldiers and not allowing yourself to be taken, enduring heat, hikes, and climbs, and *then* working the heavy bag.

This reminds me of the training I did in Kyokushin karate and Thai boxing. These methods of developing mental and physical toughness have largely disappeared from the commercial martial arts world. As one high-ranking Japanese master said to me privately, "The modern American students won't stand for it. We have to compete with the kick box-aerobics classes at the local health club."

I spoke with a student of mine currently serving in an elite combat unit. He was not at liberty to discuss his unit's work in the current conflict, but I asked him if his training adequately prepared him for war. He said it was impossible to foresee every circumstance and prepare for every combat scenario, but the mental and physical attributes that he developed in his training did properly prepare him and served him well during the conflict. In terms of the specific scenarios—there were surprises, but in terms of the individual soldier in combat, he was fully able to adjust, adapt, improvise, and accomplish his objectives.

You can never have a ready technique for every imaginable situation, you can never be sure what to expect, but you can train your mind and body to be able to respond as a warrior. You can train yourself, you the individual, to be able to cope with any situation that comes your way. I have heard this very same message from top martial artists—it is not the specific style or technique that is crucial, but the trained warrior, the individual combatant; it is his attributes, his intensity, and his spirit, that ultimately makes the difference.

Krav Maga/Warrior Fighting – The Mental Switch

Are some people natural heroes? Are some people naturally brave? I do not believe so. In Krav Maga we do not believe so. For if we did, we might cease to exist as an independent people. Anyone can be trained to be a hero. Anyone can be trained to cope with pain, loss, suffering and anxiety. It all involves a decision, or a mental switch.

In precarious situations, we humans feel fear. That fear drives some people to incredible acts of heroism and bravery while others freeze or lose control. The difference lies in our ability to control fear. In Krav Maga, we work on gaining that control. Controlling fear is a learned skill just like any other. No one is born knowing how to ride a bicycle or drive a car; we learn it. Yet some people never learn how to drive a car.

In our training, we learn to familiarize ourselves with dangerous, fear provoking, situations. Having someone come at you in the middle of the night with a real sharpened edged weapon is scary, to say the least. So we begin with a small rubber training knife. In the comfort of our training hall, under the guidance of a trusted teacher, a friend will approach you slowly with the training knife, simulating a real attack.

I have found that some adults are totally incapable of dealing even with rubber replica training knives or guns. Just the sight of them freaks them out. They say they want to learn self-defense, they want to control fear, but even the sight of such "toy weapons" makes them so uncomfortable that I must put the offending weapons away.

And yet, in rural Arizona, I have been in homes where real guns were lying around the living room and small children were not afraid; they were familiar with the weapons, they had learned to shoot them and they knew how to handle them.

Anything can be dangerous—a small cat, protruding stone on the sidewalk, kitchen utensil, lighter, bathtub, electric socket. All of these have caused serious damage to people I know, and yet we are generally not afraid of them. Fear is a product of our minds. We can all learn to handle fear better. Parents who bring their young children to me for training understand this. A frightened little child, after a few months of training, becomes a confident young adult. They have to, for in a few years they will be soldiers.

Behavior is learned. We cannot erase the fear mechanism, we do not want to, it is a God-given survival mechanism, but we can learn to channel it much more effectively. Neuroscientist, Dr. Joseph LeDoux, says with regard to fear, "Whether it proves to be one of your best survival tools or your downfall depends on your ability to control it. An effective survivor is someone who can shut off the fear alarm clanging in his head and channel the resulting motivation into purposeful action that reduces the danger."

During our full contact fighting sometimes the pain is hard to handle. Some fighters absorb so much pain that it is beyond pain. One said, "I made a switch in my head and turned off the pain." He was able to finish the fight successfully. He just "put his body someplace else." I have been told by survivors of abuse and torture that they have done exactly that, they managed to "put their bodies" someplace else and shut off the pain.

What is true for an individual is also true for a nation. Do some nations have tough genes? Are some nations better at survival? Again, this is a learned trait. The nation of Israel has survived close to two thousand years of exile, filled with every sort of suffering known to man, culminating in the Holocaust. People who lost their entire families came to Israel, started new lives, fought off endless Arab attacks, and built a new, thriving, state, one of the world leaders in hi-tech industries. Clearly we know something about shutting off the fear alarm, shutting out the pain, and channeling our energy into purposeful action.

In Krav Maga, we train our minds to be able to handle the shock of a terrorist attack, the sound of a gun going off, the sight of blood, and the feeling of having our body pounded with blows. Being able to shut off the alarm in your head, the panic button, remain calm and focused, is essential whether you are leading elite troops into Lebanon or trying to survive a traumatic situation.

The Brown Belt Test

I knew my belt test would be serious. Krav Maga expert, Itay Gil, did not give away belts for free. He would always say to me, "You and I are friends; friends can give each other many things, but not a belt. A belt must be earned."

I trained many hours a week in Krav Maga, kickboxing, judo, knife, gun, and stick defense. In addition, I worked to improve my fitness by running, sprinting up hills, jumping rope, and push-ups. The test for brown belt would include two hours of technique followed by thirty full contact fights. I knew I had to be ready. Before the fighting segment of the test, my teacher called me over. "Some of your techniques were a bit shaky, I don't know if I can pass you. You will have to prove yourself during the fights. I want to see you fight like a tiger."

"Oh God," I thought, "this is going to be even harder than I expected." The fights began. The first two guys came at me like they had a personal issue with me. The blows and throws came nonstop, relentlessly, without mercy. After four minutes, I felt like I had nothing left, but I still had to complete twenty-six more fights.

Oscar landed a back-spinning heel kick on my forehead; Ildiko hammered away at my ribs. With ten minutes to go, Itay was getting a bit worried. He turned to Eran who was sitting next to him and said, "Do you think Moshe is going to make it?"

The answer was, "No, he's wiped out. He's out of gas."

Itay came up to me as I was fighting and started breathing down my neck like a drill sergeant: "You are not going to quit, do you hear me!?" I had nothing left but willpower. I could hardly lift my leg anymore to do kicks I had done a thousand times. I relied upon knee kicks, punching, and elbow strikes, simple gross motor moves. The last ten minutes were hell: I no longer cared about pain; I no longer cared whether I passed the test. Only one thing kept me going: I am not going to let down my teacher; I am not going to let myself down.

Itay announced, "Five more seconds," but those five seconds seemed to go in slow motion, like they would never end. And then, the test was over. I was finally able to collapse to the floor. Two friends picked me up and put my head in the sink. What a relief.

One question kept floating through my head: Why was Itay making it so difficult? Why did I have to suffer so much? After the test, he answered that question, without my having to even ask him. "I was not testing your ability to fight. *I was testing your desire to live.*"

That is Krav Maga—not a tournament, not a sport, but survival. He was training me to get the beating of my life and still to hold on to life with strength that can only come from within. This is a lesson for life. I have spoken with many survivors of the Holocaust and of natural disasters; all said the same thing, "What kept me going was my desire to live."

Krav Maga Test – Make it Hard

Our belt tests are hard. For yellow belt, we require fifteen minutes of full contact, nonstop fighting. With each belt the requirements increase, and for black belt a candidate must fight forty minutes against a series of rested fighters. Even our little kids, eight or nine years old, will fight at least ten minutes of full contact fighting, most often with some tears along the way.

I watch an eight-year-old boy get kicked in the stomach and the tears start streaming down his cheeks. "Do you want to quit?" I ask him, "Do you want to stop? Are you going to give in to the pain? Are you going to fail the test and not get your belt?" No one has *ever* stopped; they have all gone the distance. They all chose to keep going, with the pain, with the tears.

When the test is over, as I award them their belt and diploma, I have them sit down for a short talk. They are sitting there drenched in sweat, eyes red from tears, and I tell them, "There is only one reason why I can stand here and test you. That is because I have done all this before you. Every blow that you feel, I have felt as well. I feel your pain as my own. I too have been hit hard, from head to toe. Why do you have to go through this?"

I turn to the proud, but somewhat horrified, parents, "Why do I make the kids go through this? Because we will all be hit in life—hopefully not physically, hopefully they will never face a mugger, hopefully no one will ever raise a hand against any of you, but life will. We all get hit." I turn to the kids, "You will apply to a college or a job and not be accepted. You will ask a girl out and be rejected. You might be fired from your job, you might get divorced, you might face any number of hardships. Life will try to beat you down and you must be strong. I want you to remember this test and the words that I tell you. Remember that you were hit, and you kept going. Remember when you were knocked down, and you got up again and you hit back. Our rabbis tell us that a man may fall down, that is pretty much a given, but the question is—can he get up again? You are still young; you have much ahead of you. I want this lesson to stick with you. Think of how strong you are today. Remember this strength; know how to call it up when you need it."

These words may seem harsh; shouldn't we protect the young ones? Shouldn't we fight their battles for them? In the film, "The Lion King," the young cub gets into trouble and his dad is mad at him. When all is well again, the cub says to his father, the powerful lion king, "So, are we good Dad?"

"Sure," the father says, "we are good."

"And will you always be there for me?" the young cub asks his dad.

No father can promise this, the cub is too young to understand that no living creature will always be there, no dad can promise this. So the older lion says, "No, but I will always watch over you."[244]

As adults, we cannot always promise to be there, all we can do is train the next generation to have warrior spirit, warrior values, to "stand up and fight your own battles," to be strong enough to face whatever our enemies, or life's own challenges, may dish out.

Israeli youth are better able to cope with challenges; they do not crumble in the face of adversity. From a young age, we know we are born to fight, we have no choice. There is no peace; there is no peace on the horizon; it is a fool's illusion. We will all be soldiers, we will all serve, and we have to have warrior spirit. In Israel, we have two common expressions, "We never promised you a rose garden." and

"Tough in training, easy in combat." No one promises us an easy, cozy life, and we better know it from the start. Warrior nations must know how to stand up to adversity, and to thrive.

Dealing with the Unknown

"The unknown scares the hell out of us." This statement explains a great deal of human behavior, or lack thereof. Much human action, whether in business, relationships, or combat, does not take place—it does not take place because we fear the unknown more than almost anything else.

We admire those who take action, those who become heroes. We describe them as "fearless," and "brave." We place them above the ordinary man and think of them as supernatural in some way. Certainly a common person could not have taken such action. But all of this is not true, and most "heroes" do not see themselves as such. They are embarrassed to be called heroes and usually say, "Anybody in my situation would have done that." Of course, most people do not "do that." Why? Fear of the unknown, fear of other people's reactions.

Effective combat training, in the IDF, in Krav Maga, or in any top military, involves scenario training. Like actors, we set up props and act out possible scenarios. We build houses, fake towns, use cars, obstacles, and even dummies to create the kind of situation we might encounter in real life combat. To the novice this is great fun; to the expert it is mind/body training. Research has shown that the mind cannot detect the difference between scenario training and real life experience. Survivors of the tsunami in Thailand intuitively acted like the superheroes they saw in movies. Studies showed that people who had watched many disaster films, and had become intensely involved in the movies, reacted as if *they* had experienced this before. Their mind reacted as if, "been there, done that, I know how to handle this situation, no problem." The lesson is clear; the mind can be fooled into thinking it has real life experience and this "experience" will help if and when a real situation arises.

Israel has an unusually high number of ordinary heroes; citizens who risked their lives to neutralize terrorists and save lives. They have *been there, done that* in their military combat training. Their fear of "the unknown" is reduced and they are able to act in a more courageous manner. Add to that a value system where each individual is responsible for the other, where we feel we are in a common battle against an evil enemy, and you have the making of many everyday heroes who are just "doing what is expected of me, anybody would have done it."

Preemptive Strikes

In 1981, Israel bombed the Iraqi nuclear reactor that was clearly aimed at producing weapons to be used against Israel. This preemptive strike is typical of the Israeli attitude. The same strategy was used successfully at the outset of the 1967 Six Day War. On the morning of June 5, 1967, amid boasts of the Arab world that the tiny State of Israel was about to be wiped off the map, the planes of the Israeli air force under the command of General Hod, took off. Before the dust settled, three hundred nine of the three hundred forty aircraft in the Egyptian air force were destroyed on the ground. Within a day, a similar fate befell the Jordanian air force. The Syrian and Iraqi air forces suffered the same, and within six days the entire Arab world had been soundly defeated. And on the seventh day the army of Israel rested.

Attitude + intensity + toughness = preemptive strikes. A key principle of Israeli self-defense is to not wait to see how things turn out; take proactive action and *make sure* things turn out right.

Krav Maga Thinking

What is Krav Maga thinking? Basically, it is Israeli thinking.

In a book about the Arab hijackings of September 1970, one of the non-Israeli passengers on the hijacked TWA flight wrote, "What could we do? The terrorists were armed. We had *no choice* but to submit."[245] Around the same time, another unit of Arab terrorists attempted to hijack an EL AL flight. They did not succeed. Why? Because Israelis do not say "What could we do?", they ask "What *shall* we do? What *will* we do about this problem?" Indeed, it was original thinking that prevented the hijacking of EL AL, despite heavily armed terrorists.

We learn to think on our feet, on the ground and in the air, we learn to improvise. In the IDF, a certain attitude develops. Each soldier is trained to be able to take over in the event that the commander can no longer function. Each soldier is taught how to modify plans and adapt to new circumstances. This training was used in the 1973 Yom Kippur War—when the invading Egyptian forces ran into trouble and got stuck—the Israeli forces adapted, adjusted, improvised, and created new plans and strategies. They had learned not to follow a textbook, but to think "outside the box."

Krav Maga thinking is also very confrontational. The philosophy is not to avoid the enemy, hoping he will go away, but to confront and *engage* the enemy. Deal with your problem now, otherwise you will have a greater problem to deal with later. Both men and women are trained this way. Israeli women are known as somewhat aggressive—hard not to be when you have been trained by the IDF in counterterrorism. This kind of thinking can help you in business and in any transaction. "No" is not the end of the discussion, it is just the beginning.

The crux of the Krav Maga practitioner's thinking is, "My situation is never hopeless, there is always a way out, no matter what the situation, I will still have options." We have learned this from our history. This behavior is part of our culture. We begin to learn it as children; we see how the adults behave. We learn to see heroic, selfless behavior as the norm. Teenagers lead demonstrations, block roads to protest dangerous political moves instigated by outside pressure, and build new settlements on hilltops.

Environmental Factors

In the training hall, a technique is performed in an ideal environment—no obstacles in the way, there is good lighting, and the practitioner is wearing comfortable clothing. The attacker is alone without backup, there are no surprise attacks, it is not raining, the terrain is smooth, and the practitioner is rested. Some modern facilities boast air conditioned training halls, ample space, and a perfectly clean environment.

In reality, things can be very different and all these factors must be taken into account. Whether by design or accident, the Jerusalem Krav Maga training center where I paid my dues and moved up the ranks, was a no-frills operation. It was far from a country club environment and was geared toward the unspoiled, serious practitioner. Hot and dusty in summer and cold in winter, you had to learn to mentally detach yourself from the environmental factors. Those who focused on their discomfort could not train properly and did not last long. One must learn to make a mental switch and ignore the heat or cold, or the other person's sweat dripping on you.

In the IDF Krav Maga program, much training is done outside in the hot sun, on bumpy terrain, and against multiple attackers. Training is done in military uniforms with heavy shoes, while fatigued. One must assume that in battle a soldier will not have optimal conditions and will not be well-rested. This is reality.

Gross Motor Moves

The moves must be the kind that you can easily use no matter how stressful the situation or how tired you are. Bruce Lee said, "I'd rather have ten moves that work for me than one hundred that work against me." The moves must work when you are fatigued and under intense pressure—hungry or thirsty, injured or bleeding, and wearing heavy military equipment.

Studies show that under stress or while fatigued, even experienced fighters cannot effectively perform complex fine motor skills. Certainly those who do not train on a regular basis have difficulty remembering techniques. The only techniques that one can count on are the simple gross motor moves.

Knowledge of Weapons

Guns can be very intimidating. The best way to defend against a weapon is to become thoroughly familiar with it. You must not go into shock when you see a gun; the sight, sounds (e.g., cocking the weapon) and smells of guns should become familiar so that they do not cause you to panic or freeze. A gun is often used to intimidate. If you can desensitize yourself to guns, you will be more relaxed in their presence. Of course, you must also respect the gun and be fully aware of the danger.

Kindergarten children see guns and they will continue to see them throughout their lives. Armed escorts accompany them on school field trips. In the army, they will become intimate with many weapons; fire them, take them apart, clean them, and reassemble them. They will sleep with them, shower with them, they will never be apart. (Otherwise they will end up in military prison.) Knowing how the weapon works and how it is used takes away the mystery and makes it easier to defend against the weapon. If a shot should go off, this is a sound they have heard before and they will not go into shock.

In Israel, many civilians carry guns. With this comes the responsibility of knowing the laws pertaining to the use of guns. For example, if you are angry with someone and want to give him a little scare by reaching toward your gun—that is considered a crime. Reaching for your gun is considered the same threat as pulling it out. Knowing this law, one understands that if an assailant even begins to reach for his weapon—this is the time to act! The threat begins with his reaching for the weapon and your response should begin there as well.

Counting on the Group – All For One

In a combat situation, every aspect of the environment must be taken into account, including the number of troops you and your enemy possess. No man is a one-man army. Every soldier knows that a time may come when his life will depend on his buddies. No soldier fights alone; your life depends on the group effort—you have to know that you can count on them, all for one and one for all.

In Israel, this attitude permeates civilian life as well. In a street self-defense situation, casual bystanders can affect the outcome of the situation. Knowing that most Israeli civilians are trained soldiers changes our set of expectations. We can expect a warrior's response, a warrior's courage, and a warrior's combat knowledge and ability. We have a saying, "All of Israel is responsible for one another." We operate on the assumption that others will join the effort. The captain of the EL AL flight, facing a terrorist threat, knew that as soon as he took action, others would follow. The bus driver knew that when he jumped the terrorist, others would join him. Perhaps there is no greater example of a fighting nation than this unwritten understanding that in times of trouble, everyone can count on everyone else.

Israeli soldiers, Lebanon, 2007

Counting on Yourself

No contradiction here—as much as we believe in, and train by "counting on the group," we also believe that ultimately you are responsible for your own life. As Itay Gil wrote, "Do not count on others to come to your aid. Assume you are facing imminent death—alone."[246] Or, as another Krav Maga instructor said, "If you will not defend yourself—you will die." Counting on others does not take the burden off of you, you must still take action.

Noncooperation

In many dangerous self-defense situations such as knife and gun threats or airline hijackings, common wisdom has been to cooperate. Israeli self-defense operates with a different set of assumptions; *never* cooperate. Like a prisoner of war sworn to try to escape, we wait for the right moment. Our bitter history has taught us not to trust the promises of our tormentors, or our friends for that matter. In the Warsaw ghetto of Poland, the Nazis promised bread and jam to those who boarded the trains for "relocation" or "resettlement." Many, weakened by years of starvation, believed them. They ended up in gas chambers. A small group realized it was better to resist. Better to die fighting than to go like sheep to the slaughter. Our operating principle is, *better to resist than to leave your life in the hands of your assailant.* Your chances will only get worse if you wait.

A fifteen-year-old Israeli girl was on her way to the mall when she was grabbed by a youth on drugs. She was in a crowded area, yet cooperated with her assailant and went with him to a quiet, secluded field. There, she was raped and murdered. Human nature is to believe the kind promises of others; cooperate and no one will get hurt. We no longer believe this. Resist now and hope for the best. Never allow yourself to be relocated; it can only benefit your assailant.

Techniques – what she could have done...

The first thing she could have done was make a commotion. In a society like Israel, such a commotion would not be ignored. Within shouting distance, she would have found police officers, off-duty soldiers, and plenty of combat trained Israelis willing to come to the rescue.

When grabbed, she could have responded with a knee kick, pointing her bony kneecap at the assailant's groin or inner thigh. Then, she could have used that window of opportunity to do a full body movement and release herself from his grip. She should have run for safety. Do not ever stick around to "finish him off." Leave that to the police or someone properly trained.

Fighting Fatigue

To fight when you are tired and have absorbed a few blows is very challenging, to say the least. For our black belt test, we fight forty one-minute fights against well-rested opponents. The point is not to see if you can fight, but to see how you fight when you are out of gas, fatigued. Krav Maga focuses on what you can do when you are fatigued, not when you are well-rested. We only trust techniques you can do when you are tired, fatigued, having been up all night and just finished hiking up a mountain.

Aggression as a Weapon

One of our security guard students had the nickname, "The Maniac." His friends told me the local Jerusalem Arabs gave him this title. He does not know that many techniques, but when he uses them, he unleashes such aggression that he is feared more than a grand master. He has confidence in his few techniques, he does not let fear enter his mind, and failure is not a possibility. He has never been beaten on the street.

Aggressiveness training is a major part of Krav Maga. After each training session, the elite security guards of Jerusalem are graded in three categories; aggressiveness, technique, and discipline. Aggressiveness means having the discipline to put the technique into action, with full conviction and determination, without hesitation, doubt, or fear.

Using What You Have

Another one of my security guard students was approached by three Arabs while on his way to his shift. They surrounded him and started pushing him around. He grabbed his spare magazine from his handgun and used the sharp edge as a slashing weapon. He cut one of the assailants on the cheek. When the assailant realized he had been cut, he panicked and ran. His friends joined him and fled.

To paraphrase an old song, "If you don't have the weapon you want, use the weapon you have." Make use of whatever you have available and turn it into a weapon of self-defense. Nearly *anything* can be used as a weapon, in the hands of a creative person.

Stay Focused

In our Krav Maga training, we often have drills involving multiple attackers or mob scenes. The idea is to train the fighter to stay focused on his survival despite the many obstacles and distractions around him.

In one drill, a soldier will be punching a shield held by another soldier while a bunch of other soldiers punch, kick, and push him. The soldier doing the drill must remain focused on the task at hand and not let the pain distract him.

No Pain

One of the first concepts I learned in Krav Maga was the concept of "no pain." The idea is that during a fight, a very stressful situation, we are trained not to think about the pain, not to let the pain "live" this moment. We put ourselves outside our bodies for the moment and deal with the task at hand: survival. We do not allow the pain to affect us. Later, there will be plenty of time to deal with that, but *not* during a fight for survival. This concept is difficult to explain in writing, but when you are in that situation, you just make a decision to not let the pain register. It works.

Training Based on Sociological Reality

Many training programs operate in a sort of vacuum, without taking the sociology of the people into account. In Israel, the training is based on reality. Techniques and training are modified as we learn lessons in the "field."

For example, in some societies, people train a great deal with knives and how to defend against knives. They ask why we do not learn and teach more of those knife techniques. In Israel, the average knife attacker is not well-trained; he is probably just some angry terrorist who grabbed a kitchen knife. Even if he is a master knife fighter, we will not fight knives with knives. Even if the terrorist stabs one person, he will soon be shot dead by some Israeli standing nearby. He will not survive the encounter. We focus on the gun training. That is the reality of our society. There is always someone nearby with a gun.

Training Based on Physical Reality

When I teach Krav Maga to new students, I often have a smaller person face a larger and stronger aggressor. I also have the opponent make life a little difficult for them. I tell them this is reality. Now, you can go to the gym, work out for a couple of years, build muscle, and improve stamina, and only then be able to contend with such an attacker, or you can learn to deal with reality *right now.*

The reality is that most people do not have that kind of time to train and the reality is that no matter how much you work out there will always be someone bigger and stronger than you. In Krav Maga, we say you must learn to deal with this fact and we must train people to overcome stronger and larger opponents. Too many styles spend years teaching techniques that have little or no chance of ever working in a real life situation. If it is not going to work—we might as well find out now so we can adjust it.

Special Circumstances

I was teaching a gun disarm technique that involved grabbing the assailant's wrist. A young, post-army Israeli woman called me over for some assistance; she was having difficulty performing the technique. I noticed the problem right away—her left arm was made of plastic. She was wearing a three-quarter length sleeve, so I could not tell where her natural arm ended and the artificial limb began, but I acted as if this was par for the course. I instantly adjusted the technique to accommodate her special needs and the technique worked.

She had a smile on her face that would not go away, her optimism would not fade. Her strength gave me courage. I wanted to say something, but I could not, so I just treated her like everyone else. That is what she wanted, to be treated like everyone else. Now, when I teach that gun disarm I always take into account the possibility that some people have an artificial arm. I can still picture her warm smile, a smile that said, "I cannot be defeated."

Fighting in Confined Quarters

Another reality we must deal with is the limitations of the physical environment. Too many schools train in "ideal environments." We do not, we train in environments that mirror reality. Fighting in confined quarters is just one of the special aspects of Krav Maga.

Nothing exists in a vacuum. And yet, the vast majority of martial arts schools I have been to, train as if that was the case. They teach techniques without taking any outside factors into account. It is as if you can choose the time and place to be attacked, and it will exactly match the way you trained at your local karate school. If you are training for sports or competition, then that is the case—your tournament setting will exactly match your training setting. However, if you are training for personal survival, you had better rethink your training.

Reality Fighting

The sad and cruel truth is you can be attacked anywhere. You can be attacked on the stairway, which completely eliminates all your fancy kicking techniques. You can be attacked in the snow by a guy wearing a heavy snowsuit, which completely eliminates your jujitsu wrist locks. You can be attacked on a small boat, in an elevator, in the bathroom, on the beach, in the mud. None of this will be at all similar to the training you did at your karate or judo school. To defend yourself, you need to get real.

Krav Maga experts address all these issues, and they should know—many have "been there, done that." In the Jerusalem training center, there is a structure set up like a house or an apartment. Some areas are too small for kicks; some areas have blind spots. Suddenly, you wake up to a whole new approach to self-defense. Unlike traditional *kata* or point sparring, you cannot know in advance what will happen; you just have to train and gain experience.

Military Krav Maga Training

What makes military Krav Maga training different from civilian Krav Maga training? The first difference is the time factor. Although all Krav Maga training is designed to allow students to gain maximum self-defense proficiency in the least amount of time, in the military this is even more so. With a civilian, both the time frame and the danger factor are broader.

The civilian fears danger, but he is not planning on entering a dangerous area at any specific time; he just wants to be prepared in general. As such, he does not have a specific time when he must be "combat ready." The soldier, on the other hand, does have a specific date when he will be "shipped out" to Lebanon or Iraq or some other hellhole. The civilian wants to learn as much as possible as soon as possible, but he still has flexibility—he does not *have* to do it all in three weeks or five weeks. If it takes a little longer, that is OK. With the soldier, he only has those three or five weeks; after that he will be put back on active duty or move on to some other aspect of training.

The second difference is "captive audience." With any commercial school, half the job is keeping students/clients motivated. If they are bored they will walk away. To keep them interested you must keep the program "interesting." This often can mean not spending enough time on any given technique. Many people become impatient, "What, this again!" An instructor often finds himself needing to introduce new techniques too soon in order to keep his clients entertained; otherwise they might walk away, and in that case they will learn nothing. With the military, you have a captive audience. They have to be there or else they will be washing the latrines. They are yours until you are finished with them. You do not have to make it interesting. You are able to drill them again and again on the basics until they get it right.

Israeli soldiers learn Krav Maga during their mandatory military service. The standing joke is, "So what did you learn today in Krav Maga?" The answer, "push-ups." The military Krav Maga training will focus on a few basic techniques, but the soldier will learn how to do them when he is tired, fatigued, worn out, and ready to collapse. He will run several miles and then have to pound the heavy bag. He will do push-ups and then face a group of soldiers who will attack him; he will hit a punching shield while other soldiers are hitting him. He will repeat this again and again. He will not forget this training and he will learn to function in the worst possible scenarios. This is military Krav Maga, and it works. Talk to any IDF soldier, even a Krav Maga instructor; ask him how much Krav Maga he knows. Most will say, "Oh, I only know the basics." It is the basics that will save you in combat.

We do not realize how things affect us. We think we do, but we really do not. Small annoyances add up to severe problems that eventually explode in our faces. Little things that we think will not affect us in a moment of truth—in fact do. We simply do not have a clue. That is what military Krav Maga training is all about. You repeat something again and again and again. You keep going when you think you simply cannot go on any further. You keep fighting when you so badly want to just give in. We will not let you give in. We insist: You will fight until you are dead. You will fight to the end. This is your best chance at survival. We learned this from experience.

In training, many people think they can take shortcuts. "Yeah, I got the idea; let's move on." These shortcuts can get you killed. It is the endless repetition that embeds the technique in your head, so that when you are dead tired, bruised, and beaten—you can still keep fighting. You have just got to keep on going.

So we do our push-ups until our muscles ache and our knuckles bleed. We ignore the pain; we rise above it. We fight back until we have no more gas left, and then we dig deep inside and find that extra reserve, that still small voice that says, "Never give up."

Krav Maga Striking Techniques

Krav Maga draws its striking techniques from the most powerful systems in the world and then adapts them for optimal street effectiveness, Israeli style.

Principles

- Every superfluous movement is eliminated. In a real situation every second counts.
- Unlike a sports fight, or grudge match, there is no place for "set ups" or strategy. Everything must be instant, this is not a game.
- Avoid all fancy moves.
- Do not turn your back on the opponent.
- Keep your feet solidly on the ground, no jumping or spinning movements.
- Strike from where you are; there is no set-up time.
- Each strike should deliver maximum power; nonetheless we train with combination strikes. We do not rely on the old Japanese saying, "One strike one kill." We rely on "Take no chances." We use penetrating blows that bring the pain deep into the muscle causing shock to the system.
- Combine hand and foot techniques for maximum effectiveness; one technique leads to the next.
- Use body momentum, not body strength, to generate quick, effective bursts of force. Use the hips, not the torso.
- Do not stop until the threat is neutralized; knocked out, disarmed, tied up and handcuffed, or...

Bag Work

Unlike traditional karate, we do not do "air punching." We do our striking techniques on pads or on the heavy bag. If you are hitting the heavy bag there is a simple way to gauge if you are doing it correctly. If the bag is swinging wildly—you are only pushing the bag, but the blow lacks punishing power. An effective, powerful strike enters the bag and "folds" it a bit, but does not cause swinging. Working with a bag allows you to strike with full power without hurting your joints.

The Strikes

- Punches – we take our punches from the most effective punching style; western boxing. We adapt the approach because unlike boxing we use kicking as well and in the street we must also protect against non-boxing techniques.
- Front kick, side kick – similar to karate.
- Low kick, roundhouse kicks – Muay Thai.
- Knee kicks, elbow strikes – Muay Thai.

Each strike is the most powerful of its kind. The program "Fight Science" scientifically examined every kick and punch and proved that these were the most powerful strikes. The western boxing punch is more powerful than the kung fu, karate, Muay Thai, or Taekwondo punch. Similarly, the Thai low kick is more powerful than any similar karate or Taekwondo style kick. It pleased me that IKI Krav had "guessed" correctly in every case.

Krav Maga incorporates these strikes as part of its gun/knife/stick and hand-to-hand defense. We do not only use them for kickboxing or sport; we use them as part of an effective, innovative survival program. We measure their effectiveness the way people measure guns; by their stopping power. Our goal is survival; all these techniques are a means to an end.

Hostage Situations

American born Nachshon Waxman was serving in the Israeli army. He had a free weekend and was eager to get home. He did not wait for the bus; he hitchhiked. The vehicle that picked him up was actually driven by terrorists looking for victims. In a tragic saga that gripped the nation, Waxman was held for days by terrorists in horrible conditions. When Israeli soldiers finally located the building and stormed it, he was found murdered.

Israeli agents have found "how to" booklets; training manuals for Arabs on how to take Israeli soldiers or civilians hostage. Hostage taking is very practical; the abducted can be traded for terrorists in Israeli jails. Israel is a nation at war. Our enemy lives not only across our borders, but within our borders as well. Arab towns are adjacent to Israeli towns and some towns are mixed. Arabs are everywhere and one never knows who is a friend and who is a foe. Your gardener might be a terrorist or just a regular guy trying to make a living. Therefore, not only soldiers on the front line have to be concerned about being taken hostage, but anyone, anywhere, at any time can be a victim, as was Nachshon Waxman who was on a street corner in Jerusalem, looking for a fast ride home.

Tragically, many Israelis have "disappeared" over the years. They were picked up by terrorists, taken to Arab villages, and murdered. All Israelis must know how to defend themselves against abductors. It is important to note that not only Jewish Israelis have been victims; Christians, pilgrims, and other tourists have been "accidentally" killed or taken hostage. On the road leading to my town, a promising young Christian clergyman was shot dead one night while driving his car. When the church protested, the terrorists issued an apology. The clergyman was wearing a skullcap, had a beard, and dark skin. It was late in the afternoon and the gunmen did not get a real close look. The Christian clergyman looked Jewish, it cost him his life. Many Christians rely on their gentile features—they fail to realize that in the eyes of some radicals they are perceived as supporters of corrupt secular western imperialism. One cannot be complacent.

Israeli self-defense/Krav Maga trains us to deal with whatever may come our way. Even though you may not be part of a special hostage negotiations team, you might find yourself in a situation where both physical and verbal skills are necessary to diffuse a situation. Many times in our history, the initial negotiations with either terrorists or deranged people have been handled by "ordinary" citizen/ soldiers. Most of us will not have to deal with hostage situations; that is usually the responsibility of police, law enforcement, and special units. In Israel, we treat the subject very seriously and it is a part of our Krav Maga gun training courses, and our Krav Maga hand-to-hand combat training as well.

Those in all aspects of law enforcement need to know these techniques, whether you are a prison guard, police officer or military, you never know when you will be called upon to handle a hostage situation. We train for situations where the hostage himself fights back and for situations where a third person is called upon to "negotiate" with the hostage-taker. We begin from a position of strength, which is the key. We do not act aggressively or submissively. We are always in control of our emotions and of the situation. We approach the person or group with confidence. We are willing to talk. When the moment of opportunity comes, we are ready—physically and mentally—to do what needs to be done. Fear and hesitation are never a part of our appearance or attitude. Our attitude, backed up by our training for this situation, gives us an immediate edge. It takes away the hostage-taker's number one weapon—intimidation.

This approach has proven itself many times throughout history. Weakness invites greater demands by the aggressors; strength makes them back down. In September 1970, when the Popular Front for the Liberation of Palestine held hundreds of Americans and Europeans hostage, only Israel took a firm stand. The other nations criticized Israel for being intransigent. Israel's approach proved itself, as gradually the terrorists began releasing the majority of the hostages unconditionally. They blinked first. It was a test of willpower. We train to never show fear, never show weakness or hesitation.

The behavior of the hostages is also an issue of training. The famous Israeli rescue of the hostages held in Entebbe, Africa, illustrates this point. When the Israeli commandos came in, they needed the cooperation of the hostages. Most of the hostages responded in a cool, disciplined way. One passenger did not. When told by the commandos to stay down so the terrorists could be dealt with, the passenger jumped up enthusiastically to greet the rescuers. Tragically, this person was killed. Military discipline and training are also important for the hostages' state of mind and their ability to endure difficult times.

Nonverbal Diffusion

Nonverbal diffusion can be defined as what Crocodile Dundee did in that classic scene where a young hoodlum wannabe pulls out a pocketknife and tries to rob Dundee and his date. The boy says, "I have a knife!"

Dundee looks at him and says, "That's not a knife, *this* is a knife," as he pulls out a knife five times the size of the sardine-sized knife the young hood is brandishing. That is nonverbal diffusion—even though Dundee was speaking, it was the large knife that did the *real* talking.[247]

As Westerners, we are taught to believe that everything can be "talked out." Reasonable people can work out their differences, that "cooler heads" and logic will prevail. Welcome to the Middle East. None of that holds true here.

When an Arab (excuse me for being politically incorrect) in the Old City of Jerusalem pulls out a kitchen knife and starts chasing a group of Jewish or Christian tourists, you *cannot* reason with him. He is not angry about being dumped by his girlfriend or being fired from his job. You cannot calm him down and tell him to consider his future. He is the product of intensive lifelong indoctrination. From his earliest days, he has been taught to chant, "In blood and fire we will liberate Palestine (sic)." His religion has taught him to hate the *infidels*. He has seen older siblings and relatives given great honor for killing Jews. He believes that what he is doing is a godly act. And you will not be able to convince him otherwise—certainly not in the next thirty seconds.

So what can you do? Well, the Krav Maga approach is, as one T-shirt reads, "Peace through superior firepower." It is the same approach as Crocodile Dundee's. The only way to prevent violence is through the threat of greater violence. Of course, there will be some news reporter, a die-hard liberal, who will report that "unnecessary, excessive violence" was employed against an "adolescent," and audiences around the world will be sitting in their comfy living rooms, shocked. There will be exceptions. There will be some martial arts guys, some law enforcement types, some former Marines, who will be sitting there with their beers, and say, "Way to go. Those Israelis know what to do." I know, because I have met them all over America.

My friend and fellow martial artist, retired NYPD detective, Louie Balestrieri, says, "As far as Nonverbal Diffusion is concerned, I believe it works. I believe that SILENCE CLAPS LOUDER THAN THUNDER. Body language has to be a part of it as well. I think that when someone begins to argue and threaten you, they are looking for a reaction and the reaction they want from you is fear. If you show no reaction by staring back at them real hard into their eyes and subtly shifting your body into your ready/fighting stance; you are showing that you are ready for what they may attempt to do. Once again this is with reasonable people. Without being political or pointing my finger at any race or creed in particular, when dealing with the terrorist mindset, you must fight fire with fire. Always carry a big gun to a knife fight. These are people that don't care. Death is an honor to them."

When you see the hatred in these terrorists' eyes, the blind faith and fanaticism, the combination of religious zeal and hate as a result of a lifetime of indoctrination, you know that it is either, "Peace through superior firepower," (love that T-shirt) or "Peace of the grave." The choice is yours.

Never Give Up

The last principle of Krav Maga and Israeli fighting is the principle that guides our lives; never give up. Giving up is *not* an option.

It was October 6, 1973. I recall it well. It was *Yom Kippur*; the Day of Atonement when Jews neither eat nor drink, but spend the day in prayer. That is the day our enemies attacked. We were surprised on two fronts; Syria attacked in the north and Egypt in the south. Iraq and Jordan sent in troops. Smaller contingents and aid arrived from Algeria, Libya, Morocco, Saudi Arabia, Kuwait, and Pakistan, as well as Arabs living in Israel itself. The attack was overwhelming. Once again we were outnumbered and outgunned. Syrian troops in the north and Egyptian troops in the south overpowered the Israeli positions and were moving deep into our territory. They had advanced Soviet weapons, antitank missiles, rocket propelled grenades, and Sagger missiles. SAM batteries knocked out Israeli aircraft. Five hundred Israeli tanks and forty-nine aircraft were lost in the first few days on the Egyptian front.

On the Syrian front in the north, one hundred eighty Israeli tanks faced off against more than thirteen hundred Syrian tanks. Syrian SAM batteries shot down forty Israeli planes; Israeli population centers were in danger. The situation was grim. Moshe Dayan was badly shaken and talked about the destruction of the third Jewish commonwealth (two Temples had been destroyed; twice before the Jewish state had fallen), casualties were mounting as men fought very bravely, but could not hold out against the overwhelming, Soviet trained, enemy forces. Individual acts of heroism were of crucial importance during those early days, holding back the enemy and allowing time for reinforcements to arrive.

One such case was "Zvika Force." Lieutenant Zvika Greengold arrived at the northern front, unattached to any unit, he fought off the Syrians with his single tank. For the next twenty hours, Zvika Force, as he came to be known on radio net, fought running battles with Syrian tanks. Sometimes he fought alone and sometimes as part of a larger unit. He was wounded and burned, but stayed in action and repeatedly showed up at critical moments from an unexpected direction to change the course of a skirmish. Such acts of individual bravery held back the enemy. Within fifteen hours, Israeli reservists were already on the front lines.

Chief of Staff Elazar had warned about this attack and wanted to call up the reserves and send the Israeli air force on a preemptive strike. The political leadership of Moshe Dayan and Golda Meir refused; they did not want the world to say that Israel provoked the war, and they were still not convinced that war was imminent. However, the key factor in Prime Minister Golda Meir's final decision was that Israel might need American assistance later on, and it was imperative that Israel not be blamed for starting the war. After the war, Meir was forced by the Israeli public to resign her post, in shame. And so, Israel found itself in a life threatening situation. It was time for a miracle.

Dado

A great hero emerged; the greatest chief of staff in the history of modern Israel—David "Dado" Elazar. He smiled and said, "We will not be defeated. Things will turn out well." It is said that his optimism was the turning point in the war. Israel had lost many of its warplanes and tanks. It was time for Israel's special weapon—the reserves.

Up to the front went our gardener, Sadok the Yemenite from Rosh HaAyin, and our neighbor, Eitan the bus driver's son whose mother still had on her arms the numbers the Nazis had burned into her, and our mailman, and all the able-bodied teachers from my school. These were the people who were going to save us. Air raids sounded at night and we all ran to the nearest bomb shelters, school was interrupted.

Dado took command of the situation, he masterminded the forces in the north and in the south; he showed no fear. Reserve soldiers heroically fought back in a thousand acts of bravery and self-sacrifice, storming the Golan Heights in the north and crossing the Suez Canal in the south. Within three weeks, Israeli forces had not only stopped the enemy's advance on both fronts, but had moved deep into enemy territory. Israeli troops were forty kilometers from Damascus and one hundred kilometers from Cairo. The Egyptian Third Army was surrounded and taken captive. This was the greatest victory in Israeli history and perhaps one of the greatest in the history of warfare. Israeli forces were ready to take Cairo and Damascus. *It was only the political intervention of the United States that prevented the complete collapse of the Arab world.* This is the spirit of the Israeli people; never give up. The battles were fought and won mostly by the reserves, ordinary people called upon to save the nation, which they did.

Biblical Concepts of Peace Negotiations

Today, many Jewish leaders in Israel and abroad are misguided in terms of how to achieve peace. If they were to look to our history, to the Bible, the Torah, they would see a clear path laid out before us, true and proven: weakness leads to war, strength leads to peace.

"Yiftah the Giladi was an able warrior."[248] The representatives of Amon, a warring nation, come to Yiftah and demand territorial concessions. These are not legitimate demands, and there is no cause for Amon to make such demands. As Yiftah points out, Israel has done Amon no wrong, and each should accept their borders as they are.

"Behold, that which Chemosh your god gives you as an inheritance, that you shall inherit, and all that our God has bequeathed to us we shall inherit."[249]

"But the king of the Ammonites paid no heed to the message that Yiftah sent him."[250]

"He utterly routed them—from Aroer as far as Minith, twenty towns—all the way to Abel-Cheramin. So the Ammonites submitted to the Israelites."[251]

CHAPTER 16

The United States, a Nation of Warriors, Again

Allies

I have two flags in my home—Israeli and American. I see our two histories as intertwined. Jews were in America from the very beginning, helping finance the Revolutionary War and fighting the battles. The ancient Hebrew was also there spiritually. Many early Americans had Hebrew biblical names. Read any account of early American history and you will come across one Hebrew name after another. The ancient Israelites served as an inspiration for the early Americans; the fight for freedom and a just cause against their oppressors. They saw themselves as the spiritual heirs, the modern Israelites.

Our two nations share a common vision, and in many ways, a common faith. Common values unite us against those who wish to destroy our way of life. We must work together. Like many of us, I shall never forget where I was when I heard the news of the attack on the Twin Towers.

Within two weeks, I was in New York standing as close to the ruins as I could get; the police were still there. I saw the smoke; two weeks had passed and the place was still in smoke. I walked around the city and saw the posters with pictures of missing loved ones and the ad hoc memorials set up for those who fell victim to this terrible crime of hate and intolerance. Americans seemed confused and bewildered; the attack had caught them unawares. For me it was clear; the age-old conflict from the Middle East, the Jihad, was simply taking one more step—Jihad was coming to the United States. It started thirteen hundred years ago with swords and men riding camels; it continues today with box cutters and suicide bombers in planes. But really, it is the same.

Once again, this was an area where Americans could learn from Israelis. The United States is over four hundred fifty times larger than Israel, with many times the population, wealth, and resources, but we in Israel are the older sibling, much older, and much more experienced. We are the seed from which America grew. It is from our Book that the founding fathers drew their nourishment; it is from our biblical warriors and heroes that they drew their inspiration.

The United States tends to act somewhat arrogant toward Israel due to its wealth and power and forgets that even in modern times Israel has given the United States a great deal—perhaps even more than it has received. "Contrary to popular lore, the equivalent of what Israel contributed to the US immeasurably surpasses, even in monetary terms, the sum total of what America gave Israel from the 1970s on (prior to that we got nothing, yet miraculously managed to thrive). America enjoyed access to Israeli intelligence, including information on Soviet weaponry, battlefield tryouts for American military hardware, their innovative improvement, etc."[252]

For the United States to become a nation of warriors again, it needs to become a little more humble and recognize

Israel as a true and equal ally. The contributions of Israel and the Jewish people to the United States include some of the most prized documents, like the Declaration of Independence and the Statue of Liberty poem—the soul of the people of Israel is engraved in the United States.

The words on the Statue of Liberty were written by a Jewish woman, Emma Lazarus, daughter of Moshe and Esther.

> Give me your tired, your poor,
> Your huddled masses yearning to breathe free,
> The wretched refuse of your teeming shore.
> Send these, the homeless, tempest-tost to me,
> I lift my lamp beside the golden door!

How tragically ironic—the Statue of Liberty, which has beckoned millions of the poor and unfortunate to come to the shores of the United States, yet ignored the Jewish plight during the genocide of World War Two, and then stood overlooking, "watching," as our enemies took advantage of American kindness and generosity and came to these shores with hate.

The smoke of the Twin Towers rising up to the heavens reminded me of the smoke from the crematoriums at Auschwitz, where Jews and others were murdered and then burned—for the crime of being "different." The United States embraces the different, and yet these people came to its friendly skies and turned the World Trade Center into a crematorium.

When Americans come to Israel to train in Krav Maga, when this cultural exchange of survival knowledge takes place, I feel it is our way of standing united against tyranny. That is what the American founding fathers did, that is what we are all doing today. Let freedom ring. The United States is the great experiment in freedom; a nation of the people, by the people, and for the people. As of late, it has come under criticism, from without and within. Let us not forget that the US flag stands for freedom and that around the world people look to that flag for inspiration and hope. The Statue of Liberty is still a beacon of hope for the oppressed, as is the spirit of the American people. Yet some have forgotten this message. They have forgotten the heroes who fought and died for that freedom. They have forgotten that freedom is never free and that many have paid the ultimate price to maintain that freedom.

Statue of Liberty, New York, © *Gary / Fotolia*

During my travels around the United States, I have found many friends and supporters of Israel. They understand Israel, support her, and pray for her people. I have found many allies who speak our language. I have found veterans of America's wars; those who have served in the marines, air force, navy, coast guard, and all the branches of the US fighting force. I have met police, FBI, SWAT team instructors, and corrections officers. There *is* a nation of warriors within the United States, there are people who still believe in freedom and are willing to fight for it, but they are not the majority.

To me, these men and women represent the finest the United States has to offer; their self-sacrifice, patriotism, and commitment to their core values are an inspiration. They give without any expectation of reward. Their only reward is the knowledge that they have served their country and that they are ready at a moment's notice to serve again.

In this day and age, such behavior is too often seen as foolish, their sacrifice is ignored or even worse, mocked, by too many in the American population, as if being a patriot is the same as being called a naïve fool who is blindly following a corrupt government. The idea of "my country right or wrong" is seen as outdated. How sad when a nation does not appreciate and recognize its protectors.

How can we change this sorry situation? One answer is to look to Israel. In September 2008, a group of American veterans, members of the Iraq and Afghanistan Veterans of America (IAVA), visited Israel. They quickly picked up on the idea of Israel as a nation of warriors, the kind they would like the United States to be once again. "Israel is a model of social involvement...it's great to be in a country where everyone is so involved, where everyone understands sacrifice and what it means" said Paul Rieckhoff, director and founder of IAVA.[253]

They were impressed with the spirit of the Israeli fighters and called them "dynamic, innovative fighters." They were also struck by the prominence of the military in Israeli culture, "You can tell from the moment you get here that Israel appreciates its soldiers, Israel supports its soldiers. **Its soldiers and its people are one**, which is very different from what you see in the US...I think the US has lost some of that appreciation."[254]

Another answer is in education and proper role models. Many people enjoy watching cop shows on TV; Law & Order,

NYPD Blue, CSI, and so forth. When they are stopped by a police officer, however, they become indignant! "How dare you delay me or interrupt my day!" They do not stop to think about this police officer's day, about his or her life. They do not think of the dangers he faces to keep citizens safe.

My friend, Louie Balestrieri, a retired NYPD detective from the Organized Crime Investigation Division, decorated multiple times for actions involving grave personal risk, served for many years with the police force. On several occasions, he would have been justified to take a human life, and yet he did not. Still, at certain times, during certain operations, he was criticized and second-guessed. We like a perfect world where no mistakes are made, where every split second decision in the heat of an operation is correct, where a good guy never accidentally gets stopped for questioning. Such is not reality. The public must understand this.

When I hear Louie's stories, told in such a humble manner, I am in awe of what he has faced, alone. The American public does not seem to know or appreciate what their boys in blue do for them, day in and day out. Their officers bear their scars—emotional and physical—alone, without appreciation. It seems as though the only actions that receive attention are when some innocent person accidentally gets pushed around. Do we understand what these public servants live with? Can we appreciate the danger they face?

This must be part of their education if the United States is to become a nation of warriors once again. They must educate people about the sacrifice, commitment, and contribution of their law enforcement and military community, those who serve and their families. They must learn to appreciate their warriors. They must show them respect.

We can all do something about this—each one of us in our own line of work. When I trained at Dr. Beasley's

Karate College in Virginia, we always ended our three days of intensive training with a salute to the United States and its heroes. We saluted the men and women who have served it through the armed forces and the security forces. Dr. Beasley would call up the members of each branch of the service, one at a time. "Will all those who served in the marines please come up front. Will all those who served in the navy please step forward and join them." Suddenly, some of our black belt instructors stepped forward; some were old men already. We had not known that they once were in the military. We gained even greater respect for them—they were true warriors. As each group marched up to the front of the room, the anthem of its branch was played. It was a very inspiring and motivational moment. We concluded with the Pledge of Allegiance.

For all the young people in the room, I am sure it awakened in them a pride for their country and perhaps a thought that someday, perhaps they too would serve their nation and be recognized for their contribution. By honoring our veterans, we set an example for the next generation.

To serve is an honor and should be seen as such. In Israel, people prematurely discharged from the army often hire lawyers to get back in. They will go to doctors to prove they are healthy enough to serve. The fellow who killed the terrorist with the tractor spent a year with a lawyer until he was reinstated in his unit. We must restore the same spirit in the United States.

Today, the US military offers benefits to encourage people to enlist; it feels that it has no choice. It is as if it is saying, "Think of your own benefit; the military can help you advance your own cause." Whatever happened to "Ask not what your country can do for you—ask what you can do for your country."?

In Israel, you must serve. If you are a pacifist, you might get away with a noncombat job, but being a pacifist is really not considered a legitimate excuse for not serving. There is a joke: A pacifist wants to get out of the draft. The recruiting officer says, "Why? Do you have any emotional problems? That is, *besides* being a pacifist?"

Some are given the choice of "national service," for instance, to volunteer in a hospital for a year or work with the disadvantaged. In either case, you must serve your country. When it comes to a job interview, the first question asked is, "Where did you serve?" Perhaps it is time for the United States to reinstate the draft, or at least require some form of service to the nation. Be proud to be an American! You will have plenty of time to complete your education.

When you have served, you will have formed a bond with your countrymen from other walks of life. You will have learned to speak a certain common language. You will have something to believe in. It is said that a man who has nothing to die for also has nothing to live for. Give American youth back their values—teach them hard work and discipline. It will create a stronger backbone for the entire society.

The founding fathers did not want a professional army; they wanted a true people's army, an army of people that cared about America—that great experiment in democracy. A nation of people that can rule themselves and fight for themselves—that was their dream. It is not too late for their dream.

CHAPTER 17

The Gaza War (Protective Edge) and the Social Media Generation

We dream and pray for the biblical words "and the land shall rest for forty years" but it is not to be. Every couple of years another battle flares up, sometimes it is called a war and sometimes only an "operation." Either way, our troops are called up, our young men die.

There were some who had their doubts about the "social media generation," the generation of smartphones, text messages, and all the new hi-tech gadgets. All these devices are geared toward the self-centered individual. Gone were the days of the pioneers who lived for the state, gone were the ideals and values of the past. So some thought. The social media generation proved them wrong. The nation rose to the occasion, perhaps as never before.

The stories that are told about the Gaza War, Operation Protective Edge (July 2014), are in proportion to every war we have fought, including back to biblical days. This war has it all: self-sacrifice and extreme heroism of soldiers, the nation coming together as "one man with one heart" and giving its all to the troops, and miracles of biblical proportions reported by secular and religious alike.

Just as in the past, Israelis showed up for reserves before they received their orders. Those that were not called in the initial call-up showed up anyway. Men in their 50s showed up to join their units, often fighting near their own sons. Israelis abroad, on vacation, for studies, dropped everything, paid for their own tickets and flew home to join their units. "No man was absent" and no woman either. Pregnant woman showed up for reserve duty. No one stayed back. Everyone wanted "in." Women distinguished themselves as well. Four female paramedics served in Gaza, treated the wounded, and marched with the troops. Under fire, they treated their patients and saved lives.

Commanders who were hurt refused to be treated before "their" soldiers were treated. Everyone gave, everyone sacrificed for the other. The spirit of these brave warriors rose to the heavens and brought untold blessings.

As always, rabbis were on the front line and the Rabbinic academies did what they could. The summer break was canceled. The rabbis said, "While the soldiers are fighting you too must fight by studying the holy Torah and praying to God." No one went home. The rabbis said, "The soldiers sleep with their boots on, so shall you." And the young scholars studied, taking only occasional naps, with their shoes on. A spiritual war was under way.

A commander comes into battle with his troops for a predawn attack, but his support troops are delayed. Soon the sun will rise; the surprise will be over. Suddenly, a great fog descends and hides the sun. As in the days of Joshua, a great miracle took place and the children of Israel were protected by heavenly forces.

The Israeli invention, the "Iron Dome" works and thousands of enemy rockets are shot out of the sky, but sometimes it did not work. The enemy said, "Their God is redirecting our rockets!" Story after story reveal cases where suddenly a great wind came and knocked the rocket off course, landing harmlessly in the sea or in open territory. One such rocket is capable of killing hundreds of people. During Protective Edge, over three thousand rockets were fired. Only one Israeli citizen was killed.

Many a soldier cried out "God is with me in Gaza!" It was felt that God marched into Gaza with His people. And the people of Israel united like never before. Truckloads of goods arrived at the front lines. There was more food and snacks than anyone knew what to do with. Restaurants served soldiers home on leave for free. Everyone was giving to the soldiers, everything was free!

The social media generation fought hard, on the battlefield and off. Many ordinary citizens became ambassadors for Israel, self-appointed defenders of our nation, posting up-to-the-minute news and commentary about the war on all social media. People dropped everything to stand up for Israel—in Israel and all over the world—as "one man with one heart." Once again Israel's sons and daughters, old and young, rose to the occasion. "Who is like Your nation Israel, one singular nation in the land."[255] Truly, we are one.

CHAPTER 18

How to Start Your Own Krav Maga Club

There was a time when the Asian martial arts were most relevant and practical. However, gone are the days of the Samurai and the Ninja. Sadly, Israel is in an era of war and terrorism. As such, Krav Maga is considered among the most relevant and practical fighting systems for today's urban population.

Police forces, the military, prison guards, and security companies all over the world are bringing in Krav Maga experts from Israel to teach them the latest, most practical method. You can be a part of this growing trend.

Information about how to start a Krav Maga club is available on the Israeli Krav International (IKI) website, (http://www.your-krav-maga-expert.com/certification. html).

Contact Moshe Katz for personal guidance and training. You will receive expert advice on how to get started and how to succeed.

EPILOGUE

Some people shy away from the word "warrior." Warriors are associated with armies and the military which have become targets of criticism for liberal minded people.

A warrior is a noble person, a person with the highest values of our society. He trains to fight not from a thirst for violence, but for our peace and security. He trains hard to be there when society needs him; his is a life of service and sacrifice. It is time to restore the warrior to his rightful place in society.

I am writing these words shortly after my first visit to Norway, where I had been invited to teach Krav Maga seminars. The word "Oslo" has a bitter taste for me. It was in Oslo that the horrific "Oslo Accords" were signed, where Israel was pressured into making suicidal concessions to our enemies, who are bent on our destruction. Too many of our people have since been murdered by terrorists, a direct result of these concessions. Oslo signifies defeat, the beginning of the end of our dream.

Most of the people I met in Oslo had never met a Jew or an Israeli, and they were totally unfamiliar with the life we lead, as I was unfamiliar with theirs. My first introduction to the Norwegian mindset was upon landing at the airport and dealing with the Norwegian security. What I found odd about Norwegian security was this—it does not exist! I walked off the plane, picked up my luggage, walked through the "nothing to declare" zone, and left! That was it, no police, no questioning, no passport control, not even the longed for stamp on my passport, nothing at all. I never even saw a police officer.

My host, Morten, explained to me during my visit that it is part of Norwegian culture to be peacemakers and go-betweens. He said, "We choose to be naïve."

But something was happening in Norway; Muslims were moving in, crime was on the rise, and fear began to take hold. But few, if any, were willing to speak up. Privately, some told me, "We are Norwegians and yet in our own country we have to watch what we say lest we offend the Muslims, who are outsiders in this land." Of course, this made no sense, but it takes people awhile to wake up. We Israelis woke up millennia ago.

The Norwegians mean well, but they do not get it. They will someday. They should not be intermediaries; they should not be involved in the so-called "peace process" because, just like most Americans, they just do not get it.

I get it. As a young child, age six, living in Israel, I was taught our history. My dad, of blessed memory, gave me a book and inscribed it with the words, "May you live Jewish history every day." And I do. I learned the words to the song, *"Ha'olam Kulo Negdeinu"* ("The Whole World is Against Us"),[256] I watched real footage from the Holocaust and saw neighbors with the numbers the Nazis tattooed on their arms to show us that we are "numbers, not men." On the way to summer camp, I saw a bombed-out house, the result of a recent terrorist attack, and in the synagogue on our holy day of *Yom Kippur* I heard that once again all our Arab neighbors launched a massive attack to finish the job that Hitler started. So I get it. It is in my blood.

People do not like wars and they want to bring the sides together to make peace. I understand, but it is not so simple. We too want peace, but as the prophet said, "Peace, peace, but there is no peace." So I remember the air raids during the 1973 Yom Kippur War. I remember my dear mom running to the bomb shelter and my dad, of blessed memory, leaving the house in his IDF uniform. I remember the last postcard one of our teachers sent us from the front lines in Sinai; the last one he would ever send. He did not make it.

So I get it. We do not have the luxury of allowing people to get off the plane and just walk out and go home; cannot be done here. We do not even have the luxury of driving more than a few kilometers without being stopped at a roadblock or walking into a supermarket without being checked. My friends, you are not in Norway anymore; welcome to the Middle East!

So I do not appreciate it when well-meaning outsiders try to push us into negotiations with an enemy they do not understand; a situation they cannot grasp. It takes a certain kind of life to understand what is going on over here and they just do not get it. Woe unto those who do not understand the nature of the enemy and the impending attack. How easy it is to become complacent and believe that one can easily achieve "peace in our times." If only it were so simple.

And so we live with the sword and the Torah; the Bible. We read the ancient words, "Have a horse ready for the day of combat and the redemption shall be that of God."[257]

And in the words of a modern poet, we vow, "We won't be fooled again."

And we pray for the words, "And the land was quiet for forty years."[258] May it be so, speedily, in our times. Amen.

We are a grateful people.
We suffer, we die, we are forced to kill,
but we are a grateful people.
We bury...unspeakable pain,
but we are grateful, even for this.
There was a time,
when even a "Jewish burial"
was denied us, not once,
not only during the Dark Years,
but during the many massacres,
pogroms, and inquisitions,
in all the lands of the exiles.
To bury, and to be able to say
the prayer for the dead,
to sanctify God's name,
even with pain, we are grateful.

As the Hebrew song says, "We are grateful for the good, for the bad, for the good" ("*Modeh Ani*," – "I'm Grateful").[259]

A melancholy smile comes across the face of a paratrooper. To the outside world this is confusing, but to us...it is the joy of liberating Jerusalem, but the pain of losing so many friends. The joy of freedom, but the sorrow of the cost. He marches forward in his red boots, but with him are the ghosts of all the friends who can no longer walk, he carries them with him, brothers in arms, forever.

We are grateful, the world forces us into an unbearable situation, they want to divide our land, and this question threatens to divide our people, but we are grateful to walk on sovereign Jewish land. We walk near the ruins of our Holy Temple, foreigners, outsiders, rule over it now, but we are grateful, to walk near it, to touch the outside stones, to feel, to remember, we are grateful even for this.

Foreigners have trampled over our Temple, the Home of Holiness, but today our feet can come close, can walk where our ancestors walked on their way to the Temple. We are grateful, despite a pain, a pain so deep it goes back two thousand years. We are grateful to be here today, there is a smile, with a tear, the heart is full and broken, all at once...all at once.

I am grateful to You, Lord of the Universe, who has kept me alive to see this glorious day.

APPENDIX A

The Future, Continually Adapting

The IDF is a leader in military innovation—continually adapting organizationally and technologically to fulfill the duty to protect our nation. In the news:

- **"IDF to Establish New Cyber Command,"** *Israel National News*, June 16, 2015, (http://bitly.com/inn-cyber)

- **"Navy's Cyber Warriors in Technological Arms Race with Israel's Foes,"** *Jerusalem Post*, April 28, 2015, (http://bitly.com/jp-navy)

- **"IDF Introduces the Commando Division,"** *Israel National News*, July 6, 2015, (http://bitly.com/inn-commando)

- **"Even if a Missile Strikes our Operations, We will Keep the IDF's Network Running,"**

Jerusalem Post, April 30, 2015, (http://bitly.com/jp-network)

- **"Getting Big Data to the Skies,"** *Jerusalem Post*, April 29, 2015, (http://bitly.com/jp-big-data)

- **"IDF's Cyber Defenders Preparing for Attacks by 'Lebanese Opponent',"** *Jerusalem Post*, May 1, 2015, (http://bitly.com/jp-cyber)

- **"US, IDF Begin Training 'Magic Wand' Operators,"** *Israel National News*, June 29, 2015, (http://bitly.com/inn-magic-wand)

- **"Israel's New 'Sci-Fi' Fighter Jet Helmet,"** *Israel National News*, June 15, 2015, (http://bitly.com/inn-helmet)

- **"New in IDF: Tactical Kamikaze Drones,"** *Israel National News*, May 28, 2015, (http://bitly.com/inn-drones)

(Links accessed July 10, 2015)

APPENDIX B

Timeline of Wars

- **Israeli War of Independence**, November 1947-July 1949
- **Reprisal operations**, 1950s-1960s
- **Suez Crisis**, October 1956
- **Six-Day War**, June 1967
- **War of Attrition**, 1967-1970
- **Yom Kippur War**, October 1973
- **1982 Lebanon War**, 1982
- **2006 Lebanon War**, summer 2006
- **Operation Cast Lead**, December 2008-January 2009
- **Operation Pillar of Defense**, November 2012
- **Operation Protective Edge**, July-August 2014

NOTES

Preface
[1]http://bitly.com/partisans-song, accessed June 30, 2015
[2]Ezekiel 13

Introduction
[3]Itay Gil and Dan Baron, *The Citizen's Guide to Stopping Suicide Attackers*, Paladin Press, Boulder, Colorado, 2004
[4]https://en.wikipedia.org/wiki/Israel, accessed June 30, 2015
[5]https://en.wikipedia.org/wiki/Arab_citizens_of_Israel, accessed June 30, 2015
[6]https://en.wikipedia.org/wiki/Gaza_Strip, accessed June 30, 2015
[7]*Ethics of the Fathers* 1:14

Chapter 1
[8]*Jerusalem Post*, April 20, 2007
[9]Psalms 121:4

[10]Ibid.

[11]*Jerusalem Post*, January 1, 2010

[12]*Associate Press Writers*, May 4, 2010

[13]*Jerusalem Post*, January 1, 2010

[14]Ibid.

[15]*Jerusalem Post*, March 23, 2007

[16]Ibid.

[17]*Jerusalem Post*, January 5, 2010

[18]Leviticus 19:16

[19]Leviticus 19:18

[20]Rambam, Laws of Gifts to the Poor 8:10

[21]Ari Yashar, *IsraelNationalNews*, June 9, 2015, http://bitly.com/ari-yashar, accessed June 10, 2015

[22]Passover *Haggadah*

[23]Ibid.

[24]Deuteronomy 20:8

Chapter 2

[25]Bamidbar 1:3

[26]*Jerusalem Post*, May 2, 2008

[27]Ibid.

[28]*Jerusalem Post*, April 27, 2007

[29]Na'ama Rak, *Israel Defense Forces website*, March 24, 2009, http://bitly.com/naama-rak, accessed June 30, 2015

[30]*Jerusalem Post*, July 27, 2009

[31]Ibid.

[32]Deuteronomy 24

[33]Maimonides, *Laws of Kings and Wars*, http://halakhah.com/rst/kingsandwars.pdf, accessed June 30, 2015

[34]*Jerusalem Post*, January 14, 2009

[35]Bamidbar 1

[36]*Jerusalem Post*, January 14, 2009

[37]Ibid.

[38]Bamidbar 15:37-38

[39]http://bitly.com/rocky-song, accessed June 30, 2015

[40]Proverbs

[41]Bible

[42]Uzi Baruch, *IsraelNationalNews*, June 11, 2015, http://bitly.com/uzi-baruch, accessed June 12, 2015

[43]*Yisrael Hayom*, April 16, 2013

[44]http://bitly.com/at-vaani, accessed June 30, 2015

[45]*Jerusalem Post Magazine*, May 8, 2008

[46]Ibid.

[47]Ibid.

[48]Joel 4:2

[49]Psalms 96:1

[50]http://hebrewsongs.com/?song=jerusalemofgold, accessed June 30, 2015

[51]Psalms 126:1

[52]Bamidbar 23:9

[53]http://bitly.com/hatikva-hope, accessed June 30, 2015

[54]*Jerusalem Post*, September 27, 2009

[55]Ibid., 11

[56]http://bitly.com/y-gaon, accessed June 30, 2015

[57]*Jerusalem Post*, April 23, 2007

[58]Ibid.

[59]*Jerusalem Post*, July 13, 2007

[60]*Jerusalem Post*, August 25, 2006

[61]*Jerusalem Post*, July 13, 2007

[62]*Jerusalem Post*, April 23, 2007

[63]*Jerusalem Post*, July 13, 2007

[64]*Yisrael Hayom*, April 16, 2013

[65]*Yisrael Hayom,* April 14, 2013

[66]Chronicles I 17:21

[67]*Jerusalem Post*, January 6, 2009

[68]Ibid.

[69]Ibid.

[70]Ibid.

[71]*Jerusalem Post*, July 12, 2007

[72]*Yisrael Hayom*, July 6, 2015
[73]*Jerusalem Post Magazine*, October 14, 2011, 11

Chapter 3
[74]Zechariah 8:4
[75]Ethan Katz, from a personal letter
[76]*Zman Maaleh*, May 26, 2011

Chapter 4
[77]Passover *Haggadah*

Chapter 5
[78]Genesis 13:17
[79]*Jerusalem Post*, July 23, 2008
[80]Ibid.

Chapter 7
[81]http://bitly.com/machar-shemer, accessed June 30, 2015
[82]http://bitly.com/ballad-medic, accessed June 30, 2015
[83]http://bitly.com/golani-damascus, accessed June 30, 2015
[84]http://bitly.com/k-shetavo, accessed June 30, 2015
[85]http://bitly.com/lashalom, accessed June 30, 2015
[86]http://bitly.com/noladeti, accessed June 30, 2015
[87]http://bitly.com/hamilchama, accessed June 30, 2015
[88]http://bitly.com/rega-echad, accessed June 30, 2015
[89]http://bitly.com/parallel-lines, accessed June 30, 2015

Chapter 8
[90]*Jerusalem Post*, August 19, 2007
[91]*The Algemeiner*, April 16, 2013

Chapter 9
[92]*Jerusalem Post*, April 22, 2007

Chapter 10

[93]Neer Korn, *National Times*, January 11, 2011
[94]Ibid.
[95]Book of Judges 7
[96]*Jerusalem Post Magazine*, June 11, 2010, 12

Chapter 11

[97]Isaiah 6
[98]*Jerusalem Post*, July 13, 2007
[99]*Zman Maaleh*, August 13, 2009)
[100]http://bitly.com/bli-lomar-milah, accessed June 30, 2015
[101]http://bitly.com/givat-hatachmoshet, accessed June 30, 2015
[102]Ibid.
[103]*Jerusalem Post Magazine*, May 8, 2008
[104]IDF Military Spokesman, January 2007
[105]*Yisrael Hayom*, June 4, 2015

Chapter 12

[106]*Jerusalem Post*, August 17, 2007
[107]Sholom Aleichem (adapted from stories), *Fiddler on the Roof*, directed by Norman Jewison, MGM, Hollywood, 1971

Chapter 13

[108]Bereshith 14:12
[109]Rabbi Abraham Ibn Ezra, Spain, 12th century
[110]Bereshith 14:15-16
[111]Genesis 32
[112]Rabbi Shimon Yitzchaki, France, 11th century
[113]Bereshith 34:25
[114]Exodus 2
[115]Ibid.
[116]Bamidbar 25
[117]Judges 3
[118]Ibid.

[119]Judges 3:21
[120]Judges 3:30
[121]Judges 4:4
[122]Judges 4:6
[123]Judges 4:14
[124]Judges 4:18
[125]Judges 4:21-22
[126]Judges 5:31
[127]Judges 14
[128]Judges 15
[129]Judges 16
[130]Ibid.
[131]Samuel I 14
[132]Samuel I 13:6
[133]Samuel I 13:19
[134]Samuel I 14:4
[135]Samuel I 13:15
[136]Samuel I 14:20
[137]Samuel I 15:28
[138]Samuel I 15:32-33
[139]Samuel I 17:12
[140]Psalms 144
[141]Samuel I 17:33
[142]Samuel I 17:34-36
[143]Samuel I 17:45
[144]Samuel I 17:46
[145]Samuel I 18:7
[146]Samuel I 19:8
[147]Samuel II 5:7
[148]Genesis 34:1
[149]Genesis 34:24
[150]Genesis 34:25-26
[151]Genesis 34:30
[152]Genesis 34:31)
[153]Rabbi Yeheskel Kahane, Brooklyn, New York, 20th century

[154]Bereshith 36:5
[155]Judges 20:5
[156]Kings II 3:19, 25
[157]Chronicles II 26:14-15
[158]Numbers 35:16
[159]Shemoth, Exodus 21:18
[160]Spain, 12th century
[161]Joshua 5
[162]Judges 6
[163]Judges 7
[164]Bamidbar 31
[165]Samuel I 25
[166]Nehemiah 4
[167]Samuel II 20
[168]Samuel I 18
[169]Nehemiah 4
[170]Samuel II 1
[171]Ibid.
[172]Samuel I 31:3
[173]Chronicles I 5
[174]Joshua 8
[175]Samuel I 17:8-11
[176]Samuel I 17:17
[177]Samuel I 17:26
[178]Samuel I 17:32
[179]Samuel I 17:33
[180]Samuel I 17:40
[181]Exodus 21
[182]Judges 15:15
[183]Samuel I 17
[184]Chronicles I 11:22
[185]Samuel I 13
[186]Exodus 14
[187]Ibid.
[188]Joshua 1

[189]Joshua 7
[190]Ibid.

Chapter 14
[191]Isaiah 45:1
[192]Maccabees 1
[193]Maccabees 2
[194]Maccabees 2:51-68
[195]Maccabees 3:12
[196]Maccabees 3:25
[197]Maccabees 3
[198]Maccabees 4:13
[199]Maccabees 4:34
[200]Maccabees 4:36
[201]Maccabees
[202]Flavius Josephus, *The Jewish War*, Penguin, New York, 1984, 8
[203]Emil Schurer, *The Jewish People in the Time of Jesus Christ*, Div 1, Vol 2, 237
[204]Josephus, *The Jewish War*, 5:11
[205]Meir Kahane, *Listen Vanessa, I am a Zionist*, Desert Ulpan, Tucson, Arizona, 1978
[206]Martin Goodman, *Rome and Jerusalem*, Random House, New York, 2007, 454
[207]Cassius Dio, *The Collected Works of Cassius Dio*, Halcyon Press, Aukland, 2010
[208]Ibid., 457
[209]Goodman, *Rome and Jerusalem*, 461
[210]Numbers 24:17
[211]Leviticus, Wayiqra 19:19
[212]Bamidmar 15:37
[213]Exodus, Shemoth 20:3
[214]Talmud, Tractate Idol Worship, Avodah Zara
[215]Schurer, *The Jewish People in the Time of Jesus Christ*, 314
[216]Kahane, *Listen Vanessa, I am a Zionist*
[217]Psalm 137

[218]Ben Abrahamson and Joseph Katz, "The Persian Conquest of Jerusalem," http://bitly.com/persian-conquest, accessed June 30, 2015

[219]Ibid.

[220]Ibid., 42

[221]Edward Kritzler, *Jewish Pirates of the Caribbean*, Aurum Press, London, 2014, 10

[222]Ken Blady, *Jewish Communities in Exotic Places*, Jason Aronson, Inc., Northvale, New Jersey, 2000, 32

[223]Jerry Klinger, "How the Jews Saved the American Revolution," http://bitly.com/klinger-j, http://www.jewishmag.com, accessed June 30, 2015

[224]Karen Sutton, *The Massacre of the Jews of Lithuania*, Gefen Publishing House, Jerusalem, 2014, 31-32

[225]Vladimir Jabotinsky, *The War and the Jew,* Altalena Press, Tova Press, Inc. 1987, 25

[226]Ibid., 26

[227]Lester Eckman and Chaim Lazar, *The Jewish Resistance*, Shengold Publishers, New York, 1977, 11

[228]Ibid., 15-16

[229]Ibid., 16

[230]United States Holocaust Memorial Museum, Washington, D.C.

[231]Marek Edelman, *The Ghetto Fights*, Bookmarks, 1990

[232]Ibid.

[233]Moshe Arens, *Flags Over the Warsaw Ghetto*, Gefen Publishing House, 2011

[234]http://bitly.com/partisans-song, accessed June 30, 2015

[235]Robert Rozett, *Conscripted Slaves*, Yad Vashem Publications, Jerusalem, 2014, 112

[236]Ibid., 152

[237]Ibid., 237

[238]Nahum Bogner, *At the Mercy of Strangers*, Yad Vashem Publications, Jerusalem, 2009

[239]Yehoshua Buchler, *The Profile of the Jews in Slovakia after World War II*, Yalkut Moreshet, 65, 1998, 119-32

[240]David Bankier, editor, *Probing the Depths of German Antisemitism*, Berghahn Books, 2000

[241]Menachem Begin

[242]Chaim Herzog, *The Arab – Israeli Wars, Vintage, 2005,* 46

[243]Edward Black, *Banking on Baghdad*, Dialog Press, Westport, CT, 2008, 313

Chapter 15

[244]Irene Mecchi and Jonathan Roberts, *The Lion King*, directed by Roger Allers, Rob Minkoff, Walt Disney Pictures, Burbank, 1994

[245]David Raab, *Terror in Black September*, Palgrave Macmillan, New York, 2007

[246]Itay Gil and Dan Baron, *The Citizen's Guide to Stopping Suicide Attackers*

[247]Paul Hogan and John Cornell, *Crocodile Dundee*, directed by Peter Faiman, Rimfire Films, Australia, 1986

[248]Judges 1:1

[249]Judges 11:24

[250]Judges 11:28

[251]Judges 11:32

Chapter 16

[252]*Jerusalem Post Magazine*, April 2, 2010

[253]*Jerusalem Post*, September 17, 2008

[254]Ibid.

Chapter 17

[255]Chronicles I 17

Epilogue

[256]http://bitly.com/haolam, accessed June 30, 2015

[257]Mishlei, Proverbs 21:31

[258]Judges 5:31

[259]http://bitly.com/m-ariel, accessed June 30, 2015

BIBLIOGRAPHY

Arens, Moshe, *Flags Over the Warsaw Ghetto*, Gefen Publishing House, Jerusalem, 2011

Bankier, David, editor, *The Jews Are Coming Back*, Berghahn Books, Yad Vashem, Jerusalem, 2005

Bankier, David, editor, *Probing the Depths of German Anti-semitism*, Yad Vashem, Jerusalem 2000

Begin, Menachem, *The Revolt*, Steimatzky, Bnei Brak, Israel, 1990

Black, Edward, *Banking on Baghdad*, Dialog Press, Westport, CT, 2008

Blady, Ken, *Jewish Communities in Exotic Places*, Jason Aronson, Inc., Northvale, New Jersey, 2000

Bogner, Nahum, *At the Mercy of Strangers*, Yad Vashem, Jerusalem, 2009

Buchler, Yehoshua, *The Profile of the Jews in Slovakia after World War II*, Yalkut Moreshet, 65, 1998

Dio, Cassius, *The Collected Works of Cassius Dio*, Halcyon Press, Aukland, 2010

Eckman, Lester, and Lazar, Chaim, *The Jewish Resistance*, Shengold Publishers, Inc., New York, 1977

Edelman, Marek, *The Ghetto Fights*, Bookmarks, 1990

Fisch, Harold, *The Koren Jerusalem Bible*, Koren Publishers, Jerusalem, 2008

Gil, Itay, and Baron, Dan, *The Citizen's Guide to Stopping Suicide Attackers*, Paladin Press, Boulder, Colorado, 2004

Goodman, Martin, *Rome and Jerusalem*, Vintage, London, 2008

Graetz, Heinrich, *History of the Jews*, The Jewish Publication Society of America, Philadelphia, 1967

Herzog, Chaim, *The Arab-Israeli Wars*, Vintage, London, 2005

Jabotinsky, Ze'ev, *The War and the Jew*, Altalena Press, New York, 1987

Josephus, Flavius, *The Jewish War*, Penguin, New York, 1984

Kahane, Charles, *Torah Yesharah*, Solomon Rabinowitz Book Concern, New York, 1963

Kahane, Meir, *Listen Vanessa, I am a Zionist*, The Desert Ulpan, Tucson, Arizona, 1978

Kritzler, Edward, *Jewish Pirates of the Caribbean*, Aurum Press, London, 2014

Lazar, Chaim, *Destruction and Resistance*, Shengold Publishers, Inc., New York, 1985

Raab, David, *Terror in Black September*, Palgrave Macmillan, New York, 2007

Rozett, Robert, *Conscripted Slaves*, Yad Vashem, Jerusalem, 2000

Schurer, Emil, *A History of the Jewish People in the Time of Jesus Christ*, Hendrickson Publishers, Peabody, Massachusetts, 1993

Sutton, Karen, *The Massacre of the Jews of Lithuania*, Gefen Publishing House, Jerusalem, 2014

Yadin, Yigael, *Bar-Kokhba*, Random House, New York, 1971

ACKNOWLEDGMENTS

My Dad – Rabbi Paul M. Katz, of blessed memory

My father always taught us to stand strong, to be proud of who we are, to embrace our heritage. He was a proud Jew and a proud American. He was an American Eagle Scout and an Israeli soldier, a community leader, and a family man. He was a man who lived his life by his principles. His beliefs were translated into action throughout his life. He took up the pulpit to preach for Israel and to mobilize support. When Israel was attacked in 1967, he packed up his young family and moved to Israel.

He taught us not to run away, not to back off from a fight or any challenge. When he knew he was right, he would not accept "no" as an answer. He believed in being a "majority of one." He led by example and he was proud when we followed his example, just as he had followed the example of his dear father, Moe Katz, for whom I am named.

When we embraced Jewish activism—he was there; for moral support, to bail us out of trouble, to pick up the pieces. He may have been worried, but he never showed it; he only showed pride.

In the 1973 Yom Kippur War, he answered the call to arms and joined the IDF, serving with the home front, doing his share. I can still picture him in his uniform. In his later years, as a retiree, he volunteered with pride with the Jerusalem police force, patrolling the Old City of Jerusalem. He passed on suddenly in April 2004.

He is with me with every step I take, with every challenge I face, and with every obstacle I overcome.

My Mom – Honey K. Katz, may she live for many more years in good health

Behind every warrior, and next to every warrior, is the woman who makes it all possible. From taking several buses to visit my brother, Ethan, while he was serving in some isolated base in the middle of the Negev desert, to packing cookies to send to my nephew, Yitzi, serving in the paratroopers, to sleepless nights while my nephew, Arie, fought in Lebanon, my mother has been the cornerstone and rock of the family.

More than that, it is the confidence one is imbued with from a loving mother that makes all accomplishments, and sacrifices, possible. The daughter, wife, and mother of rabbis, she embodies all the virtues of the classic "woman of valor."

My Brother – Ethan Joel Katz

Ethan always wanted to serve the people of Israel. In his high school yearbook, his personal page was devoted entirely to guns and Israel. One of his friends said, "I don't know if Ethan included all the family members, but he certainly included all the family guns!" The yearbook staff wrote, "Ethan will certainly go far, probably the Syrian-Lebanese border."

As soon as Ethan graduated high school, as his classmates were off to study, he flew to Israel and volunteered to join the army. He served in the combat unit *Nachal Mutznach* (infantry, paratroopers), a highly respected unit known for combating terrorists in Arab-controlled cities—Hebron, Jenin, Bethlehem. The unit earned recognition for having badly hurt the infrastructure of the Hamas and Islamic Jihad in these towns.

Ethan always responded to the call when it was time to report for reserve duty, considering it an honor and a privilege to serve. He chose the difficult path, walking in the footsteps of ancient Hebrew warriors. He was raised with the stories of the Maccabees, the Bar Kochba revolt, and the freedom fighters for Israel. He continued their battle; he embraced their struggle.

Today, he serves as a role model for youth; teaching and inspiring them to walk in the footsteps of giants. He brings to life the lives, stories, and sacrifices of those warriors who came before us, inspiring the future and setting an example. His passion for the cause has earned him widespread recognition and respect; more importantly, he has shaped the lives of many—young and old.

My Nephew – Arie Yehuda Katz

Arie is named for his great-grandfather on his mother's side, who was taken away by the Nazis in Poland. When Arie visited Poland as part of the March of the Living program, he recited the *Kaddish*, the Jewish mourner's prayer, in memory and in honor of his namesake. The true honor, I believe, is the life he leads and the service he performs for our people. Arie served for five years in the *hesder* program, combining intensive religious studies with combat service in the IDF.

To him, it is an honor to serve. He has never shown any fear, any hesitation, or any doubt. He has never bragged about his accomplishments nor complained about any difficulties—he carries himself like a true warrior.

He is a member of the 101 Paratrooper unit, a unit that played a key role in the Second Lebanon War. He suffered the loss of two brave and honorable commanders—Yiftach Shrier and Ilan Gabai, of blessed memory. Arie participated in some of the toughest battles of the Second Lebanon War, but did his best to hide this from the family, to spare us the worry.

After completing his obligatory military service he traveled to many countries to teach Jewish youth and inspire them with our heritage. He continues to serve in the reserves. May God always watch over him and protect him.

To all these and so many more, I dedicate this book. For it is an ongoing battle, an unfinished story. May we soon be able to say, in the words of the Bible, "And the land was quiet for forty years."

ABOUT THE AUTHOR

Moshe Katz was born in Cleveland, Ohio, and has lived in Maaleh Adumim, Israel, for many years. He is a graduate of UCLA (BA) and Bernard Baruch Business School (MBA). He served in the Israel Defense Forces (IDF) – Infantry.

Katz has over thirty years martial arts experience. He is the founder of Israeli Krav International (IKI) and serves as Head Instructor. In addition to teaching in Israel, he tours the United States, Canada, Europe, Asia, and South America teaching Krav Maga/Israeli Self-Defense.

- 6th dan black belt Krav Maga
- Only 4th dan black belt certified by Itay Gil, former trainer of Israel's elite counterterrorism force and trainer of elite units
- Member Masters Council, Black Dragon Fighting Society International, Dr. Lawrence Day, Prof. Joe Cayer
- Certified by Wingate Institute – Israel's national

sports center, martial arts department
- 2010 European Krav Maga instructor of the year
- 2014 Black Belt Hall of Fame International Krav Maga instructor of the year
- Certified – handgun, Urban Combat Shooting

The author doing military service, 1993

Experience Israel for yourself. Immerse yourself in two weeks of Krav Maga training, Jewish/Israeli history—in the land of Israel where it all took place.

Visit the IKI website: http://www.your-krav-maga-expert.com